RESCUE—PRAIRIE FIRE STYLE

While Cobra Two sprayed HE rockets around the large field, I pulled out my binoculars and focused on the gully. Our boys were crouched just below the rim, out of the direct line of fire. But as I watched, a steady barrage of bullets kicked up dust along the crest. We were definitely out of time.

Cobra Two and I got our signals straight. I put the pipper on a grove of small trees concealing one of the patrols. As we closed at practically zero dive angle, we were so low that my first rocket hit the ground with its motor still running. The rocket snaked wildly through the weeds like a big Chinese firecracker. The second rocket hit a glancing blow and ricocheted back into the air, sailing over the target and finally exploding several hundred meters away.

My radio blared, "We're almost in. Keep it up, Covey. You've got 'em all shooting at you!"

As we came back around for another run, the downed pilots bolted from the gully just as Cobra Two touched down . . .

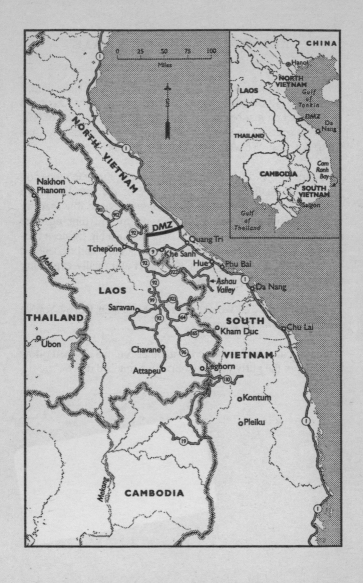

DA NANG
DIARY

A Forward Air Controller's
Gunsight View of Combat in Vietnam

TOM YARBOROUGH

St. Martin's Paperbacks

DA NANG DIARY

Copyright © 1990 by Thomas R. Yarborough.
Revised edition copyright © 2002 by Thomas R. Yarborough.

Cover photo © U.S. Air Force.

"The Ballad of the Green Beret." Copyright 1963, 1965, 1966 Music, Music, Music Inc. Reprinted by permission.

ISBN: 0-312-98493-6

Printed in the United States of America

St. Martin's Paperbacks edition / September 2002

St. Martin's Paperbacks are published by St. Martin's Press, 175 Fifth Avenue, New York, NY 10010.

10 9 8 7 6 5 4 3 2

This book is dedicated to the memory and fighting spirit of all
the United States Air Force
Forward Air Controllers who were lost in battle in the
skies over Southeast Asia.

"Give honour to our heroes fall'n, how ill
. soe'er the cause that bade them forth to die."

William Watson
"THE ENGLISH DEAD"

CONTENTS

PREFACE

When I first wrote *Da Nang Diary* in 1990, my intent was to use my personal experiences as a vehicle for examining some of the extraordinary activities of the ultrasecret "Studies and Observations Group," the most clandestine U.S. military unit to serve in the war in Vietnam. As an Air Force pilot flying for SOG, I was in no position to address the operational ground details of those incredibly harrowing "Prairie Fire" missions into Laos, Cambodia, and the DMZ, but I had hoped to flesh them out by adding the perspective of the Air Force forward air controllers who supported SOG reconnaissance teams on their dangerous journeys behind enemy lines. Within obvious limits, I think I was successful. Yet I have always harbored some nagging feelings of dissatisfaction and frustration about not being able to tell the "whole story."

For one thing, I feel compelled to point out that the "whole story" is an evolving one, as evidenced by the fact that as a nation we once again find ourselves embroiled in an unconventional war, a battle forced upon us by the horrific terrorist attacks of September 11, 2001. And as in Vietnam, United States Army Special Forces troops in Afghanistan are at the point of the spear, operating in total secrecy and without recognition for the incredibly dangerous missions they perform. I suspect that current reporters and historians sifting through the limited information available on special operations in Afghanistan will chafe, due to security restrictions, at not being able to get at the "whole story." But when they do, it will be clear that a direct link

from the Green Berets in Vietnam to the new generation of
Special Forces in Afghanistan was fully operative, forged
in the same professionalism, dedication, and sacrifice.
Hopefully, historians will not be forced to wait thirty years
before the veil of secrecy is lifted and information is made
available for study, analysis, and the telling of another epic
chapter of the "whole story."

In that respect, the decade that has passed since publi-
cation of the first edition of this book has fortunately witnessed an astonishing increase in the amount of information
available in the public domain about even the most secret
operations of the Vietnam War. The end of the Cold War
and the declassification of millions of documents have, in
many cases, literally eliminated the security restrictions
through which we were once forced to view the official
American experience in Vietnam. Those same classification
filters had also hampered and hamstrung those of us within
the military who wrote about that war. Although we had
firsthand knowledge about many of the war's secrets, in
most cases we respected the requirement, if somewhat reluctantly, to protect classified information, even though it
meant leaving out salient facts and key components of the
story. Now, the filters are gone and the restrictions are off.

Two authors in particular have pushed the envelope and
opened the files on SOG. In his *The Secret War Against
Hanoi*, Richard Shultz concentrates on the broader picture
and has produced a thoroughly researched and highly an-
alytical policy study of SOG's covert operations against
North Vietnam. At the operational level, John L. Plaster's
SOG is the definitive account of the extraordinary courage
and dedication displayed by Special Forces-led reconnaissance teams going in harm's way "across the fence" into
Laos, Cambodia, and North Vietnam.

Because of the pioneering efforts of Plaster and Shultz,
I have been inspired to revisit my own aerial account of
supporting SOG reconnaissance teams. While it has been a
matter of quiet satisfaction to me that the main outlines of

Da Nang Diary require little or no revision, I nevertheless welcome the opportunity to refine and expand my treatment of Operation Prairie Fire by including additional background and details previously locked away in some dusty Pentagon safe marked "Top Secret." The forward air controllers—Prairie Fire FACs—had a god's-eye view of the action, and their missions and experiences in SOG's covert war are an integral ingredient of the "whole story." I am proud and honored to tell their part of it.

This project could never have been undertaken without the support and encouragement of many friends, colleagues, and scholars across this wonderful country. I owe a debt of gratitude to Mark "Papa Wolf" Berent, whose persistence inspired me to "get the Vietnam experience recorded on paper by those of us who did the fighting, the bleeding, and the sacrificing." Among those warrior-friends who contributed firsthand accounts of episodes, both serious and humorous, are Kim Budrow, Carl D'Benedetto, Sonny Haynes, Don Jensen, Sherdeane Kinney, Norm Komich, Jim Martin, Evan Quiros, Tom Stump, and John Tait. I owe particular thanks to Dr. Wayne Thompson and his staff in the Office of the Air Force Historian, who helped me sift through mounds of classified "SITREPS" and unit histories. That same thanks goes out to Colonel Elliot Converse at the USAF Historical Research Collection at the Air University, Maxwell Air Force Base, Alabama, and to all the dedicated folks at the National Archives for their assistance and patience as I proceeded to drive them to fits of distraction with my constant demands for more information. I am also indebted to Bill Forsyth, POW/MIA Analyst at the Joint Task Force Full Accounting, and to Roxanne Merritt at the John F. Kennedy Special Warfare Center Library, for their professional assistance. And one of the true gems in this process has been my very capable, vivacious, and long-suffering secretary, Terry Jennings, who took care of me and endured my mood swings and intemperate language as I navigated through the trials of teaching and writing at

Indiana University. Additionally, a host of students and audiences to whom I have lectured on this topic also contributed to the enterprise.

My incomparable literary agent, Ethan Ellenberg, was one of my biggest supporters throughout this project. Through Ethan's help, I was especially fortunate to have teamed up with several remarkable professionals at St. Martin's Press, including Jerad Kieling and Marc Resnick. As senior editors, they guided a novice author with an iron hand in a velvet glove. Without their wisdom and advice, I would still be fumbling through a first draft.

Finally, my wife, Jane, is the source of all my successful endeavors. She fought the Vietnam War just as surely as I did, and hers was the tougher battle; at least I had the entire U.S. Air Force behind me. Her love and encouragement have always been boundless, and when I became discouraged, it was her steadying influence and faith in the project that kept me working late into those long nights as *Da Nang Diary* took shape. As evidence of her undying support, she will claim that this book is error-free. As much as I would like to agree, I know better. The inevitable mistakes and misinterpretations that remain are my responsibility alone.

Tom Yarborough
West Springfield, Virginia

April 9, 1973

Several other pilots had joined me for dinner at the well-appointed officers' club at Ubon Air Base, Thailand. It felt great to relax over a couple of beers and a good meal, especially since my day had started with a 0430 takeoff, some fourteen hours earlier. Even though the war in Southeast Asia was winding down, you would never know it from the intense combat missions being flown by a handful of Air Force forward air controllers (FACs) stationed at Ubon. As one of those FACs, I had started my day by directing five hours of air strikes in Cambodia, landing my OV-10 aircraft at Phnom Penh to refuel and rearm, then logging another four-and-a-half-hour mission before landing back at Ubon.

As part of that afternoon mission, I had been checking out the results of a B-52 Arc Light strike when Cricket—call sign of the airborne battlefield command-and-control center inside an orbiting Air Force EC-130 aircraft—sent me to respond to an emergency call for help from Hotel 21 at Kompong Thom, about eighty air miles north of Phnom Penh, Cambodia's capital. Once we established radio contact, Hotel 21 (nicknamed Sam) informed me that one of his outposts, about fifteen kilometers southeast of Kompong Thom, was under heavy attack and in danger of being overrun. The kicker was that the outpost commander spoke no English or French, so all our conversations were to be relayed for translation through Sam. As I approached the target area, the thought of controlling air strikes relying on Sam's English comprehension and translation abilities, not to mention his removed location, left me in a cold sweat.

In spite of my concerns, identifying friendly and enemy positions turned out to be a piece of cake. In the deep shadows just before sunset, I could make out three distinct streams of what appeared to be green tracers slamming into the friendly outpost. An occasional 82mm mortar round added to the colorful but deadly scene. By contrast, the good guys returned fire with their own barrage of white-hot tracers from M16s and M-60 machine guns. From what I could see, the closest enemy position was about 150 meters south of the friendlies; the other positions were 200 meters east and 300 meters west, respectively. Judging from the light show below me, nobody seemed to be running short of ammunition.

As I sorted through the ground situation, one other disconcerting variable complicated the equation. April in Cambodia is the height of the dry season, but the heat and convection occasionally produced fair sized cumulonimbus (CB) cells late in the afternoon. Unfortunately, one of those rogue CBs drifted into the area, its leading edge just a mile or so west of the battle. This beauty almost totally blocked out light from the setting sun, forcing a premature darkness on the area. Adding an air of supernatural imagery to the strange scene, the bottom half of the CB turned an ominous black color, while the anvil top glowed an incredible pink.

At that point Bertha Flight, a two-ship of F-4 Phantoms, arrived overhead, fat on gas and loaded with wall-to-wall 500-pound Mark-82 bombs. They agreed to drop their stuff in pairs, so I started them off on the southernmost target. Rolling into the semidarkness to mark the fortified fighting positions, or FFPs, I confess to being unnerved when the sky filled with .51-caliber machine gun fire from all directions, most of the enemy tracers glowing in that eerie green color. Several well-directed bursts streaked over my canopy as I executed a hard pull off to the south, just tickling the edge of the thunderstorm still sitting on the flank of the battle area. As I fretted about running Bertha Flight on restricted headings from east to west—right into the storm—

Sam came up on Fox Mike radio and broke the tension with an incredible story.

In an excited voice, Sam shouted, "The ground commander says please hurry with your bombs. The Khmer Rouge are throwing hand grenades into his position."

If the bad guys were indeed that close, we were in big trouble, so I asked Sam to verify the nearest enemy position. When Sam confirmed the location at 200–300 meters, I started smiling, wondering about these superhuman enemy soldiers who could toss a grenade three lengths of a football field. Still chuckling, I asked him, "Sam, do you really think the bad guys could throw a hand grenade 300 meters?" Without missing a beat Sam replied, "Well you know, some of the Khmer Rouge are very strong." In spite of the situation, I howled with laughter.

After being severely hosed by every automatic weapon in the area, Bertha Lead and then his wingman each dumped a pair of Mark-82s on the southern FFP. With the CB now blocking any east-west run-ins, we all moved to the eastern target, where once again we were greeted by some of the heaviest small arms and machine gun fire I had ever seen. In spite of the hail of red and green tracers, Bertha gave me three more north-to-south passes, silencing the enemy position and cooking off one medium secondary explosion and several sustained fires, all brilliantly orange and yellow in the fading light.

Two down and one to go. I could still see sporadic fire from the bad guys to the west of our friendlies, but there was no way to work fighters because of the towering CB almost directly overhead. Instead, I held Bertha Flight high and dry to the east while I armed up the M-60 machine guns and dove under the weather to fire two pods of marking rockets and lots of strafe at the offending enemy positions. In the darkness the lethal explosions of white phosphorous made for an impressive sight and seemed to do the trick; the bad guys didn't fire another shot—or throw another hand grenade.

On the night flight back to Ubon I began to relax, think-

ing with some satisfaction about the mission and how our
efforts had hopefully made a big difference to the besieged
Cambodian ground commander. I also thought about the
strange assortment of colors I had observed at various times
during the battle. As I approached the downwind entry for
Ubon's runway 05, I recall being struck by the panorama
of white runway lights and blue taxiway lights. Slowing
below 155 knots, I dropped the gear, threw down the flaps,
and began turning right base. At that point the radios died
and the cockpit went completely black—the only docu-
mented case of complete electrical failure in the history of
the OV-10. There was no time to grab a flashlight; I simply
held the landing picture I had used a thousand times before
and let aircraft 830 settle gently on to Ubon's runway. After
I taxied in, the crew chiefs found three AK-47 bullet holes
stitched neatly across the right side of the nose compart-
ment.

It had already been a hard day's night, so I was looking
forward to some socializing and dinner at the Ubon Officers' Club. At the table next to me, a group of newly assigned pilots talked somewhat boisterously among
themselves. They had just reported to our squadron and had
yet to fly their first combat missions. Like so many before
them, the young lieutenants tried to mask their nervousness
with bravado and macho talk. Though not meaning to
eavesdrop, I couldn't help overhearing their conversation.

Their talk focused on the war and what it would be like
to go up against the highly trained and experienced North
Vietnamese antiaircraft gunners, and they speculated on
various tactics and maneuvers for avoiding the deadly flak.
Predictably, the discussion turned to Lieutenant Joe Gambino, one of my squadron mates and close friends, who had
been shot down and killed near Kompong Thom just two
days earlier—on his twenty-fourth birthday. They had
heard that Joe was one of the best, and if it could happen
to him, well. . . .

As I sat listening to the new pilots, my thoughts drifted
back to when I had first arrived in South Vietnam as a new

FAC, almost three years earlier to the day. Eager but green, just like the kids at the next table, I would have given anything to have one of the "old heads" sit down and tell me what an actual combat mission was like. I had wanted to know everything at once. At the time it had seemed vitally important to me to know if the North Vietnamese gunners actually used red and green tracer ammunition, if they truly hated FACs as we'd heard, and if captured FACs were summarily executed or tortured to death. I wanted to hear firsthand from a veteran which type of fighter aircraft dropped the most accurate ordnance, how close to friendly troops you could realistically work an air strike, and how low an FAC should fly to be really effective. And although I would have never considered asking anyone, I also wanted to know if there were tricks or gimmicks to control the fear and emotions.

After my friends and I finished dinner, I called over the young Thai waitress and ordered a Sing Ha beer. When it arrived, I took a long sip, then a deep breath, and walked over to the next table. The new guys looked up and immediately fell silent. I suspected word had gotten around that I was the instructor pilot who would train them. As an old head and the only two-tour FAC in the squadron, I had the dubious distinction of having seen lots of action. Evidently that status made me somewhat of a celebrity to some of the pilots, and perhaps certifiably crazy to the others. Regardless of what the new troops thought of me, their upturned faces radiated a strange mixture of suspicion, awe, and anticipation. Looking down at them, I felt old—at twenty-nine!

"Anybody interested in hearing a few war stories?" I asked. The faces collectively broke into wide smiles; someone scooted up an extra chair, and a barrage of questions began.

Everybody talked at once. "Tell us about the SA-7 Strella." "Do the Cambodian ground commanders speak English?" How much flying time will we get?" "What do you think is the best pattern to fly when you're working fighters?" "What happened to Joe Gambino?" "Are there restrictions on strafing with our machine guns?"

Over the din I gave the time-out sign. I chuckled to myself, recalling how I had asked similar questions as a new guy but had never received a straight answer. When it quieted down, one of the lieutenants, looking a bit more reserved than the others, asked cautiously, "I'd like to know what you think it takes for new guys like us to become combat-ready FACs?"

Good question. To myself I thought, "Time—time and the knack to anticipate the unexpected," but from my own experiences I knew the young Air Force pilots sitting around that table didn't want to hear double-talk or abstract philosophy on acquiring combat sense and judgment. They wanted practical answers in terms they could relate to, from a pilot who had been there. The only way I knew how to answer the question was by telling them what it had been like for me, three years earlier, when I stepped off the airplane in Vietnam as a nervous young lieutenant about to begin my combat tour as a forward air controller.

April 1970

INDOCTRINATION OF A ROOKIE

A gloved hand reached out and gently shook my right shoulder. Opening my eyes, I found myself staring into the boyish face of a young Air Force staff sergeant. "Sir," he said, his left hand cupped against my right ear to block out the sound of the jet engines, "the aircraft commander says we're getting ready to start our descent into Cam Ranh Bay. The jump seat's all yours if you want it."

"Thanks," I answered groggily. "Tell your boss I'll be right up as soon as I grab a cup of coffee." The young load master smiled and shuffled off in his faded green flight suit, trailing a long black cord connected to his headset and boom microphone, the other end attached somewhere inside the large C-141 jet transport aircraft.

I stood up, stretched, and took a look around the interior that had been our home for the three hours since the pre-dawn takeoff from Clark Air Base in the Philippines. Fifty or so military men sprawled sleepily in the rear-facing airliner seats. Behind the seats, toward the rear of the aircraft, three large pallets of cargo filled the remaining available space. An intricate weave of canvas webbing held the contents of each pallet neatly in position. There seemed to be boxes and crates of every size and description, all of it priority cargo headed for the war effort in South Vietnam. The fifty of us on board constituted the priority human cargo.

Standing there watching the other men sleep, I stole one last glance at the third pallet. Although it was partially obscured by the other pallets, there was no mistaking the distinctive shapes stacked three high: satin-finished aluminum military caskets. I wanted to shift my gaze, but I couldn't. The metal boxes held my eyes captive, and with no one watching me, I stared shamelessly at the third pallet. The caskets represented an abstract concept I wasn't prepared to confront, much less deal with. I was going to Vietnam as duty and honor demanded and to fulfill my childhood dream, my big adventure, my rite of passage, and my trial by fire. But buying space in one of those caskets wasn't my destiny; I could feel it. With only the slightest hesitation, I snapped out of the momentary trance, turning away from the scene as easily as I might have switched channels on a television set.

As a young Air Force pilot anxious to get into combat before the war ended, I wasn't at all sure where reality and my destiny would cross. The next few days would clarify where I would fit in. And fitting in was indeed quite problematic for those of us about to go into battle. At the macro level, the war had already ripped American society apart, and that same war had become far more about the United States than about Vietnam. Armed with ample historical precedent, our leaders had witnessed the French debacle in Indochina, and from all indications, we Americans turned a deaf ear to the warnings of French military intellectuals who eagerly pointed toward the disasters to come. While France may have glimpsed a foreshadowing of our fate, none of it filtered down to the working level—to my level. As a young pilot, I glossed over the rather murky national security policy issues and facts; my job was to fly and to fight. In the meantime, one fact *was* perfectly clear: In April 1970 there was a lot of war raging all across Vietnam. In spite of President Richard Nixon's announcement of the Vietnamization program for turning the fight back over the South Vietnamese, there were still 429,000 U.S. troops in Southeast Asia. As a forward air controller about to be stationed right in the middle of the war, I felt certain I would see my share of the fighting.

Walking toward the flight deck, my ears popped as the

cabin altitude surged, probably because the pilot had reduced power to start the en route descent into Cam Ranh
Bay. As I climbed into the jump seat between and just
behind the two pilot seats, the flight engineer handed me a
headset. When I was wired for sound, the pilot pointed to
the TACAN set and announced, "We're 180 miles out of
Cam Ranh, descending through flight level three-one-zero.
We should be on the deck in about thirty minutes. This
your first time in-country?"

Without waiting for a reply, the aircraft commander continued, "Somebody on the crew told me you're gonna be a
FAC. Sporty job. Let me be the first to welcome you to the
war."

With that, the pilot turned back to the controls and began
hand flying the big silver Starlifter toward the approach and
landing at Cam Ranh, one of the key aerial supply ports in
Southeast Asia. As we approached to within a few miles
of the runway, the high-pitched whine of the hydraulic
pumps told me the copilot must have activated the landing
gear and flap levers. Slowing to 135 knots, the pilot picked
up a two-and-a-half degree visual glide slope and deftly
planted us on the centerline of the big runway, a little over
three hours after our "oh-dark-thirty" departure from Clark
Air Base.

Waiting in the passenger terminal for my B-4 bag, I hid
my nervousness and apprehension by watching the steady
stream of soldiers, referred to as "grunts," milling around.
Most wore soiled, sweat-stained fatigues and "boonie" hats.
A few were even covered with red clay, which had dried
to dust. It was obvious they had just come in from the bush,
the infantryman's pet name for the jungle. To me, they all
looked mean and irritable. Ironically, they were leaving
Vietnam and should have looked happy. In terms of numbers, the departing troops equaled the well-dressed, well-
scrubbed new arrivals. If the scene in the passenger
terminal represented the U.S. troop drawdown, the plan was
already in trouble—I seemed to be part of a one-for-one
swap.

Within a short time, my small group of pilots linked up with a passenger service noncommissioned officer who loaded us into a fifteen-passenger van for the short ride to our temporary barracks. From there the NCO hustled us across the street to a tin and sandbag hut for administrative processing and briefings.

In a small, stuffy briefing room, the young Air Force major standing before the group of new pilots made a lasting impression. Looking professional yet relaxed, he fit my mental image of a Vietnam combat veteran—suntanned, short blond hair, a faded K-2B flight suit with subdued black rank insignia, pilot wings, and name tag. To me, the most striking visual cue of all was that he sported well-worn jungle combat boots with canvas inserts, not the plain black leather boots that marked the twenty or so of us in the briefing room as new guys and rookies. All of us felt a strange combination of envy and anxiety as we watched the major deliver his welcome briefing. In front of us stood a combat-ready forward air controller who knew what being shot at felt like, who had probably handled air strikes all over Vietnam against enemy positions just a few yards from friendly troops. Watching him stand beside the podium, I couldn't help wondering how I would react to actual combat. The bottom line was that he had been there; we hadn't. Our briefer's attitude suggested arrogance and superiority. The intimidation was unspoken but very real.

"Okay, gents," he said, hands on hips, looking supremely confident. "I know you're all tired from Jungle Survival School at Clark and from chasing women in Angeles City, but now you start earning your sixty-five-dollars-a-month combat pay. While you're here at Cam Ranh, the 504th Tactical Air Support Group will be your home. The Group owns all FACs in Southeast Asia, so after five days of indoctrination with us, we'll assign you to one of the FAC squadrons. Most of you will stay in-country with either the 19th, 20th, 21st, or 22nd Tactical Air Support Squadrons, TASS for short. A few of you lucky souls will be on your way to a hardship tour with the 23rd TASS at

Nakhon Phanom, Thailand. But before we really get into the assignment thing, let's see what you guys know about the vocabulary of the trade in South Vietnam. I just happen to have a short pop quiz for you—a real chance for you to excel."

The briefing room echoed with groans of disbelief and protest. Some major sitting near the front piped up with a very rude, "You gotta be shitting me!" The briefer flashed his best "Steve Canyon" smile and passed around mimeographed sheets. The questions, about ten of them, were actually terms for which we were to supply definitions or explanations. I knew a few of them and could guess at a few more, but on the rest I drew a complete blank. My ignorance made me laugh right out loud. If my future assignment in any way hinged on the results of the test, I was destined to spend a year in the grungiest hellhole in Vietnam. I had seen Morley Safer from CBS News broadcast from "War Zone C," but I couldn't remember exactly where it was. VNAF was easy—the South Vietnamese Air Force—but "playmate" baffled me. I knew "Panama" didn't refer to the country but had no idea what it was, and there was no telling what "QC" signified or what a "Dust-Off" was.

After the quiz we all breathed a collective sigh of relief when "Steve Canyon" informed us that it wouldn't count; we didn't have to put our names on the test. Had he stopped right there, his point—we were green and ignorant—would have been made. Instead, he looked slowly around the room for dramatic effect, then announced in deliberate, clipped words, "This little exercise was meaningless as a test. Its real purpose is to bring you prima donnas back down to earth, to take the wind out of your sails, and to prove to a bunch of cocky pilots that you really don't know as much about fighting this war as you think you do."

He lost me at that moment. Here we were, our first day in Vietnam, crammed into school desks designed for sixth graders. Our black boots were an embarrassment, and our flight suits, covered with regulation Tactical Air Command insignia and unit patches with every color of the rainbow, marked us as being right off the plane from the States. We all knew we were novices and just wanted to shed our new-guy image and blend in. The major was our bridge; he had the answers but wouldn't share them with us. As if we didn't already sense the gulf between old heads and rookies, he seemed to enjoy making us feel like FNGs—f——ing new guys.

The briefing droned on for another thirty minutes, but I tuned it out. All I could think about was getting over to Supply and drawing my jungle boots and subdued black rank and wings. Then some irrational compulsion would probably force me to find the nearest tailor shop and bribe someone to sew the insignia on while I waited. It was all very unsettling. This was my first day in a war, so how could I be so totally absorbed with something so trivial as insignia and boots? All other explanations aside, it came down to one selfish notion: I may not have been a combat veteran, but I sure wanted to look like one.

Steve Canyon was only one of many briefers we endured that day, April 19, 1970. An assortment of colonels, intelligence specialists, administrative clerks, and finance wizards trooped across the stage in succession, each intent on convincing us that his bailiwick was the real reason the war was being waged. But the grand prize for the day went to the medics. A kindly looking Air Force flight surgeon took the podium just before lunch. He had silver hair and wore gold wire-rimmed glasses. He projected a great fatherly image but seemed too old to be only a captain. While several of us commented under our breaths about how many times he'd been passed over for promotion, he turned on the 35mm projector and flashed the first slide on the screen. The room instantly fell silent. On the screen was a sickening photograph of what appeared to be a man's genitals, turned purple and literally rotting off. Slide after slide followed, each more graphic and grotesque than the one before. The flight surgeon rambled on about the social diseases rampant in Southeast Asia, but he needn't have. If ever a picture was worth a thousand words, there it was, in living color.

The doc wound up his presentation as all the other briefers had, with a slide of a gorgeous, naked, large-breasted young lady right out of the pages of *Playboy*. When the oohs and aahs died down, the doc smiled and said, "Gentlemen, this is what you're fighting for." Loud applause filled the briefing room. He continued, "If you're gonna fool around, do it with a round-eye like this. Don't get mixed up with the local Vietnamese women. When the horny factor starts to take over your intellect, try to remember the pictures I've shown you today, and then ask yourself if it's worth it. For those of you who will totally disregard the things that I've said, don't wait too long to come see us. We'll probably say we told you so, fill your ass full of penicillin, then send you back to duty." Nervous laughter greeted his prediction. He ended with, "Any questions? If not, let's break for lunch."

After the doc's show-and-tell, our appetites weren't very keen, but we gaggled over to the dining hall just to see where it was. After waiting in line for a few minutes, I was the first of the new pilots to reach the cashier table. An airman first class, obviously bored with the whole process, demanded sixty-five cents. When I handed him a crisp dollar bill, the world came crashing down. The airman turned red with anger and shouted, "Jesus Christ, what are you trying to do to me? I can't take green. Scrip! Don't you have any scrip, you know, MPC—military payment certificates?"

From the blank look on my face the airman must have sensed my dilemma. In a calm but sarcastic tone he continued the tongue-lashing. "Jesus, don't tell me you're one of the new turkeys from the 504th. We've told them a hundred times to convert your money before you clowns come to the dining hall. Why can't they get it right?"

Just as I was about to stammer out some kind of explanation, a crusty old major named Mac, who'd been with us all through the pipeline training preparing us for duty in

Southeast Asia, stepped forward. Mac scruffed his short-cropped red hair with his fist, wrinkled his forehead into a hundred deep furrows, then fixed the mouthy young airman with a glare that would have frightened Boris Karloff.

"Let us through this line right now, or I'll personally kill you where you sit. Then I'll court-martial your dead ass and send it home to your mother in body bag with a dishonorable discharge! So what's it gonna be? You gonna let us through the line, yes or no?"

The airman mumbled yes, and Mac replied, "Wise choice. Just put this on my tab." With that, we eased down the cafeteria line and loaded our trays, not out of hunger but out of spite for dining hall bureaucracy.

My first night in Vietnam was made a lot easier than I deserved. My father-in-law, Lieutenant Colonel Ken Wood, was stationed at Cam Ranh as chief of maintenance for the 483rd Tactical Airlift Wing, equipped with the C-7 Caribou. His job became a nightmare when the F-4-equipped 12th Tactical Fighter Wing packed up and went home, leaving behind all the jet-trained maintenance troops to work on reciprocating engines. In spite of the obstacles, Ken Wood was one of the best; this was his third war, and he was able to work miracles on the Cam Ranh flight line.

That night we had a quite dinner at a Navy club right on the water. After six months in Vietnam, Ken looked tired and skinny, but the old spark and constant work ethic were still there. I filled Ken in on the latest from home, and he gave me his insights into the war effort at Cam Ranh. It was the same old story—trying to keep enough airframes flying to haul the massive amounts of supplies and equipment necessary all over Vietnam. Scheduling was a guessing game because Ken never knew where or when a big supply push might be needed. The tactical situation drove the requirements, and all too often, the Viet Cong dictated the tactical situation. In a war without any defined fronts, a trouble spot could pop up anywhere in the country at any time. Ken's Caribous had to be ready to respond with the trash haulers' motto: "You call, we haul." In Vietnam, tactical airlift was critical because it was the only reliable way to avoid the very real danger of enemy ambushes along the road.

As Ken and I talked, the ocean breeze tempered the tropical heat, so all in all it was a very pleasant evening. We might have been sitting anywhere in the States having a few beers and talking over old times. But as night began to fall, the immediacy of the war crept back into my conscious thoughts. I kept thinking about one of the briefings that afternoon in which the group intelligence officer relayed a story from April 1st about several Viet Cong sappers attacking a fuel tank farm at Cam Ranh, blowing up three 10,000-gallon fuel tanks in the process. As if to play on my jitters, at frequent intervals security posts around the air base perimeter fired flares into the night sky. Each flare exploded with an audible pop and then drifted slowly to the ground, suspended under a small white parachute. The flares gave off a flickering sort of illumination, an eerie yellow, wavering cast. When the flare burned out, the area was plunged back into total darkness. At that instant it was easy for me to imagine Viet Cong sappers hiding from the light, then scurrying forward in the darkness. At any second I half-expected a firefight to erupt right in front of us. I felt almost disappointed the next morning when I realized that not a single shot had been fired overnight.

The following day, our combat indoctrination began in earnest. Since all of us came from different flying backgrounds, our instructors leveled the playing field by walking us through a brief history of forward air controlling. The basic concept of spotting enemy targets from an aircraft began during World War I, but the airborne control of aircraft delivering ordnance against tactical targets first took root during Korea. There was always a critical need to pinpoint the exact locations of both enemy and friendly troops, yet the fast-moving jets flashed by targets at a tremendous speed and were therefore unable to identify intricate details on the ground. As a result, episodes of "short rounds," or bombs dropped on our own troops, occurred all too frequently. One answer to the problem involved placing a pilot on the ground with a radio where he could see the front lines, discuss targets with the operational ground commander, then direct strike aircraft against the target. The concept worked up to a point, but there was one sizable drawback: The ground FAC was never really sure that the target he was describing was in fact the same "target" the fighter pilot saw from the air. The element of positive control was obviously missing.

The solution was relatively simple: Place a pilot in a low-flying, slow-moving aircraft and keep him in constant radio contact with both the friendly ground troops and the fighter aircraft. First tried in July 1950 using the venerable North American T-6 Texan as the aerial platform, the concept led to the establishment of the 6147th Tactical Control Group operating under the radio call sign of "Mosquito." Eventually armed with smoke rockets, small numbers of Mosquito FACs marked targets all over Korea for Air Force, Navy, and Marine Corps fighter aircraft engaging the enemy in close proximity to friendly troops.

The FAC mission came into its own during the war in Southeast Asia, and in Vietnam the FAC was a key figure in the employment of all tactical air power, serving as the controller and link between forces on the ground and strike aircraft. When air strikes went in anywhere in South Vietnam, Laos, or Cambodia, there was a high probability that the action was being controlled by a FAC flying just above the treetops to perform the mission. He was literally the airborne eyes, ears, and strategist of the tactical battlefield, often making critical decisions that determined the very nature and outcome of the battle. Even more amazing, in most cases the FAC was a young lieutenant on his first operational assignment after graduating from pilot training!

U.S. Air Force involvement first began in February 1962 with the covert introduction of FACs dispatched to Vietnam as advisors under the code name JUNGLE JIM. Later changed to FARM GATE, the program was gradually replaced by a full-scale deployment of FACs dedicated to specific U.S. Army units as the American troop buildup kicked off in 1965.

As we listened to the briefing, each of us in the room, sitting in our sixth-grade desks, began searching the faces of our fellow pilots for any hint of reaction when the teachers touched on two subjects. First, it was clear that a hierarchy had been established. The Army demanded that FACs supporting its units had to be fighter pilots. Obligingly, the Air Force poked bunches of us through a fighter lead-in program, blessed us as fighter pilots, and anointed us with the coveted "A" FAC designation. In contrast, a non-fighter-qualified pilot was designated as a "B" FAC, and was only allowed to work close air support missions with Allied forces—primarily ARVN or Korean troops. In reality there wasn't a bit of difference, but the bureaucracy won out by continuing to apply a silly rule whose original intent had been lost in the haze of time.

While a few of the new FACs squirmed slightly at the mention of the "B" FAC designation, all of us squirmed noticeably with the introduction of the second topic. Since FACs flew so low, slow, and so often, per capita they drew more continuous ground fire than almost any other Americans in the war, and because of the increased exposure, their aircraft took lots of hits. Even more sobering was the statistic on losses. The FAC casualty rate was staggering in comparison to other Air Force unit losses. Trying to absorb the message, we all looked at each other in a new light. While each of us thought he was invincible, we had to face the fact that quite a few other pilots sitting in the briefing room would never make it home.

During the afternoon session, we were briefed on how FACs had worked with the famous 101st Airborne Division during the assault on Hamburger Hill, located in I Corps's infamous A Shau Valley. We learned about the heavy enemy infiltration and bloody fighting going on in the Central Highlands of II Corps. Key battles around Kontum, Pleiku, Dak To, Ben Het and Kham Duc always involved savage action for our troops on the ground—and for their FACs.

Next, we found out about the frustrating battles raging in III Corps's War Zone C, where enemy troops retreated across the border at will to sanctuaries in Cambodia. We also heard about the activities in IV Corps—known to everyone as "The Delta"—where seesaw battles around places like Can Tho, Ben Tri, and Vinh Long tested American nerve and courage on a daily basis. Finally, we held our collective breath as the briefer described incredibly dangerous FAC missions just above the Demilitarized Zone in a section of North Vietnam designated "Route Package One." The area was simply referred to as "Tally Ho."

With so much to learn and so little time, our teachers at the 504th used the firehose approach: They stuck the nozzle down our throats and turned the flow up full blast, hoping we'd retain enough of the information to be effective—and to survive.

Four days later, resplendent in our new jungle boots and subdued insignia, twenty of us took our customary seats at the sixth-grade desks in the now-familiar briefing room. Rumor had it that the powers that be had finally decided on our assignments. We weren't sure that the powers had given it much thought, but we mortals had kicked it around a great deal, especially over cold beers at the bar.

Our small group ranged in rank from second lieutenants to one lieutenant colonel, with a few first lieutenants, captains, and majors thrown in. We had been in training together for a long time, in some cases over eight months. Most of us had started as fledgling fighter jocks in the 27th Tactical Fighter Wing at Cannon Air Force Base, New Mexico. From there we had moved on to Hurlburt Field, Florida, for FAC training in our assigned aircraft: the O-1 Bird Dog, the O-2 Skymaster, or the OV-10 Bronco. After completing Jungle Survival School at Clark Air Base in the Philippines, we were about to split up and go our separate ways. We each hoped a few of us would stay together, but we were ready to take whatever came—as long as we got our first-choice assignment!

Each of us had his own idea about the perfect FAC job.

I desperately wanted to fly in III Corps with the famous 25th Infantry Division, known throughout the Pacific as "Tropic Lightning." My second choice was to fly for the Americal, the 23rd Infantry Division at Chu Lai in I Corps. In the FAC community, the Americal had a reputation for being hard-nosed, tough fighters, always in the thick of something—which meant lots of action for their FACs. Unfortunately, the tragedy at My Lai had tarnished the Americal's otherwise outstanding combat record, which stretched back to Guadalcanal during World War II.

In either case I would be assigned the classic FAC mission of directly supporting the Army. It would be a steady diet of visual reconnaissance, close air support, and the ultimate challenge: troops in contact, where the FAC controlled air strikes in the immediate vicinity of friendly forces. My strong attachment to the Army probably stemmed from my own background as an Army brat. My father was a retired colonel and, in my estimation, one of the most dedicated officers in the U.S. Army. My younger brother was an active duty grunt lieutenant with the 82nd Airborne Division at Fort Bragg, so my empathy for the troops on the ground was genuine if not obvious. Additionally, the rules specified that FACs supporting U.S. troops had to be fighter pilots, and as one of the few young fighter-qualified jocks available, I thought getting one of my choices was a shoo-in.

Virtually our entire group agreed on one thing. We didn't particularly aspire to jobs with the 20th TASS "Coveys" or the 23rd TASS "Nails." Those squadrons flew a special FAC mission called SCAR—strike control and reconnaissance. The mission was interesting, but where they flew it was unsettling. Coveys and Nails flew over the Ho Chi Minh Trail in Laos, interdicting supplies being shipped south along a twisting network of dirt roads and paths. Laos, best described by Bernard Fall as a "political convenience," had become a quagmire of intrigue as various factions within Premier Souvanna Phouma's Royal Lao government vied for power. In that vacuum, the North Vietnamese and the Laotian Communist Pathet Lao virtually owned the Trail from North Vietnam south through Laos and into Cambodia. Their logistics infrastructure included 100,000 troops. Consequently, there were no "friendlies" on the Trail, no close air support, and no troops in contact. It was a secret war over one of the most remote areas of the world—and it was brimming with weapons. The ground fire in South Vietnam, where pilots flew through a hail of small arms and automatic weapons fire, was plenty dangerous, as loss rates showed. But in Laos, low-flying, slow-moving FACs not only flew against deadly concentrations of small arms and machine guns, but they also faced the same big guns that defended Hanoi: murderously accurate 23mm, 37mm, and 57mm antiaircraft artillery—"triple A" for short. The stakes for Covey and Nail FACs rose dramatically with the termination of Operation Rolling Thunder in 1968, which virtually ended U.S. bombing in North Vietnam. Safe from that threat, the NVA simply moved two thousand of their triple A weapons from the North to locations along the Ho Chi Minh Trail. A single round from any one of them could blow an aircraft to bits—and from what we heard, the gunners on the Trail had plenty of ammunition.

The Trail just wasn't my idea of a good time. On top of that, the Coveys at Da Nang lived on a virtual ground zero, with the VC lobbing rockets indiscriminately into the base at regular intervals. Da Nang came by its nickname honestly—Rocket City.

The rumor mill had been correct—our assignments were firm. Our old friend Steve Canyon did the honors, dutifully reading off each man's assignment in rank order. When he got to me, I heard no sound at all but simply stared in abject disappointment as his lips formed the words "20th TASS, Covey Da Nang."

That afternoon I hurriedly packed, all the while trying to convince myself to make the best of a situation I considered patently unfair. I managed a quick call to my father-in-law and a brief goodbye to my buddies who were scattering to every corner of Vietnam. By late afternoon six of us had thrown our B-4 bags into the back of a C-130 transport and were airborne on the two-hundred-mile flight north to Da Nang, the second largest city in Vietnam, situated just seventy miles south of the demilitarized zone along the 17th parallel—the infamous DMZ.

The name Da Nang really applied only to the old Vietnamese city of Tourane, but the name was commonly used for everything in the surrounding area. Starting with the big U.S. buildup in 1965, Da Nang had mushroomed into a sprawling series of military installations clustered around the port facilities and the two long north-south runways. The Marines and the Military Airlift Command's aerial port occupied the west side of the airfield, while a conglomeration of ARVN, Special Forces, and Navy units were packed onto the two-mile-wide spit of land between China Beach and the I Corps bridges. Air Force units operated from the area immediately adjacent to the east runway. The largest outfit, the F-4-equipped Gunfighters of the 366th Tactical Fighter Wing, owned most of the real estate, but 20th TASS had carved out a nice chunk of land occupying the northern section along the east runway.

The Coveys, so named because of their radio call sign, lived in an old French area of the base known as the main compound. Surrounded by high walls, the buildings were right out of *Beau Geste*, with tile roofs and thick, white stucco walls. The Covey FACs occupied the second floor of the large H-shaped building just inside the compound gate, while the "Jolly Green" rescue helicopter pilots shared the ground floor with a detachment of A-1 pilots from the 56th Special Operations Wing. The main compound also housed a dining hall, small theater, post office, officers' club, nurses' quarters, and a number of trailers that housed the senior officers. Such was the setup that greeted me on April 23, 1970.

My accommodations in the Covey hooch were nothing to write home about: a small ten-by-twelve bare room with no windows, one desk, two metal wall lockers, and a set of bunk beds, all painted gray. The similarity to a prison cell was unmistakable. As a first lieutenant about to make captain, I technically outranked my new second lieutenant roommate, but since he had arrived two weeks earlier, according to the "newbie" pecking order and the law of the jungle, I inherited the top bunk.

My roomie turned out to be an interesting character who talked constantly and came across as a bit of a blowhard. He had already flown two or three combat training missions, which, in his mind, entitled him to link himself with the in crowd of old heads, throwing around insider terms and saying things like "we do this on a mission" or "we've found it best to do that." He seemed just a little too sure of himself, and within two days it was obvious the veterans had no use for either of us until we could pull our own weight as combat-ready FACs.

It took only a few more days to decide I didn't want to spend my entire tour with this guy. Besides the incessant talking, two other things about Roomie bothered me. First, when sitting around in the barracks, most of us wore our flight suits or just our underwear. Not my roomie; he always wore faded Levis and a white T-shirt with a pack of cigarettes rolled up in the sleeve. He was harmless enough but looked for all the world like a hood out of *West Side Story*.

My second gripe involved noise. Roomie had just bought himself a brand new Akai tape deck, which he played at full volume. And he played only one song, Creedence Clearwater Revival's "Proud Mary." Now, I was a devoted CCR fan and had spent many happy hours at the Eglin Beach Club rocking the night away with my wife while a local band valiantly tried to imitate John Fogerty and the real CCR, so Roomie's choice of music was no problem. The kicker was that he insisted on running the volume up to the point where the eardrums bled, then he would back off a decibel to show how considerate he was. I would come strolling into the room only to be flattened by the sound ricocheting off the four walls, and when I complained, Roomie couldn't hear me. Polite requests and irrefutable logic had no effect, so I was forced to take drastic action. Using my best Major Mac glare, I yelled, "Turn that damned thing down right now or I'll kill you where you sit. If you think I'm bluffing, just try me!" The shocked expression on Roomie's face quickly turned into a pout, his lower lip poking out like a small child's. I had to turn away to keep from laughing, but Roomie obediently cranked the volume down and left it down.

Things settled into an all too familiar routine of in-processing and administrative briefings. Each day I'd watch the other Coveys go out to fly combat missions while I remained behind, filling out one bureaucratic form after another. Yet a few of those forms provided their own adrenaline rush and struck me as being downright provocative, as well as somewhat unnerving. On the "Escape and Evasion" form I had to provide a series of personalized questions and answers designed for use in case I was ever shot down. In order for the rescue pilot to confirm that he was indeed talking to the right person on the ground, he would ask one or more of my previously supplied questions: "What's the name of you family cat?" To which I would answer over the survival radio. "Fluffy," thus verifying my identity. The second form was even more troubling. I was required to present Air Force Form 137 to the flight surgeon who placed the document on the floor, inked the bottoms of my bare feet, then had me stand on it. The object of this morbid little exercise was to provide a footprint for identification purposes, since after a crash, the soles of the pilot's feet were often the only identifiable parts remaining.

Somewhat surprisingly, the grisly subject matter of the forms only whetted my appetite to find out from the pros what really transpired on a Covey mission. In my mind the aura surrounding the combat veteran Coveys imbued them with genuine hero status. But when I tried to draw the old heads out on what it felt like to fly against the big guns on the Ho Chi Minh Trail, they'd respond with an amazingly similar refrain: "Oh, you'll get all that during your checkout. Right now, just enjoy the time off while you can."

The Covey intelligence officer was a little more talkative. Since he wasn't a pilot, he couldn't supply the stick-and-rudder perspective; he was, however, very helpful with background information. One afternoon following an aircrew briefing, the intel officer sat down with me and launched into a thumbnail sketch of the operation. He explained that the very unconventional air war over Southeast Asia had produced some strange but very effective hybrids. One of the many innovative ideas used in the Vietnam War was the introduction of the FAC into the politically sensitive command-and-control system in Laos. Because of the murky political-military situation there, the restrictions on U.S. bombing seemed to outnumber the people. Known as rules of engagement, or ROE, these dos and don'ts were so convoluted that nobody could understand them, much less apply them. Evidently many higher-ups in the Air Force felt that the former American ambassador to Laos, William Sullivan, a hard-nosed infighter who was paranoid about maintaining absolute control over the military in "neutral" Laos, was directly responsible for creating the mess. The Sullivan influenced bureaucrats had devised some real doozies: You could drop bombs only within two hundred meters of a major line of communication—a road, trail, or river; you could not fire unless the enemy fired first; pagodas couldn't be bombed, even though the North Vietnamese Army's 316th Division had its headquarters in one. Frustrated Air Force and Navy fighter pilots rightfully felt hamstrung as a result of all the restrictions promulgated by all the verbalized jitters and "what ifs" some nervous straphanger had dutifully recorded as ROE.

Enter the FAC. To regain control of an admittedly tough situation, USAF commanders inaugurated a program in which FACs flew daily missions over designated sectors of the Ho Chi Minh Trail. The FAC became the on-scene strike controller and referee. With firsthand insights into the situation, the FAC, orbiting above the target in his slow-moving aircraft, could work out the political kinks of the air strike through direct radio contact with Laotian ground commanders and with the U.S. Embassy in Vientiane. The program worked so well that, beginning in 1968, planners devised Commando Hunt operations, an air campaign designed to place a constant air umbrella over the roughly two-thousand-square-mile sector of the Trail contiguous to South Vietnam. That section of roads running down the southern Laotian panhandle was codenamed "Steel Tiger," and the Da Nang Coveys were one of the FAC units assigned to work Steel Tiger around the clock, with the OV-10 Broncos handling the day duty and the Cessna O-2s fighting the battle at night. With the NVA capable of moving thousands of troops a month down the Trail, along with supplies to support them, the FACs definitely had their work cut out for them.

After hearing the intel officer's story, I was ready to go and itching to get back into an OV-10 after a six-week layoff. Finally, on April 28, I flew the first of four local refresher rides with a squadron instructor pilot (IP).

Until then I had compiled a grand total of forty-three hours in the OV-10, so I wasn't a pro by any stretch of the imagination. All of the new local procedures, coupled with my own rustiness from lack of stick time, made the need for going up with an IP to work out the kinks painfully clear. Fortunately, my instructor pilot for the day, Captain John Tait, a West Point graduate who had taken his commission in the Air Force, was a patient soul with lots of empathy for new beans like me.

As John and I walked up to the sandbag-and-metal revetment sheltering our assigned aircraft, number 654, he gave me some advice on the plane's aerodynamics: "Take a good look at this little beauty in the clean configuration. You won't see her that way often, much less fly her that way. The bird is sleek looking today, just like you flew in training back at Hurlburt. But within a week you'll be flying her loaded down with a 230-gallon centerline fuel tank and all kinds of rocket pods. With all that stuff hanging, the frontal drag is tremendous. It'll be like switching from a sports car to a truck."

I was hanging on John's every word while drinking in

the view of the machine I was about to spend the next year
flying and fighting in. The Bronco was a relatively new
aircraft, first flown in 1967. That made it all the more appealing to me. Originally designed as a counterinsurgency
light attack aircraft, the OV-10 entered the Air Force inventory in the forward air controller mode in April 1969.
With its twin turboprop engines, four machine guns, ejection seat, and great cockpit visibility, the Bronco was a
perfect addition to the FAC inventory. For me, being able
to fly the OV-10 was like a dream come true.

The Bronco was deceptively large, measuring forty-one
feet long, fifteen feet high, and sporting a forty-foot wingspan. Sitting on the ramp in its gray war paint, the OV-10
conjured up two vivid memories for me. First, it looked
mean, like a praying mantis about to spring. Second, with
the fuselage and cockpit suspended between twin booms
and twin tails, it reminded me of the legendary P-38 Lightning of World War II fame. As a kid, I had devoured every
airplane book in the libraries, and some of my favorite stories were about the exploits of the P-38 pilots of the Southwest Pacific, men like Dick Bong, Tom Lynch, Tom
McGuire, and Tom Lanphier and his incredible interception
and shoot-down of Admiral Isoroku Yamamoto. I used to
fantasize that it was more than mere coincidence that I
shared the same first name with most of them and that there
was a direct link flowing from past to present. But the tangible link lay in the similarity between the two airplanes. I
may have been born too late to fly the P-38, but the OV-10
was all mine, and it was a love affair from the beginning.

John Tait introduced me to the line chief and to several
of the crew chiefs. He didn't make a big deal about doing
it, but the gesture told me a lot about John and his respect
for the hard-working maintenance troops. I made a mental
note to copy John's style of talking to the crew chiefs often
and of sharing a few details about the missions.

The moment had finally arrived. Following a lengthy
preflight, I strapped into the front ejection seat while John
did the same in back. Fumbling around with the maze of

switches and controls, I silently chided myself for being so nervous, as sweat poured off me in buckets. I wanted to get off on the right foot with John and to make a good impression on him. My future reputation in the squadron might well hinge on whether John Tait thought I was a good prospect or a doofus klutz.

After running through the rest of the checklist, I signaled the crew chief by extending my right index finger in a twirling motion. He repeated the signal, so in sequence I cranked the right, then the left Garrett turboprop engines. As the engines spooled up to speed, I kept watching the young crew chief and the CO_2 fire extinguisher he held. For some crazy reason I caught myself thinking about a conversation I had heard two days earlier between two old heads. The gist was that if an engine caught on fire during start-up, the pilot was pretty much on his own. Rumor had it that most of the extinguishers were only half-charged because the young maintenance troops used them to cool down hot cases of beer. Fortunately, both of 654's engines cranked perfectly, so I released the brakes and we taxied out of the revetment area and within minutes were airborne.

Using my new call sign, Covey 221, I checked in with "Panama," Da Nang's tactical radar control center. We started a climbing turn to the east, which carried us across the narrow strip of land between the runway and the beach. There wasn't much opportunity for sightseeing though: My head was on a swivel because the air was filled with every conceivable size and shape of aircraft. I counted at least a dozen helicopters in the immediate area, all swarming around like bees at a hive. A flight of F-4 Phantoms arched gracefully in front of me, leaving an exhaust trail of black smoke visible from ten miles away. The MIG pilots up north didn't need good eyes; the Phantom's black smoke was a dead giveaway. Sandwiched in among all those war birds, a C-7 Caribou at my altitude droned slowly south along the coastline, and an O-2 slightly below me cruised in directly over the twin spans of the I Corps bridges. I asked John over the intercom, "Is it always this crowded?" As he keyed his intercom button, I watched in the mirror as he nodded yes.

"That's one thing you'll have to get used to about Da Nang. You've really got to stay alert with all this traffic. But it's not always this bad. Check your clock." Puzzled, I glanced at the instrument panel. It was about 12:10. John smiled and continued. "Lunch time. Everybody comes back into the pattern at once. We must be having something really good at the dining hall today. Hell of a way to fight a war, isn't it?"

Climbing through fifteen hundred feet, we crossed the coast and went "feet wet," the radio term used to signify that we were flying over the warm waters of the South China Sea. In one of our intel briefings, the briefer had solemnly advised us that, given a choice, a feet-wet bailout was preferable to one over dry land, because there were "no bad guys to speak of, and no ground fire. It makes for an easy helicopter rescue." As I thought about his advice and looked down into that incredibly blue water, I wondered about sharks.

It was a perfect day for flying. Visibility was clear and a million miles in bright dazzling sunshine. In our sector there wasn't a cloud in the sky. Far to the east I could see a squall line moving toward shore, and by late afternoon a few of those cells would top forty thousand feet, but at the moment, they were no threat to us. All I could think about was how great it was going to be to go upside down again and pull Gs. When we were about ten miles off the coast, John seemed to read my mind. "Okay, Tom, I know it's been a while. Go ahead and wring her out. Just don't break anything." He didn't have to say it twice. I rolled the aircraft inverted into a split-S and off we went. Coming out at the bottom of the maneuver, heading in the opposite direction and doing well over 250 knots, I sucked in four Gs and pulled us up into a loop. As we zoomed straight up through the vertical, I tipped my head back to pick up the horizon, then eased the OV-10 over the top on her back, using the inverted horizon as a reference to keep the wings level. Coming down the back side, I fed in the back pressure with just a little too much "ham fist," causing a mild bucking action called a buffet or burble, the airplane's aerodynamic way of telling me to ease off the Gs or we'd go into an accelerated stall. At the bottom of the loop it felt too good to stop, so I pulled us right back up into a Cuban eight, followed by all four leaves of a clover leaf, and finished off the series with an Immelman. Reluctantly, I had to give in when John insisted we get on with the profile. I demonstrated a traffic pattern stall series and some slow flight, then we headed back to Da Nang for some practice instrument work.

As we coasted back toward Da Nang Bay, I spotted a lone O-2 about a mile to my left on a parallel course but slightly lower. It was the perfect setup for an old-fashioned bounce. Briefly, I considered the wisdom of showing my fanny on my first ride, but on the other hand, the IP might think less of me for not being aggressive. Mind made up, I dropped behind the O-2 and closed in from his six o'clock position. Closing in for the kill, I couldn't be sure if my "victim" had ever "rat raced" before—he might embarrass me big time. But at Hurlburt I had hassled with a few O-2s, and although they could be a handful with the right pilot at the controls, they were generally no match for the OV-10. Known affectionately as the "Oscar Deuce," the O-2 was essentially the military version of the Cessna Skymaster, a light aircraft with one 210-horsepower recip engine in the front and another at the rear. Among some O-2 jocks, the unique engine placement spawned another nickname, "Suck and Blow."

As I pulled up beside my target, I could see it wasn't a FAC-configured O-2 but rather the psychological warfare version equipped with a vent for dumping propaganda leaflets over the enemy and with a loudspeaker for audio appeals for enemy troops to defect to the South. Throughout Southeast Asia, everybody referred to them as "bullshit bombers."

John must have known what I had in mind, but he never said a word. He simply watched intently as we slipped into a wide route position beside the O-2. I waggled my wings to get his attention, and when the pilot looked at me, I started the rat race by executing a barrel roll over the top of him. Watching from the inverted position out the top of my canopy, I knew he had played the game before when he pitched out into a hard left bank and dived for the deck. I dished out the bottom of the barrel roll at full power and closed the distance between us in no time.

The O-2 jock responded by performing a series of abrupt clearing turns called a scissors maneuver, first to the right, then back to the left. Rather than match him move for move, I hung back several hundred feet and just below him, safely tucked into his natural blind spot. Each turn finally became less severe until the O-2 gradually settled into wings-level flight. Dumb. The guy didn't deserve to be let off the hook, so I moved directly in trail with my gunsight pipper superimposed on his rear engine. Switching my radio to Guard emergency transmit, I blasted him with a loud "tac-tac-tac-tac-tac," simulating machine-gun fire. Everyone listening to Guard frequency instantly recognized the sound and probably chuckled at the humiliation they knew the bounced pilot must be feeling. When I moved back into a route position off his left wing, we had a clear view of the pilot staring at us, but I couldn't see his eyes because his dark visor was down. A boom microphone attached to his helmet partially hid his moving lips, but it didn't take a genius to figure out what he must have been muttering. As confirmation of his bad mood, the O-2 jock pressed his gloved left hand, middle finger extended, against the window, then rolled into a gentle right bank for his unceremonious departure from the scene.

With the fun and games over, John and I pressed on with the rest of the training mission. For starters, Da Nang Approach Control cleared me for a straight-in TACAN approach to Runway 17 Left. I was supposed to fly strictly on instruments while John kept a sharp eye out for other traffic, but that was harder to do than it sounds. Sitting in the front cockpit, focusing on instruments and concentrating on my crosscheck, I could still see everything going on around us through my peripheral vision. I couldn't resist peeking as two helicopters crossed my final approach course. Then John warned me about a VNAF A-37 turning final in front of me. Just when the distractions were about to drive me into a fit of frustration, Approach Control sent us around for two F-4s behind us who had declared emergency fuel.

The same sort of thing happened on a radar approach. The controller finally broke me off at two miles from touchdown. As the controller radar vectored us away from the field, John explained that Da Nang was the busiest airport in the world, with more takeoffs and landings each year than Chicago O'Hare. We decided to give it one last try. Finally, we got clearance back to the beacon for an ADF approach. I screwed up the holding pattern entry royally, but eventually we managed to shoot the published approach all the way to a touch-and-go landing. Rather than press our luck, we stayed in the closed pattern for six more touch-and-goes. After the novelty of the first few wore off, I mentioned to John that the takeoff roll seemed a little too long and the plane felt sluggish at lift-off. With just the slightest edge in his voice, John explained, "You're not in that balmy weather at Hurlburt. Runway temperature here is over one hundred degrees, so the engines aren't cranking out as much shaft horsepower. Accept the longer takeoff roll, and let her get a few more knots before you lift off. Just wait till you fly this baby at max gross weight. The roll is so long you've got time to sing all four verses of the Air Force song." Embarrassed at not having thought about the effects of high temperature, I let the subject drop. John took the full-stop landing, and we taxied back to the Covey revetments.

When we climbed out of the cockpit, I was soaking wet and really tired. John looked fresh; his hair wasn't even messed up. He must have seen the expression on my face because as we walked back to operations to debrief the ride, John told me, "You should carry some water with you. I use a baby bottle, but anything unbreakable will do. This heat will really dehydrate you fast, so take a few big gulps now and then and you won't get so worn out." I never flew another mission without a baby bottle full of water.

May

FLYING OVER THE HO CHI MINH TRAIL

On the first of May I flew a morning training mission with John Tait. We had concentrated on the basics yet, for some reason, my flying had been sloppier than on our ride three days earlier. After the flight, as I sat listening to John recite the litany of my mistakes and foul-ups, another IP came crashing into the room.

In an excited voice, he asked, "Hey, did you guys hear the news? Armed Forces Radio just announced we've invaded Cambodia. It's about damn time. Now we start kicking ass and taking names!"

The IP's enthusiasm wasn't because of the invasion itself, or the associated fighting and dying. It had more to do with a feeling of relief and a sense of fair play. Finally, old nagging frustrations would give way to a surge of optimism. No longer would U.S. troops in War Zone C be forced to fight with one hand tied behind their backs. The political wall protecting the enemy in his Cambodian sanctuary had been shattered and, for the first time in the war, American ground forces had been allowed to attack in strength across an international border in order to destroy NVA base camps and supply caches. For the first time, there was no place for the bad guys to hide. Units from the 1st Air Cavalry Division; the 4th, 9th, and 25th Infantry Divisions; and the 101st Airborne Division could take the fight to the enemy right in his own private game preserve.

President Nixon's decision to cross the border was a bold one and a radical departure from the previous administration's hands-off policy on sanctuaries. Of course, the

political climate had shifted dramatically in mid March
when General Lon Nol had ousted neutralist Prince Siha-
nouk, opening the way for the U.S. incursion. Militarily,
the decision gave a big boost to the morale of U.S. troops
and gave fair warning to Hanoi that the American president
meant to give his Vietnamization program every chance of
working.

For the Coveys, the Cambodian incursion was welcome
news. As the man said, it was about time our side could
kick ass. Of more immediate concern, the invasion of the
Cambodian sanctuary meant that Laos became the only
route the North Vietnamese could use to infiltrate troops
and supplies south. Business on the Trail was bound to pick
up.

That same afternoon, armed with a new sense of urgency, I flew an ordnance training mission with Major
Norm Edgar. For the afternoon go, Norm and I headed for
a deserted rock in the ocean about fifteen miles east of Da
Nang. We were armed with four LAU-59 rocket pods, each
containing seven white phosphorous rockets. Called "willie
pete" for short, these rockets were the stock-in-trade of the
FAC. When a willie pete detonated on the ground, the
white-hot lethal explosion produced a large snow-white
cloud of smoke easily visible to fighter aircraft circling the
target area. If a FAC sang out, "Hit my smoke," the orbiting
fighters knew exactly where to put their bombs. If the
rocket was a little off, the FAC gave a correction, such as,
"Hit fifty meters west of my smoke." In such a case, frame
of reference became the toughest variable. To the FAC flying at two thousand feet above the ground, fifty meters was
a clear and definite measurement. Besides, it was his yardstick. For the fighter pilots circling the target at twelve
thousand feet, however, fifty meters was an indistinguish-
able blur, at best a "wag"—a wild ass guess. If the FAC
really wanted to get good bombs from the fighters, he
would pick some ground object, regardless of its actual
size, and make that his base reference. "Okay, Gunfighter
Flight, see that straight stretch of north-south road just east

of the target? I'm calling that road ten meters wide. Put your bombs fifty meters west of my smoke." From the cockpit of Gunfighter Lead's F-4, the road might look like a pencil line on the ground, but he could now imagine five pencil lines west of the willie pete, and he would be right on the FAC's target.

As we approached the island, I carefully set my switches on the armament panel and turned on the gunsight. In the mirror I could see Norm looking around the back of my ejection seat to make sure I had the switches in the correct position. In plenty of cases, an eager student had inadvertently set the toggle switch to "drop" instead of "fire." Any IP would feel sick when the stud in the front seat had a good run on the target and squeezed off that first rocket, only to have the whole pod drop off the bottom of the plane. I wasn't about to let that happen.

The switches were good, so I rolled in on the first pass. Once established in a forty-five-degree dive angle, I placed the gunsight pipper below the target and let it track up to the outcropping. When the pipper was superimposed on the target, I quickly confirmed that the ball in the turn and slip indicator was centered, then fired the rocket and pulled the stick back into my lap in a healthy four-G pull-off. Everything felt right on the pass, so I was pleased but not surprised when the willie pete hit the target dead center. Norm grunted a little under the G forces but came on the intercom with, "Not bad. Can you do it again without a long setup? Keep pulling her up through the vertical, then whifferdill right back down for a second shot while the bad guys are reloading."

After coming over the top inverted, I rudder-rolled her right side up and made a couple of coarse stick-and-rudder corrections to put the pipper back where I wanted it. I fired number two and pulled off. Beautiful! Another direct hit. Laughing, I asked Norm, "Any other questions?" He laughed too, seeming to enjoy my success as much as I did.

We attacked the rock repeatedly, trying different tactics and dive angles on each pass. Norm seemed to know a hundred different tricks and techniques, including a "stand off" lob from several miles away or a curvilinear approach to the target where the aircraft never traveled in a straight line. Norm hinted that in high threat antiaircraft areas, like the Ho Chi Minh Trail, such tactics could mean the difference between life and death for the slow-moving, vulnerable FAC. I was more than willing to take his word for it.

Finally, he took the aircraft and announced, "Now we get serious. Loser buys the beer tonight." In the OV-10 the backseater couldn't fire ordnance, so we went over the procedures. Norm would do the flying and when he gave me the signal, I would fire the rocket for him. As I watched intently from the front seat, Norm set up the pass. We were tracking nicely when he came on the intercom: "Ready, ready, fire!" I squeezed the pickle button on my stick, and the rocket roared away, impacting on target just a few feet left of center. It was a remarkable shot, especially since Norm had no forward visibility to speak of and no gunsight. He was using the old "TLAR" method—that looks about right. Then it was my turn. The way my blind luck had been running, I just knew I had him. Sure enough, my rocket went right down the stovepipe. It was a great feeling, particularly after my less-than-sterling performance earlier in the day. As we cruised back to Da Nang, I could already taste that ice-cold beer.

I completed the phase 1 refresher checkout with a night sortie the following evening. The flight consisted of flare drops and night rocket firings followed by some touch-and-go landings. The mission was uneventful until we returned to the Da Nang traffic pattern, where I saw my first ground fire. For some reason, Da Nang tower had us enter downwind on the west side of the field, about a mile in trail behind an O-2. All I could see were his position lights and his red rotating beacon. Suddenly, two distinct streams of tracers arched up out of the darkness at the unsuspecting Oscar Deuce. The sight of the bullets made my pulse shift into high gear. I thought to myself, "This is the real thing. This is a shooting war, and I'm actually in it!" At that moment I experienced strong feelings of excitement and dread, but the sensation had a mystical, detached quality about it, not at all unpleasant or unnerving. Then the sound of my IP's voice brought me back to the present.

"Did you hear what I said? Those idiots are shooting at us. Turn off the goddamn lights!" Barely stopping for breath, he screamed over the radio, "O-2 on right downwind, you're taking ground fire. Break hard left." Without having to be told again, I immediately turned off all our outside lights. For some unknown reason, the O-2 continued to drone on straight and level, drawing several more long bursts from his assailants on the ground. My instructor was livid. "That stupid SOB must have his head up and locked. Look at him just fly through the stuff like he was on a picnic." I was about to chime in with an agreement when the IP clicked the mike button. "Tower, that O-2 getting ready to turn final just got hosed by about a hundred rounds of M16 fire from the Marine compound. You better get on the horn and tell those morons to knock it off."

After a short pause, the tower responded, "Roger. We'll notify Gunfighter Operations. They'll have to relay the protest, not us."

I couldn't believe what I was hearing. Over the intercom I asked the instructor, "You mean those are our own people firing at us? What kind of games are they playing?"

His voice heavy with disgust, he answered, "What makes me so mad is that this isn't the first time it's happened. Periodically those dudes get all liquored up and try their hand at night target practice against aircraft in the pattern. It's a good thing they're probably drunk, or we'd really be in a world of hurt."

With nothing to prove by staying in the shooting gallery, I told the tower we were breaking out and reentering the traffic pattern for the other runway. We completed our touch-and-goes on the east runway without incident. Initially, I considered the episode my baptism of fire. It was my first time under the gun, and I hadn't panicked or become flustered. But it wouldn't sell—they weren't really firing at me. And besides, I didn't want my initiation to come from my own troops shooting at me.

Since I had over 750 hours total flying time, the squadron considered me to be a high-time pilot. For that reason, my phase II checkout was the short version, consisting of two back-seat rides watching old heads work the Trail and four front-seat rides under the watchful eye of an IP. If all went well, I would get a final check ride and be certified as combat ready. My first chance to fly an actual mission over the infamous Ho Chi Minh Trail came on May 5, when I jumped into the back seat of First Lieutenant Homer Pressley's OV-10.

Homer was from Alabama and had an easygoing approach to almost everything. He was a super pilot and one of the most experienced Coveys. I couldn't have teamed up with a better role model. Unfortunately, Homer's best efforts couldn't make up for the miserable time I had in his back seat.

First there was the constant "jinking" to throw off any North Vietnamese gunners who might have been trying to aim at us. Homer abruptly changed directions and altitude more times than I care to remember. Most pilots pride themselves on maintaining perfectly coordinated flight, but on the Trail, that kind of predictable flying could get you killed in a hurry. So we went through an endless succession of skidding or slipping turns, climbs, and dives. We must have exceeded the wildest expectations of any gunners watching, because they didn't fire a shot.

The jinking was bad enough, but when coupled with constantly looking at the ground through high-powered binoculars, the effect was almost nauseating. As I intently watched the road four thousand feet below, Homer caught me off guard more than once with an unexpected reversal of direction. In all its magnified glory, the lush Laotian jungle rushed past my field of vision, producing uncontrollable waves of dizziness. Up until then, I had never been airsick in my life, but Homer's jinking was about to do me in. The sensation was totally miserable, and I would have been just as happy to cruise straight and level and let the enemy gunners have at us.

Just when I thought I couldn't stand another second of the roller coaster ride, something on the ground caught Homer Pressley's attention. "Tom, I think we got something. See that football-shaped clump of trees just south of where the road forks? We just may have ourselves a couple of trucks." Using Homer's directions, I focused on the target. The trucks weren't clearly visible to me at first, but then I made out the straight lines of the bed and the unmistakable shape of the cab—two camouflaged trucks deep in the shadows along the tree line. The lingering dizziness was gone in an instant. As Homer checked the map coordinates, I picked out two more shapes. Trying to cover my excitement, I nonchalantly announced my discovery. Homer shot back, "Good peepers. With eyes like that, you're gonna be a natural in this business."

Within minutes, two flights of F-4s carrying five-hundred-pound MK-82 bombs rendezvoused with us. Homer gave them the standard briefing, and before I could digest it all, the strike was on. With the fighters covering us, Homer rolled in and put a willie pete right into the tree line. Flight Lead called in from the north, but I never saw him until he pulled off. The next instant all eight MK-82s went off around Homer's mark. The explosions and concussion waves were tremendous. I was totally enthralled, having never seen live ordnance dropped that close. Back at Red Rio Range in New Mexico and at Range 73 at Hurlburt, we had dropped only BDU-33 practice bombs. My experience from the States also explained why I couldn't pick up the fighters visually as they rolled in to drop their bombs. The dive to the target was known as "coming down the chute," and I was conditioned to looking just above the horizon for propeller-driven A-1 Skyraiders or for other OV-10s.

On the next pass, I watched Homer's head tilt back and look out the top of the canopy. I followed his gaze and there, almost vertically above us, I saw the wingman coming down the chute. No wonder I couldn't find Lead on the first pass. Two's bombs exploded about where his leader's had, but the smoke and dust were so thick that it was impossible to make out anything on the ground. Quickly, Homer worked the second set of fighters and had them orbit the target "high and dry" while we took a close look at the results. Because the bombs had been right on the mark, I fully expected to see four smashed trucks or what was left of them. When the dust finally cleared, every tree in the target area had been completely blown away or splintered. Yet miraculously, all four trucks, as well as two trailers we hadn't seen before, were still sitting there, looking no worse for the ordeal. We knew they had to be badly damaged, but I couldn't imagine how they had survived that pounding intact.

We loitered in the area for another thirty minutes, hoping for more fighters, but no flights were available. In that part of Laos, an airborne battlefield command-and-control center inside an Air Force EC-130 parceled out the limited fighters to the sector FACs along the Trail. Operating under the tactical call sign of "Hillsboro," the command center evidently felt that Homer had received his quota for the day. It was a classic case of supply and demand. Hillsboro promised to keep us in mind if any stray fighters showed up, but my front-seater was less than optimistic about the prospects. It seemed such a waste to leave those trucks sitting there. I couldn't help thinking that the other targets on the Trail that day must really be doozies for Hillsboro to pass us by in favor of someone else. Since it was my first true combat mission, it seemed compellingly important to me that we bag those trucks. The bitter disappointment sapped the interest right out of me. Homer felt it too as he reluctantly broke off the vigil and headed north to continue the visual reconnaissance.

At that point we were more than two hours into the mission, the longest single stretch I had ever spent in the OV-10. With the excitement of the trucks and air strikes behind us, I found myself once again dwelling on creature comforts—or lack of them. The rock-hard ejection seat was giving my butt rough sledding. No matter how I squirmed around trying to get comfortable, it still felt like I was sitting on a bed of nails. The midmorning sun didn't help either. Blazing through the canopy into the cockpit, the sun rays gave a good imitation of being the high-temperature setting on a very efficient convection oven. Finally, my armor-plated helmet seemed incredibly heavy. In reality it weighed only a few ounces more than a regular helmet, but I could have sworn it weighed at least fifty pounds. The fit wasn't exactly right either, resulting in a "hot spot" on the back of my head that was killing me.

It seemed my whole thought process was negative and self-defeating. Angrily, I told myself to stop bellyaching and get on with the job. My circumstances weren't perfect, but they were considerably better than the mud and slime those Army and Marine grunts crawled around in. So I concentrated on map reading and on asking Homer about tactics and visual reconnaissance (VR) techniques. Gradually, I forgot my discomfort and even managed to pick up some good tips from my very capable teacher. Exactly 4.8 hours after takeoff, Homer set us down for a perfect landing back at Da Nang. It was only 10:50 in the morning, but it had already been a long, exciting day.

Back in Covey Operations, Homer debriefed the flight, describing sights, sounds, and nuances I hadn't even noticed. At one point, as he talked about the bombs missing the trucks but probably blowing the drivers away, a strange feeling came over me. Until that moment I hadn't really thought about the people in the target area, only about the inanimate trucks. I had no hang-ups or moral aversion to killing those drivers—they were the bad guys and would have iced us if given the opportunity. Still, the notion of actually killing another human being bothered me, making me feel uncomfortable with myself and with the impersonal nature of the air war over Laos. Today's bombing mission had been my first exposure to inflicted death. It affected me in another way too. I couldn't stop thinking about the grunts slugging it out in the jungle face-to-face with their bad guys.

The next day, after an uneventful second back-seat ride, I was delighted to see from the yellow grease penciled names on the scheduling board that Captain Albert D. Jensen was going to be my IP for my first front-seat ride over the Trail. Any organization informally rates its own people, and while all the Covey IPs were capable pros, Don had the best reputation among the young pilots. He was about average size with slightly thinning sandy-colored hair. Don was outgoing and good natured, but there was an intensity about him that convinced you he knew his stuff.

On the morning of May 7, we discussed the mechanics of the flight, then walked out the back door of Ops and across the Covey compound to the intelligence shop for our formal briefing on targets, threats, and weather. Inside, a large floor-to-ceiling map showed every geographic detail of the southern panhandle of Laos, code-named Steel Tiger. Every segment of the Ho Chi Minh Trail had been carefully overlaid with clear acetate. As elaborate as it was, one feature on the map was more eye-catching than any of the others. A series of red circles covered the Trail, each representing a triple-A gun that had recently fired at one of our FACs. The effect was immediate: The whole map was nothing but red circles! For comic relief, and in the best traditions of war and gallows humor, some wit had sarcastically written in grease pen across the top of the map: "Send your favorite zip gunner on an all-expense-paid vacation to visit Buddha. Donate a MK-82 to a worthy cause."

The briefer gave all the latest data, including extensive warnings about every gun up and down the Trail. He cautioned us, "Be very careful flying around Delta 86. There are two active 23mm guns in that area; they seem to have an unlimited supply of ammo. The gun right here on the east side of the road is real bad news—a nine-level gunner if ever there was one. From other pilot debriefs, we've been able to determine that this joker knows how to lead a target. His buddy on the other side of the road is probably a trainee. He's wild in his shooting, but he could always get lucky."

After painting the threat picture, the briefer moved on to specific duties. As part of the mission, we drew two "preplanned strikes"—dedicated fighters assigned to targets picked by the planners down at Seventh Air Force Headquarters in Saigon. Other targets, generated by the FACs, were called "immediate requests" or "targets of opportunity." After our mission data cards were filled with all the essentials, the briefer sent us out the door with a cheerful "Have a good mission." Don and I strolled across the street and picked up our survival vests, helmets, and .38 revolvers from the personal equipment shop, then headed out to aircraft 799.

John Tait had been right. With four rocket pods, two pilots, and that monster centerline tank, the takeoff roll of the Bronco seemed to take half a day. At a gross weight near fourteen thousand pounds, the plane's climb rate was not impressive either. To compensate, the initial turnout of traffic was to the east, rather than west toward the Trail. After gaining a few thousand feet of altitude over Da Nang Bay, we circled back over the airfield and headed for the Laotian border, eighty-five air miles away. At the border I gave Panama the traditional "across the fence" call, the code phrase that let them know we were leaving South Vietnam and crossing into the secret political-military world of Laos. Next stop, Ho Chi Minh Trail.

After we checked in with Hillsboro, we learned the fighters for our first preplanned strike had arrived an hour early; Hillsboro wanted to know if we could hack it. The race to the target would be tight, and my overall lack of familiarity with the region and procedures would slow things down even more. Rather than let some other FAC have our fighters, Don relayed an optimistic "Can do." We were still ten minutes away when the fighters checked in on our discrete UHF radio frequency and, much to my relief, Don decided to "demonstrate" the first strike. I knew he was just being kind so I wouldn't embarrass myself. Everything had happened so fast—my mind was still back in the arming area at Da Nang—but the quick turn of events had little effect on

Don. Because he knew the area like the back of his hand, he briefed the fighters as all of us converged on the assigned visual reconnaissance area. The target was a suspected truck park just off a main segment of the Trail. With the four ship of F-100s orbiting impatiently overhead, Don quickly circled the scene, navigating around scattered clouds hanging over the target. He located his objective and rolled in for the mark. We were using the same system Norm Edgar and I had used a few days earlier: While Don flew, I would fire the rocket for him. While we were still at the top of the chute, the radio crackled.

"Covey, Litter 31. You're taking ground fire from your nine o'clock. Keep it moving."

Don answered, "I copy, Lead. See if you can pinpoint the gun." Switching to the intercom, he told me, "This is great. You get to duel with a gun on your first mission. Some people are just born lucky. Okay, get ready, ready, fire!" With a flick of my thumb the rocket swished out the tube and was on its way. Don sucked in about six Gs and racked us hard right, then back to the left. He came back on the intercom in an excited tone: "Tom, look out to our left, just a little above over level. See them? See those gray-colored puffs? That's 37mm, about two clips worth or ten rounds." I searched the horizon and picked out a couple of small clouds drifting by, but I wasn't at all convinced they were man-made.

Litter Flight had a visual on our smoke, so Don cleared them in on the target. As each camouflaged Super Saber rolled in and dropped his ordnance, we kept our eyes peeled for ground fire but, strangely, saw none. Through it all, I kept wondering if any of the pilots might be former squadron mates from back at Cannon Air Force Base. I was also fascinated by the way Don probed the triple-canopy jungle, trying to find and hit trucks that could not be seen from the air. After Lead dropped, Don directed: "Two, put your bombs on the west edge of Lead's bombs"; "Three, give me a pass one hundred meters south of Two's bombs."

In spite of the methodical probing, the strike turned up

nothing. We spent the next few minutes looking at the destruction through our binoculars but saw only clouds of red dust and busted trees. Don sent Litter flight home with a less-than-spectacular bomb damage assessment (BDA): "100 percent of the ordnance on target, but no visual results due to smoke and foliage." I watched in the mirror as Don used his grease pen to write all the strike data on the side of his canopy. Homer Pressley had done the same thing; I had incorrectly assumed it was a technique unique to him. When I asked about it, Don laughed and explained, "If a FAC loses his grease pen, he declares an emergency and calls it a day. Besides, writing on the canopy keeps your head out of the cockpit and makes you concentrate on what's happening outside."

As we moved north along the Trail, Don pointed out some of the landmarks that would help me navigate in VR-6, the Covey portion of the route structure. Paralleling the main Trail, the Xe Kong River meandered along, twisting and turning to form some strange figures with its bends and cutbacks. With a little imagination it was easy to visualize the most prominent ones: Snoopy's Nose, the Man's Head, the Twin Boobs, and the Dog's Head. On a clear day, high-flying fighters could see those features from miles away, so the river sculptures made great spots for FAC and fighters to rendezvous.

Our second preplanned strike involved a road cut where Route 96 crossed a fairly large stream. The idea was to crater the road approaches to the ford, making it impossible, or at least difficult, for enemy trucks to cross the stream. Don told me the strike was all mine. He would back me up with suggestions and ultimate safety of flight authority, but the basic decisions and fighter control were up to me. Armed with that guidance, I headed for the target twenty minutes before the scheduled rendezvous with the fighters, figuring it would be easy enough to find the spot where the road crossed the stream. When we arrived in the general area, I was shocked to see at least four roads or trails crossing the stream! Three of the four weren't even on the

1:50,000 scale map I had spread out all over the cockpit like I intended to wallpaper the place. Through an agonizing backtracking process that took every second of the twenty minutes, I finally identified the correct ford. While I was still folding maps and trying to get organized, a two-ship of Navy A-4 Skyhawks checked in. This particular flight was from one of the aircraft carriers of Task Force 77, the US Navy armada cruising on "Yankee Station" about one hundred miles east of Da Nang.

Because of the long flight to the target, my fighters were low on fuel and ready for an immediate strike, so I took a deep breath and gave the A-4s my best briefing, desperately trying not to sound as nervous as I felt. Any mistake of omission or commission on my part might cost one of those pilots his life; I definitely felt the pressure. My fighters seemed to absorb my briefing without difficulty, so I continued my orbit until in position to roll in from the south, parallel to the road four thousand feet below. Lining up the road in the gunsight, I fired the rocket and announced, "Mark's away." Pulling off target, there was no apparent ground fire, but I kept jinking, just in case. Looking back over my shoulder, I saw the white smoke from my rocket drifting up from the north bank of the stream, just on the edge of the road. Not bad for my first try in actual combat. I flew in a loose orbit directly over the target, then advised my fighters, "Okay, Lead, hit from my smoke to fifty meters south anywhere along the road. You're cleared for random headings, just call the direction you're in from and FAC in sight." In a high-threat area, Don had told me that random headings gave the fighters the option to attack from any point on the compass, making it tougher for the gunners to know where to aim. I assumed that because of the orientation of the road the Skyhawks would use a north or south run-in. It was a major confidence builder when Lead rolled in from the north and put his bombs right on my smoke. To get the biggest craters, I had directed the fighter jocks to arm up their bombs for delayed fusing. As a result the whole area was obscured by red dust from the detonations. Lead pulled off to the east, directly into the late morning sun, making detection even harder for any ambitious gunners who were hoping to pop off a few rounds at these very professional Navy pilots. Because of the dust, the wingman continued around and came in from the south and put a beautiful string of bombs on the south ford, blowing away a large chunk of the road. Preoccupied with watching the dust clear over the target, I was somewhat surprised to glance up and see Two pull off to the west instead of into the sun as his leader had. Almost on cue the white puffs of 23mm exploded just below and several hundred feet off Two's right wing tip. Before I could react, Don came up on the radio and shouted, "Two, break hard left. You're taking ground fire!" Without acknowledging, Two executed a crisp left turn and within seconds was out of danger, continuing his climbing turn around the circle to rejoin his leader.

When we landed back at Da Nang, Don talked to me at length about the fine points of controlling air strikes. He complimented me on my handling of the strike, noting that the mechanics had been just fine. He went on to remind me that my responsibility included the fighters' safety as well as their effectiveness. Don pointed out that once the bombs had been released, there was nothing I could do about it; when the Navy wingman had taken the ground fire, I should have been monitoring the wingman instead of worrying about where the bombs hit. Being a good FAC involved a lot more than marking targets and having guts. The key was in developing situation awareness, a sort of sixth sense for evaluating everything going on around you.

The next day we tried it again. Without a lot of prompting, I managed to get us to the target and to run a reasonably smooth strike against a suspected storage area and transshipment point. For the remainder of the mission, Don Jensen put me through some tough navigation problems. He would find some obscure point on the map, read off the coordinates, and tell me to take him to it. We were en route to the third practice target when Don let out a yelp from the back seat. "Tom, bring her back around to the right. Now look at that straight stretch of road cut into the face of that bright red-colored cliff. Got it? Now tell me what you see." I immediately saw the shape he was talking about but couldn't believe my eyes, so I took out the binoculars and looked closer. Sure enough, it was a large truck right out in the open. Don couldn't believe it either. Dayshift Coveys rarely saw trucks at all, since virtually all movement on the Trail occurred at night to take advantage of the darkness. And since trucks almost never ventured out in the daylight, OV-10 jocks relied on sharp eyes or blind luck to find vehicles parked and hidden under the dense, green, triple-canopy jungle.

We asked Hillsboro for help, and twenty minutes later I contacted Wolfpack 41, a flight of four F-4s from the 8th Tactical Fighter Wing at Ubon, Thailand. "Wolfpack, Covey 221," I announced proudly. "Say your mission number and type ordnance, over."

I was mildly shocked by their response: "Roger, Covey. We're mission number 632. Lead, Three, and Four are each carrying one 'Pave Way.' Two is the designator ship. We can give you ten minutes of play time."

Pave Way was the code name for a highly accurate weapon, a laser-guided two-thousand-pound bomb. Because the system was so new, most FACs and fighters had never used Pave Way, and as a rookie I was certainly no exception. Under the right conditions, the process was relatively simple, although it required a lot of choreography. The early concept called for the designator ship to circle the area, with the back-seater employing a Buck Rogers hand-held device to illuminate the target with an invisible laser beam. The other strike pilots maneuvered their aircraft so as to roll in and come down the chute directly over the top of the designator. If all went well, the free-falling bomb would intercept the reflected laser beam and track all the way to impact. Accuracy of Pave Way was reported to be uncanny, but because of the rigid parameters the pilots had to fly, they were all sitting ducks for any proficient gunner who felt lucky and had a lot of ammunition stored up.

As I marked the target for Wolfpack 41, a strange thing happened. When my rocket fired, evidently one of its four folding fins failed to open, sending it careening off at a ninety-degree angle to our flight path. I quickly pulled up into a vertical climb in order to reposition for a second shot. Hanging at the top of the whifferdill, slow and very unmaneuverable, the vulnerable Bronco was evidently more temptation than the gunners could stand. Two guns opened up from the top of the next ridge to our east. Within seconds, we were bracketed by 23mm airbursts, all very close and very ugly looking. Instinctively I kicked hard bottom rudder to get the nose below the horizon. With the help of gravity and both engines screaming at 100 percent power, we gained flying airspeed quickly. In short order I reengaged the target and had the pipper back on the truck. Just before I fired, the guns hosed us a second time. By pure chance, I happened to glance directly at the southernmost gun when he fired, so I got a good fix on his position. I pulled off the pass with some inspired jinking and climbed back to altitude. My mark wasn't great, but the F-4s picked out the truck with no difficulty.

As was customary on a Pave Way strike, I was about to turn control over to flight lead when I had second thoughts. The idea of attacking the truck while the bad guys used us for target practice didn't sit well. Instead, I found myself saying, "Hey, Lead. I just got a good tally on that south gun. I'm game to go after him if you are." I thought I heard a small groan from Don in the back seat, but he choked off any comment and just gave me a "thumbs up" signal.

Lead came back with the answer I had hoped for: "Covey 221, I didn't get a fix on either one of the guns, but if you mark 'em, we'll blow 'em away."

"Roger that, Lead. FAC's in to mark. Keep me covered." Rolling in from the east almost directly out of the sun, I roared down the chute for a quick attack. As we pressed in, it seemed oddly unreal to be going head to head with a gunner who was intent on killing me, yet there was a strange excitement, an exhilarating feeling about it. Up till now the gunner had had his way but, with any luck, I was determined to change that.

Easier said than done. A couple of flak bursts off our left wing shattered my concentration, and I fired before I had the sight picture nailed. Right away I knew the rocket would be short, so I squeezed off a second one and pulled off to the south in a gut-wrenching high-G turn that tunneled my vision.

Don came on the intercom instantly. "Keep it turning to the left. That other gun is tail-shooting us. That's it, keep it turning. Now, break back hard to the right!" Stick full against my right leg, we were in ninety degrees of right bank in a heartbeat. Out the top of the canopy, I could see a line of nasty-looking little puffs. Surprisingly, they were quite a distance away. I unloaded the G forces so we could accelerate and then eased back toward the ridge where the guns were waiting. Neither of my rockets scored a direct hit, but they formed a nice bracket around the suspected position. There was nothing left to do but turn control over to Lead and move out of the way.

"It's your show, Lead. Go get him."

"Rog, I got control. Nice work, Covey."

With Lead's verbal pat on the back, my spirits soared. It wasn't a gushing tribute; still, I sensed the bond between aviators, I sensed Lead's admiration for us slow-movers who ran the gauntlet of fire to get the job done, and I sensed some things about myself that had worried me but would no longer. At that moment, any self-doubts about my ability to handle the stress of combat evaporated.

The designator ship was doing his job at about twelve thousand feet when Lead called in from the southeast. The gunners must have known their stuff was weak because neither opened up. Lead called off, and ten seconds later a huge explosion ripped the jungle wide open exactly where the gun pit had been. Since nobody had pinpointed the northern gun, Lead moved his traveling laser show back to the red cliff where the truck still sat. A few seconds later,

Three dropped his bomb into the imaginary basket to score a direct hit on the large truck. When the smoke cleared, Don and I couldn't believe it. There was absolutely nothing left—not a wheel, a fender, or a single scrap of metal— just a large, smoking hole. After a short discussion with my IP, I passed the BDA to the fighters. We settled on one truck destroyed and one 23mm gun silenced and probably destroyed. Wolfpack 41 went home happy, and I felt like I had learned a lot about the war and about myself.

A few minutes later, just before we started back to Da Nang, the bubble burst. I heard Don talking to another FAC on our Covey FM frequency, and I turned up the volume to listen. The voice asked, "Hey, Jensen, did your stud just put a strike in on a truck at the red cliffs?"

Don answered, "Roger that. A direct hit. We put a Papa Whiskey on it, and there was nothing left of the mother."

There was a long pause before the other FAC responded. "There was nothing left because it wasn't a real truck. It was a fake, just a flak trap, and you dumb shits fell for it! It's been sitting there for a week. Where have you been? Boy, this is rich. Just wait till the guys get wind of this. You'll be buying the bar for a month."

It was like someone slapped me in the face. I felt myself flush as the anger and embarrassment welled up inside me. It wasn't so much that I had been suckered in by the fake truck; my IP had fallen for it too. The sting and bitterness came from hanging it out for no good reason. For the life of me, I couldn't figure out how the fake truck had gone unreported, how it could have been passed off as a joke, just waiting for some fool to stumble across it—especially when I was the fool. The truck on the red cliffs most certainly was a flak trap, and a bunch of us had just put our butts out in the breeze so somebody could have a good laugh at our expense. I shuddered to think what the price could have been. As we headed for home, all I could think about was punching out the imbecile who had masterminded the prank.

On May 11 Norm Edgar gave me my combat-ready

check ride. We were scheduled for one preplanned air strike against a suspected truck park out in the middle of nowhere. The mission was totally uneventful, but my handling of the air strike generated a mild controversy.

When I finally located the target coordinates, they turned out to be in the middle of the jungle, far from any roads, trails, or dry streambeds capable of supporting truck traffic. Norm and I spent thirty minutes staring through our binoculars from every conceivable angle, trying to find any clue that a truck might be hidden under those thick trees. It had to be a mistake, so I widened my search pattern and finally came across another clump of trees almost a thousand meters west of the preplanned target. A small, dusty trail ran along the tree line and then ducked into the woods near a small stream. It looked a lot more plausible for a truck park than the other spot. I thought about playing it straight, just hitting the original coordinates and letting Seventh Air Force do the explaining. I also considered talking the situation over with Norm, but that would have been the easy way out—it was my decision, and he wouldn't be in the back seat for my whole tour. When the fighters showed up, I directed their bombs against the point where the trail entered the trees. We probed all around the area but came up empty-handed. As the fighters left the scene, I gave them the BDA and evidently left them with the impression that they had hit the preplanned target.

On the way home, Norm quizzed me about my decision. "Tom, you know you put that strike in west of where you were supposed to. How come?" Somewhat defensively, I outlined my reasoning, to which Norm responded, "I agree. If I'd been in your shoes, I'd have probably done the same thing." Norm thought I'd done everything else well, so I figured the episode was closed.

That night an impromptu party developed in the hallway of the Covey barracks. One of the old heads had finished up his tour, and the celebration included generous portions of French 75s, a killer concoction of cheap champagne and brandy. In a fairly short period, nobody was feeling any pain. In celebration of my own new combat-ready status, I managed to do a good job of keeping up with the most ardent of the revelers. To my surprise, few if any of the Coveys showed the slighted interest in my accomplishment. To them, I was still just one of the new guys.

At some point in the evening, a captain named Mike pulled me off to the side. He was the same pilot who had called on the radio about the fake truck, so I wasn't kindly disposed toward him at the outset. I had a sneaking suspicion that he was one behind the embarrassing and potentially deadly episode. We were standing just outside the community shower room, and Mike had one foot resting on a bench as he started talking. "I was out in the area today when you put in that air strike. You weren't even close to the coordinates you should have hit. I don't know what your problem is. Maybe you can't read a map, or maybe you're just sloppy. Either way, that kind of behavior won't hack it in this outfit."

I felt the same flush I had experienced a few days earlier. Angrily, I shot back, "Let me get this straight. You were sneaking around out there watching my strike without checking in with me like you were supposed to? How about explaining that little breach of flying safety?"

Mike then said exactly the wrong thing. In an arrogant tone, he hissed, "I just wanted to see how Jensen's star pupil handled himself without Daddy Don there to bail him out."

I literally saw red. I shouted back, "You asshole!" Then my right fist slammed into his left cheekbone, sending him sprawling onto the shower room floor. He landed like a sack of potatoes, then groggily shook his head. He propped himself up on both elbows but made no other effort to get up. I knew this round of the fight was over.

Mike looked at me for a couple of seconds, trying to get his eyes to focus, probably more from the effects of the French 75s than from my less-than-ferocious right lead. He said, "What the hell did you do that for?"

I walked over to the shower and turned the cold water

on him full blast. As he tried to squirm out of the way, I yelled, "You're a creep. If you ever play games with me out in the area again, the next time I'll take your whole head off."

As far as I could tell, Mike never said a word about the fight, but the news spread through the Coveys like wildfire. The next day I figured it was all over when the Covey commander, Lieutenant Colonel Edward P. Cullivan, called me over to his table in the officers' club. He had a sly smile on his face as he started talking. "Don't you get enough combat out over the Trail?" He grabbed my right hand and inspected my bruised knuckles, then motioned me a little closer. "Just between you and me, that SOB's had it coming for a long time. Don't do it again, though."

In spite of the unpleasantness with Mike, I felt I'd reached a milestone. I was extremely proud of becoming a combat-ready FAC. I certainly didn't feel disturbed about flying combat missions—no nightmares, no chills, no guilt-ridden anxiety attacks. Yet somewhere in the back of my mind, amid the jumble of new emotions, I wondered if I ought to be feeling something negative. After all, *Stars and Stripes* ran daily articles on the antiwar outcry over the assault in Cambodia. Could it be that I was out of step in approving of the incursion? By approving, did that mean I felt no sense of loss or shame over the terrible shooting tragedy at Kent State? It might have been a cop-out, but I slid through the process without answering my own questions. I decided to leave morality to the folks back home who had the time and luxury to consider it. My waking moments seemed to have room for only one reality—the trucks and the guns on the Ho Chi Minh Trail.

I enjoyed flying more than I ever could have hoped. Being alone in the Bronco provided me with an incredible sense of freedom and an enormous feeling of satisfaction. The immersion was so complete that I found myself existing in a world where everything outside that bubble seemed abnormal. Yet there was a price to pay. Time and missions became open-ended and consequently a heavy physical

drain. The grind came from having no sense of calendar.
Even as a new guy, I rapidly found myself losing all track
of time. I could always count on logging four hours of
combat time over the Trail, but the missions started running
together, just like the days of the week. I had hoped to
improve as a FAC by analyzing every mission. It didn't
work. I could vividly recall some events but had blurred
recollections of others. Some anonymous sage captured part
of the feeling with some latrine-wall graffiti when he observed, "A Covey mission is four hours of boredom punctuated by a few minutes of stark terror." I wasn't sure about
the stark terror, but the rest struck a familiar note. I could
vouch for one thing: After a hot gun battle out in Steel
Tiger, the letdown following that adrenalin surge was exhausting. And we went out and did it again the next day
and the next and the next.

Except for brief notes scribbled in my journal, memory-
jogging events replaced days of the week as a means of
tracking time. "Those were fresh eggs at breakfast this
morning." "That gunner by Snoopy's Nose is really getting
good." "Did you see the set on that new nurse?" "*M*A*S*H*
is playing at the flick tomorrow." Unfortunately, some of
the events were traumatic, not necessarily the sort of things
you shared with family and friends back in the States. Toward the end of May, several memory joggers shook me
out of my rut.

About four o'clock on the afternoon of May 22, I
strolled into Covey Operations to pick up my mail. Un-
characteristically, the place was packed. Half the people
were scurrying around, while the other half just stood there
dazed. Usually a few people were hanging around playing
darts, but it was obvious that nobody was in the mood for
games today. At that moment the duty officer sprinted in
the back door and began nudging his way through the
crowd. I tapped him on the shoulder and asked, "Bill, I just
got here. What's going on?"

Bill's eyes met mine briefly, then his stare dropped down

to his boots. "Rick Meacham's been shot down. He bought the farm."

I didn't know what to say. It was an awkward moment. I heard myself ask, "How? Where?" My voice echoed as if I were talking in a barrel.

Bill answered, "We don't know any of the details, but he went down in the triborder area near Khe Sanh." Bill looked back up at me, then continued to elbow his way through the crowded room.

My mind raced, confused. I had barely known Rick; we had talked only a couple of times. Still, it was a shock to be told he was dead. Then a thought struck me. What was he doing up at the triborder? That wasn't even part of the assigned Covey area. Then I remembered Rick was part of a "sneaky pete" flight within Covey, a small group of six pilots who flew some supersecret mission about which the rest of us knew nothing. The six of them kept pretty much to themselves and took a lot of good-natured kidding from us because they were always off in some corner whispering. Everyone knew them as "Prairie Fire" pilots.

I'd heard the Prairie Fire pilots on the radio with Hillsboro once or twice. They talked about "playing" some ball game or about a certain area being "hot," obvious code words with no meaning to an outsider. In our preflight briefings before each mission, the intel officer always went to great lengths to point out a series of square boxes on the map called "no bomb lines" or NBLs. The NBLs were located in some nasty areas just inside the Laotian and North Vietnamese borders, with the largest concentration located in the DMZ, the no-man's land dividing North and South Vietnam. Rumor had it that the NBLs had something to do with Prairie Fire pilots.

Although none of us knew the Prairie Fire pilots that well, Rick's shoot-down and death had a sobering effect on all the Coveys. Initially, it made most of us stop a minute to reflect on our own mortality. But the scope was wider than that; the impact on the unit as a whole was more profound. Rick's death was the first Covey combat loss in nineteen months. Statistically, we were long overdue, and everyone had been expecting it. Now the unspoken question was, would we go another nineteen months, or were the floodgates open? Somewhat guiltily, I figured I was the only one thinking along those lines until I heard one Covey tell another, "We're really in for it now. Bad things always happen in threes." As if in fulfillment of that prophecy, later that night over the Trail, the NVA shot down the first AC-130 Specter gunship of the war.

As a measurement of roster strength, Rick's death represented only a small decrease in the percentage of available manpower. But the deep emotion everyone felt at losing a gifted pilot, one of our own, hit much harder and in ways not quantifiable on a morning strength report. Rick's death proved beyond any shadow of a doubt that in a close-knit flying unit, a synergistic effect was at work: The total amounted to more than the sum of the individual parts. The missing man diminished us but at the same time made us stronger.

Rick was gone, but life went on. A few mornings later, I had the day off. Just like in the popular fighter pilots' song, I was "not on the schedule, not earning a dime." Blissfully tucked into my top bunk, I was attempting to "sleep late on the taxpayers' time." At some point I heard someone rattling around the room. No blaring "Proud Mary," so it wasn't my roomie. Through bleary eyes I saw our Vietnamese maid squatting in the middle of the room, polishing my boots. She already had my dirty laundry piled on the floor beside her. Even in the flattering soft morning light, Mamma San had to be one of the most unattractive women I had ever seen. Somebody had her in mind when they coined the old saying, "Beauty may be only skin deep, but ugly goes all the way to the bone." She was short and pudgy, with long, black hair combed back into a tight bun. The effect emphasized her very square face covered with unsightly zits. Her perpetual smile revealed teeth stained black by years of chewing betel nut. Mamma San wore a white blouse and classic black pajama bottoms, standard garb for civilians—and the Viet Cong. Watching her, I couldn't help staring at her bare feet. Her toes looked like a man's gnarled fingers, spread wide apart. She had probably never worn real shoes in her life. On the plus side, Mamma San was cheerful and tried her best to take good care of us.

I jumped out of bed and ambled down the hall toward the community shower, with Mamma San right behind me carrying an armload of sweat-stained flight suits. Standing under the steady stream of cool water from the shower nozzle, I began to revive. The brownish water spraying all over me felt great. Everyone from the flight surgeon on down swore that Da Nang's rust-colored water was fit for human use, so I numbly accepted the oaths as gospel. I accepted the water, but even after a month at Da Nang, I was still somewhat self-conscious about taking a shower while all the maids watched.

Mamma San and two other maids squatted directly outside the gang shower room, stacking laundry into piles and chattering away to each other in Vietnamese. As they gossiped and sorted clothes, all three kept their eyes glued on whoever happened to be in the shower. If I made eye contact with one of them, she would smile and all three would break into uncontrollable giggles. I wasn't sure whether to be flattered or embarrassed by the unwanted attention. Fortunately, one of the nightshift Coveys staggered into the shower room and was greeted by the same giggles. I convinced myself that Mamma San and her buddies were watching the other guy or that they paid no real attention to our naked young bodies. It worked until I walked out of the shower room. At that point one of Mamma San's friends added to my self-consciousness by pointing vaguely at the lower half of my torso. Fearing the worst about where her gesture might lead the conversation, I was relieved when she cackled in broken English, "How you call that line? Suntan?"

Almost as a badge of honor, each of our dirty flight suits sported a huge sweated-in salt stain on the back. A few

days earlier, I'd heard a couple of pilots complain that their
flight suits never seemed clean. Coming out of the shower,
I found out why. As I stood there shaving, Mamma San
gathered up about twenty-five flight suits and laboriously
stuffed them into one automatic washing machine designed
for less than one-third that load. Fascinated, I watched as
she produced a giant box of Tide from the Covey supply
locker and then measured out one tiny cupful into the over-
stuffed tub. She pushed the right buttons, and the machine
rapidly filled with brown water. When the wash cycle finally kicked in, the agitator in the overloaded machine
moved only about an inch in either direction. I started to
say something to her, but she looked so pleased with herself
that I didn't have the heart. Late that afternoon Mamma
San neatly stacked my less-than-clean but beautifully
ironed flight suits on the corner of my desk, then proudly
walked out of the building with an almost full box of Tide.

On May 28, after preflighting aircraft 693, I gained an
appreciation for why nobody liked to fly late-afternoon sorties. The hot afternoon sun reflecting off the concrete ramps
transformed the whole place into an inferno. My sympa-
thies went out to the crew chiefs who were forced to endure
the searing heat over twelve-hour shifts. Stripped to the
waist, climbing all over the scalding hot metal surfaces of
the OV-10s and O-2s, the young airmen did their jobs ef-
ficiently and still managed to be fairly cheerful as they
helped me strap in.

The other reason nobody cared for the afternoon go also
stemmed from the weather, but for a different reason. With
the temperature, humidity, and convection building
throughout the tropical day, a line of hefty thunderstorms
would likely be in their usual spots along the mountain
range separating Vietnam and Laos. Picking your way
through the bottoms of those monsters in a light aircraft
with no radar was definitely sporty.

Dripping wet from sweat but glad finally to be airborne,
I headed for the "fence." From my cruising altitude of
eighty-five hundred feet, I could clearly see a solid wall of

thunderstorms waiting to test my skill and nerve. The tops of the largest cells, already towering thousands of feet above me, appeared to be building faster than my aircraft could climb, so I knew my choices in the Bronco were limited: go home, go under, go through, or go around. Forget the first choice. Going under might be an option over flat terrain, but in the mountains strong down drafts could slam an aircraft into a peak without warning. Punching through a storm was risky and dumb, so I struck off to the south, hoping to end-run the ominous looking cells.

After about fifteen minutes on a southwesterly heading, I stumbled across the most awesome sight I had seen in years. Seemingly out of nowhere, a five-mile-wide corridor opened up in the solid line of thunder bumpers. Through it I saw beautiful, dazzling sunshine. The sun hung there like a huge orange-red ball, shimmering thirty degrees above the western horizon. The scene took me back to my senior year at Tamalpais High School when I had witnessed an identical spectacular sun hanging over Stinson Beach, just north of San Francisco. Snapping out of the reverie, I hesitated a second, wondering if the corridor might be a temporary sucker hole, but as if drawn by some uncontrollable force, I pushed both power levers up and plunged into the breach.

Flying between the huge, boiling walls of clouds, I kept thinking about the scene in *The Ten Commandments* when Charlton Heston parts the Red Sea. At any moment I half-expected the spell to break and the whole shooting match to come tumbling in on top of me. Pressing on through the canyon, I was fascinated by the light show flickering about on either side of me. Lightning strikes deep inside the cells produced a continuous pulsating series of glowing discharges of static electricity. In spite of their eerie beauty, I knew that in a matter of seconds the awesome power inside any one of those babies could transform my airplane into a pile of junk.

And suddenly I was out of it. The storm was behind me, and before me was nothing but sunshine and deep afternoon shadows. My attention turned to the Trail, but in the back of my mind I knew I would have to face the thunderstorms again on the return trip—only then it would be pitch black.

On each of the last few missions, the intel types had been asking us to watch a suspected enemy headquarters complex and truck park along a particularly hot section of the Trail. All the indicators of enemy activity were there: a nearby water supply, plenty of cover, and lots of dust on the trees lining the road, strong evidence that trucks were in the immediate area. In an earlier probing strike, one of the Coveys had encountered stiff ground fire, another indication that the bad guys were hiding something worth protecting. As I flew over the suspect area, all seemed quiet. I circled for about fifteen minutes, but if there was anything down there, I couldn't see it. The long shadows made it especially difficult to pick out detail. Just as I was about to leave, a mirror-like reflection from the ground caught my eye. It disappeared in a split second, but it had been there long enough to convince me it was a reflection from a glass surface—maybe a truck windshield. I concentrated my search on the small valley where I had seen the flash. My excitement faded, however, with the passing minutes because all I could see was an endless sea of green trees. I thought about requesting an air strike from Hillsboro, but the chances of my target making the priority list seemed slim at best. I decided not to bother.

Flying north along the Trail, I was lost in my own thoughts when the radio startled me. "Covey 221, Hillsboro. We've got a divert flight of F-105s. You got a target for them?"

"Funny you should ask, Hillsboro. There's a suspected truck park I'd like to probe. Send them to the Dog's Head for a rendezvous."

"Roger on the Dog's Head. You'll be getting Bear Flight. They're on the tank right now topping off with gas and should be with you in about twenty minutes."

While waiting for my fighters, I scoped out the area one

last time, then moved several miles north so as not to tele-
graph my intentions to bomb the place.

I set up an orbit over a wide spot in the road called
Chavane. The place was short on looks but long on history.
Our maps showed Chavane to be an active airfield, but it
was actually nothing more than a large, relatively flat
meadow. During World War II, the Japanese had a fighter
outfit stationed at Chavane. As I looked down on the abandoned grass runway, I could visualize a flight of Zeros
bouncing across the rough ground on a formation takeoff,
scrambling to intercept a gaggle of Allied bombers intruding into the Chavane sector. I wondered if those young
Japanese pilots of my imagination were successful in their
intercept. Did they die? Was it just another mission? Ultimately, the answers seemed unimportant, and the questions
timeless. Thirty years later, a backwater known as Chavane
was still caught up in war.

"Covey 221, Bear Flight checking in over the Dog's
Head with four of the world's finest. Everybody's got four
Mark-117s and twenty mike-mike. Over."

"I copy your lineup, Lead. Take up a heading of due
east for ten miles. I'm orbiting directly over the first stretch
of dirt road you come to. I've got a suspected truck park
for you. Target elevation 2,150 feet. Highest terrain in the
area goes up to 4,750, about twenty klicks to the northeast.
We've got two known 23mm guns in the area, and you can
also expect small arms and automatic weapons fire. Nobody's shot at me so far, but they're probably saving it for
the world's finest. How copy so far?"

Lead answered, "Real funny, Covey. Keep going—
we're all ears."

"Okay, gents, if you get in trouble, your best emergency
bailout is heading 045 into the high mountains. This close
to sunset, you can count on spending the night if you go
down. Your best emergency airfield is Ubon, 135 miles due
west. There are no, repeat, no friendlies in this area. Once
I mark, I'll hold over the target, and you'll be cleared for
random headings, and I want delayed fusing. If anybody

pinpoints a gun, you're automatically cleared in on him. The surface wind appears to be from the southwest at less than ten knots. Unless you've got questions, let's do it."

To start the rocket pass, I rolled the Bronco almost inverted into 135 degrees of left bank, then applied back pressure to the control stick to pull the nose below the horizon and down toward my target in the center of the small valley thirty-five hundred feet below me. Before I could roll back to wings-level, a stream of tracers raced toward me from a saddleback-shaped ridge just to the east. The tracers looked different from those I had seen on earlier missions. These seemed to be moving much faster and glowed with a deep red, almost burgundy, color. The first half of the stream passed well in front of me, left to right, but the last few rounds streaked directly over the top of my canopy at a tremendous rate.

Whoever that gunner was, he caught my attention; I kept one eye in his direction and the other on the target as I lined up and fired. The rocket evidently penetrated to the jungle floor before exploding, so that only small whiffs of white smoke seeped up through the foliage and trees. Bear Lead rolled in to give it a try, but halfway down the chute, he came up on the radio. "Covey, I'm taking it through dry. Lost your smoke in the shadows. How 'bout putting down another mark?"

As Lead pulled off to the south, I kept my eyes glued on the general area where I had received the ground fire. Not so much as a whimper came from that gun, but when I glanced back to check on the lead F-105, half a dozen airbursts strung out behind the rapidly climbing Thud. I had no idea where the new stuff came from.

"Any of you Bears get a fix on that second gun?" I asked.

"Covey, this is Three. He's over to the west of us somewhere. I saw the tracers but no muzzle flashes."

"Thanks, Three. Okay, gents, I'm back in to mark. Keep your eyes open."

I pressed in out of the west at a fairly low dive angle,

hoping to keep the sun directly behind me. The guy on the saddleback wasn't fooled a bit. Looking into the dark shadows, I could see his muzzle flashes for a split second. I had the sensation of flying right down his gun barrel. The tracers, reddish brown this time, floated directly at me, then speeded up as they zipped by the right side of the cockpit.

I really sucked in the Gs pulling off the run. To keep the blood from pooling in my legs, I pushed out as hard as I could with my stomach muscles and grunted loudly. Flight surgeons called it the "M-1 Maneuver," a technique used to fight against blacking out under heavy G forces. The M-1 wasn't for use in polite company, but it definitely came in handy in combat.

It was a relief to see a thick white cloud of smoke billow out of the small valley. Before I could give any verbal instructions, Bear Lead cut off my radio call. "Lead's in from the north. I'm going after your gun. Covey, move a little to the west. You're right in my flight path." I racked it around hard to the west as Lead barreled down the chute, just missing a collision by less than two hundred feet. Muzzle flashes once again lit up the tree line just as Lead pickled off four 750-pounders. The bombs fell in perfect formation toward the trees, then exploded in a giant fireball on a slope just above the gun. The blast probably hadn't killed the gunner, but he obviously had one hell of a headache—not to mention two busted eardrums.

Before anyone could interrupt me, I keyed the mike button. "Two, go for the tree line one hundred meters north of Lead's bombs. You're cleared in hot. Go get him!"

The tree line offered no resistance as Two dived on his target. I watched through my binoculars searching for a gun pit, but the overhangs and trees cast such dark shadows that it was impossible to make out any detail along the ridge. As Two climbed away, the ground just north of where I thought the gun was erupted in a wall of dirt and flames. Close but no cigar. I thought about having Three split the difference, but the gun appeared to be out of commission, and I needed some bombs to probe the original target. The

smoke from my second willie pete had completely dissi-
pated, so for the third time I rolled in to mark the target
for the orbiting Thuds.

Nobody fired a shot as I lined up west to east and
squeezed off three rockets into the little valley. Three
evenly spaced white puffs filtered up through the jungle,
providing all the reference my fighters needed. Bear
Three's bombs hit dead center, and Four's overlapped to
the west, blowing gaping holes in the stand of trees. Circling the area, I strained to see into the craters. Finally, on
the very edge of Four's last bomb hit, I made out some sort
of structure. The thatch building was rectangular, with the
long axis oriented north to south. The west wall had blown
in, causing the roof to collapse. A well-used trail, easily
capable of supporting vehicles, led to the south.

Bear Flight still had five more minutes of play time, so
Lead asked permission for one strafing pass each before
heading home. I wasn't keen about the request because, to
be effective on a strafe run, the fighters had to press in to
a fairly low altitude. The target didn't seem worth it, but I
was still too green to have the good sense to tell them no.
Lead had made the suggestion, so what the hell.

With reservations, I cleared them in. The big F-105s
sprayed the Trail with withering 20mm cannon fire, the
impact generating hundreds of bright sparkles as the rounds
exploded on the target.

After Bear Flight departed for their base in Thailand, I
eased out over the Xe Kong River to relax for a few
minutes before continuing with my reconnaissance. With
the sun teetering just above the horizon, I would have to
move quickly to get a look at one more possible target
before darkness set in. As I glanced out at the right engine,
something unusual caught my eye. Three feet outboard of
the engine in the leading edge of the wing, I saw what
appeared to be a black spot about the size of a silver dollar.
I banked around to the west to get a little sunlight on the
wing, and sure enough, the black spot turned out to be a
very real bullet hole. Funny, I had never heard it or felt

anything when it hit. Then, in a panic, I thought about the fuel tanks in the wing. A quick check of the gauge showed no fuel loss. Thankfully, I remembered that the tanks were self-sealing. As I stared helplessly out at the wing, it occurred to me that if there was one hole, there could be another.

Being strapped into an ejection seat definitely limits a pilot's options for checking over the exterior of his aircraft. I twisted and turned in my seat as much as possible, then manipulated the mirror in an attempt to search back along the booms and tail. Something didn't look right on the top of the wing. Using the electric motor to run the seat up to its full height, I ended up pinning myself against the top of the canopy. From that contorted position I had a clear view, and it wasn't pretty. In the center of the right wing I could make out a jagged hole about three feet in diameter. Sharp metal pieces stuck up into the wind stream, indicating the skin had been blown out rather than pushed in. Since the fuel tanks seemed okay, my major concern was damage to the main wing spar, the long piece of beam that held the wing to the fuselage. If that baby buckled, the only choice was a long step over the side.

My first instinct drew me toward home plate at Da Nang, but one look at the line of thunderstorms blocking my flight path convinced me that a divert to Thailand was the smart decision. In the rapidly approaching darkness, my chances of finding another miracle corridor through the storms were slim. Then there was the small matter of bouncing my way through severe turbulence with a structurally unsound wing. I called Hillsboro and told them of my decision to divert.

I then tuned in channel 93 on my TACAN and received a good azimuth and a distance of 125 miles to Ubon Air Base. At sixty miles I called Ubon's tactical radar site. "Lion, Covey 221 on primary uniform, over."

"Covey 221, Lion. Squawk two-one-zero-zero ident and say your altitude." Without having to look, I reached to my right and momentarily hit the toggle switch on the transponder, a black box of electronic magic that sent encoded signals to the radar controller's screen at Ubon. "Lion, I'm at six point five requesting radar vectors to a straight-in approach to Runway 23. Be advised I've got battle damage and am declaring an emergency. Just to be on the safe side, I'd like to keep any maneuvering to an absolute minimum."

"Copy your emergency, Covey 221. Radar contact on the zero-nine-five degree radial for fifty-two miles. Say your fuel, souls on board, and nature of your difficulty."

"I've got nine hundred pounds of fuel, one soul on board. I have battle damage and possible severe structural damage to the right wing."

Actually, I didn't want to panic myself into believing the situation was all that threatening. After all, the wing had held up even after some fancy high-G maneuvering. Still, by declaring the emergency, I would get priority handling over other traffic. I just wanted to get myself and aircraft 693 on the ground in one piece. Lion asked a few more questions and at thirty miles turned me over to Ubon Approach Control. The night weather was good but hazy, so I didn't pick up the runway lights until five or six miles out on final. In spite of approach control's offer of a GCA, I opted for a visual straight-in. I was tired and didn't feel up to flying precise instruments.

At two miles out, I knew the landing would be a piece of cake. The only distraction was that every fire engine and crash wagon on the base seemed to be positioned along the edge of the runway. They were there to assist if I had trouble and for that I was grateful, but to look down into the darkness at all those flashing red lights was unnerving. I almost wished the crash crews didn't seem quite so eager.

I touched down on centerline five hundred feet down the runway and rolled out to the midfield taxiway—with all the fire trucks chasing along beside me. I felt almost guilty about disappointing them. After clearing the runway, I sat patiently through the drill while the de-arming crew put large safety pins attached to red streamers into each rocket pod, a precaution intended to prevent an inadvertent firing into the heavily populated base. Then a truck with a flashing yellow "Follow Me" sign led me to a parking spot in front of the control tower.

I felt stiff and exhausted sitting in the cockpit, and it was great to stretch and move around once I climbed out. Before I had time to collect my thoughts, a colonel, a lieutenant colonel, and two majors, all dressed in 1505 tan uniforms, tried to hustle me over to the TOC, the tactical operations center. Pulling away from them, I grabbed a big flashlight from one crew chief and jumped up on the ladder with the line chief who was already up on the aircraft sticking his head and shoulders into the ugly rip in the top of my wing. He gave a low, mournful whistle as he backed gingerly out of the hole. Shaking his head and pointing at the jagged mess, he drawled, "Lieutenant, I sure as hell hope they don't make you pay for this. Your wallet could be light for the next twenty years." As I sat there on the wing wondering if the line chief knew something that I didn't, someone from flying safety climbed up the ladder with a caliper and began measuring the hole in the leading edge. I wasn't at all surprised when it turned out to be a perfect fit for a 23mm round.

Reluctantly, I climbed down from the wing and followed the four impatient officers into the TOC, where everyone on base had some form or another for me to fill out—intel report, battle damage report, incident report, air traffic control report, maintenance report. It was a glorious day for the bureaucracy. Just when there seemed to be a light at the end of the administrative tunnel, a lieutenant colonel with knife-edge creases in his 1505s lowered the boom on me. Leaning forward with both hands on the table where I sat, he started lecturing: "You know, the only way you could have taken a hit like that was to be down in the weeds trolling. I don't know what kind of rules exist in your squadron, but around here we observe certain minimum altitudes which, incidentally, go a long way toward preventing what I've seen here tonight."

Déjà vu. Could this guy be related to Mike, my antagonist back at Da Nang? He sure had the same arrogant, self-righteous, confrontational style. I frowned, trying to make some sense out of his ridiculous accusation. My first response was rage. Then I glanced up at a couple of F-4 jocks leaning against the far wall. They just smiled and rolled their eyes. With their unspoken support, I mellowed. Lieutenant Colonel Knife-Crease was probably just a harmless "wing weenie" who had forgotten or had no idea that a 23mm's maximum effective range was over fifteen thousand feet. To hide my disgust, I laughed and asked the colonel to call Bear Lead over at Korat Air Base for confirmation that I had simply been doing my job. On that note I got up, grabbed his hand and shook it like he was an old buddy, then stomped out the door to shouts of "Wait a minute, I'm not finished yet."

My troubles weren't over. I dropped into the officers' club to grab a hamburger only to encounter the reverse of the money situation I had run up against at Cam Ranh. My MPC scrip wasn't negotiable at Ubon—only good old American "green" was acceptable. I had about had it with administrative hassle when I literally ran into an old friend of mine from Hurlburt. Vern loaned me some real money and even found me an empty bunk to sleep in. One cheeseburger and two beers later, the world seemed a lot brighter. Vern and I were at the bar on our second scotch when the assistant club manager walked up. "There's a phone call for you. Some colonel over at the TOC needs to talk to you about some battle damage."

We chugged our drinks and stood up. I asked Vern, "Is there a place I can hide out?" He nodded yes as we bolted for the side entrance. I yelled back to the manager, "Tell him I said to get screwed." Howling with laughter, we stumbled out the door and headed for the 497th "Night Owl" Squadron party hooch to continue the festivities.

Late the next afternoon, a Covey O-2 flew in to take me back to Da Nang. The crew kindly brought along a spare parachute, buckled me into it, and crammed me into the very cramped back seat. Once we were airborne, the ride east wasn't too bad, even though my knees were directly under my chin. My cordial pilot appeared unconcerned as he punched through the heavy line of afternoon thunderstorms near the fence. The turbulence slammed us around but only lasted a few minutes. Watching him maneuver between the cells, I wondered how my wounded OV-10 would have stood up under a similar pounding.

On short final approach at Da Nang, the pilot turned the controls over to his navigator, who did a decent job landing from the right seat. The nav flared just a little high and dropped us in with a thunk, but it was good to be back home in anybody's airplane with any kind of landing. As we taxied into the revetments, I stared at the empty spot where 693 normally parked. The regular crew chief, a young airman named Bennie, stood forlornly in the vacant revetment, arms folded across his chest. As I climbed out of my cramped seat in the O-2, he loped across the ramp with easy, athletic strides. Bennie had been a star basketball player at McClymonds High School in Oakland with aspirations for a college scholarship. Unfortunately, everybody thought Bennie was too short for even the collegiate ranks.

Eyes squinting in the sunlight, he asked, "Lieutenant, are you okay? We got worried when you didn't show up last night."

"I'm fine, Bennie. Sorry about messing up your airplane." Bennie's face tightened with concern.

"How bad was it?" I told him about the dud 23mm round cracking the spar in half then ricocheting out the top of the wing. Bennie looked away for a second, his mind's eye contemplating every detail of the damage—and imagining what might have happened had the shell exploded. He looked back at me, then his expression eased into a broad smile. He shook my hand and said, "How that wing stayed on I'll never know. You must be one lucky dude! And we'll get my bird back in no time." He was right about being lucky, wrong about the plane. Neither of us could know it would be another eight months before aircraft 693 was repaired and back in the war.

June

In a war with no front lines, American soldiers, sailors, and airmen had no place to hide. Even the rear echelon troops might come under sniper fire or rocket attack at any moment. Ever since the Tet offensive two-and-a-half years earlier, everybody serving in South Vietnam knew the score. Although the government boasted about secure areas, we knew differently. "Charlie" had the capability to swing into small-unit action at will.

Since we couldn't hide, the next best thing was to forget—and one way to forget involved a change of scenery. Thanks to the foresight of some anonymous morale and recreation officer, Vietnam offered the American soldier in-country R and R, and one of the favorite R and R spots turned out to be Da Nang's own China Beach.

On June 3 I flew the early go and returned to the Covey hooch by 11:30 A.M. One of the advantages of flying a dawn patrol mission was having the rest of the day off. It was a beautiful day, so rather than sit around, four of us struck out for an afternoon at China Beach. The logistics of getting there became half the fun, and since all the Covey M-151 Jeeps were in use, we decided to hitchhike.

The main road between the air base and the beach bustled with the heavy traffic normally found in a large city. The difference was that virtually every four-wheeled vehicle was U.S. military. A bewildering assortment of trucks, buses, jeeps, and carryalls bounced along at a steady clip from sunrise to sunset; with darkness came curfew, effectively eliminating all movement except for military police jeeps or an occasional truck convoy. Sharing the road during the day with the heavier motorized traffic, a steady stream of pedestrians and Vietnamese motorbike riders snaked along in the oppressive heat. Many of the hikers were GIs hoping to hitch a ride with a buddy or some member of their outfit. As the four of us trekked along beside the busy road, almost all the troops immediately in front of us and behind us got rides in a matter of minutes. Evidently four pilots in flight suits with towels and swim trunks under their arms didn't evoke sympathy from the drivers of the passing vehicles. Finally a three-quarter-ton carryall with a young Marine lance corporal at the wheel pulled up. In a loud, confident voice, he shouted, "Good afternoon, Sir. May I interest you in a ride, Sir?"

As we walked up to the front door, our Marine's stiff manner gave way to a slightly more casual attitude. His right hand was on the wheel, his left arm draped comfortably out the open window. Something in the expression on his old-young face left no doubt that everything was negotiable. We eyed each other cautiously for a few seconds; then I asked, "What's this gonna cost us?" His face took on a pained look, then he broke into a wide smile.

"That depends on where you're going. If I had to guess, I'd say China Beach. Sure is hot out here, isn't it, Sir? Me, I got no time to go swimming, but something to drink would hit the spot. Only, I'm not old enough to buy myself what I had in mind."

With that revelation, we knew where the conversation was going. Everything in Vietnam was rationed—cigarettes, stereo equipment, booze. Each of us had a ration card entitling the bearer to limited purchases in each category; the whole exercise had been designed to curb the thriving black market. The kicker was that underage enlisted troops weren't allowed to buy booze anyway.

The lance corporal sensed we understood his dilemma. "Here's the deal," he said in a low voice, his eyes darting around like those of a con artist making a back room deal in a scene from a B movie. "We stop at the Class Six store.

One of you gentlemen gets me a bottle of Southern Comfort with your ration card. Then I'll take you all the way to China Beach. Okay?"

Thirty minutes later, we piled out of the carryall at the front door of the beach snack bar. We sent our happy driver on his way with a promise not to open the bottle until he was back in his company area.

China Beach was no Waikiki, but it had possibilities. The beach itself was relatively narrow and steep, with lots of small-grained yellow sand. On that particular day, over-crowding was no problem: there were only about twenty of us as far as the eye could see. The height of the surf surprised me, although the big waves didn't break until almost at water's edge. The only reminders of the war zone were the multiple strands of concertina wire blocking either end of the designated swimming area and the steady procession of low-flying Huey helicopters scoping out the beach for Air Force and Army nurses who might be sunbathing. When the Hueys came in on their low-level reconnaissance runs, the rotor wash whipped the sand around like a Sahara dust storm. In spite of that annoying distraction, the beach was still a great place to relax, a reminder of calmer, simpler times.

Even though my morning mission over the Trail had been relatively quiet, I felt tired and drained. It was a relief to sprawl on the warm sand, put my mind on hold, and soak up the rays. I wasn't the only one who was dragging, since all of us had been shortchanged on sleep the night before. At about 2:30 in the morning, the VC had treated me to my first rocket attack.

I sat bolt upright as soon as the first piercing siren wail sounded over the compound speaker system. Within five seconds I heard the dull but loud "kah-woomp, kah-woomp" as the first of two 122mm rockets exploded some-where on the west side of the airfield. It probably would have been a good idea to take cover, but climbing out of my top bunk seemed like too much trouble. Besides, I had never experienced a rocket attack before, and my idea of how to react wasn't firmly established. When the rockets hit, a few guys swaggered around for the macho effect and a few others went to the opposite extreme, grabbing flak vest and helmet and diving under the nearest bunk. Both types were genuinely frightened; they just showed it in different ways. The majority of the Coveys acted indifferent or curious. The story going around was that the bad guys firing from the hills west of Da Nang couldn't aim at specific targets—they just pointed their rockets and hoped for the best. Their chances of scoring a direct hit on me seemed pitifully small, so I lay back in my top bunk and wondered why I was hearing two distinct sounds when each rocket exploded. In the midst of the noise and confusion, the security police came on the public address system and announced, "Condition Red. Da Nang is under attack." The voice repeated the warning over and over, long after the last rocket blew up.

Judging from the number of people running around in the hallway, few others had taken cover either. Finally I jumped out of bed and looked down the hall. At a small open stairwell at the far end, a crowd of wide-awake Coveys filled the doorway, half of them with cameras taking pictures of the fires burning across the runway. The scene reminded me more of a circus than a war. The animated group finally dispersed when the PA system announced the all clear. By then it was after 3 A.M., and since I had to get up at 4:30 anyway, I pulled out a trashy novel to kill the time before my mission.

Stretched out on the hot sand of China Beach, I forced myself to block out any more thoughts of rocket attacks and missions over the Trail. Before we started back to the barracks late in the afternoon, I managed to finish the trashy novel, take a couple of refreshing dips in the ocean, and down a few beers with my fellow pilots.

There was a price to pay for the few hours of relaxation at China Beach. The next morning, as I flew down the Trail searching for trucks, the harness and straps holding me tightly in the ejection seat cut painfully into my sunburned shoulders. The Air Force nurses had been kind enough to donate some Noxzema to the cause, but it really didn't help, even though I had smeared on a whole jar of the stuff. The body heat from my sunburn matched the heat in the cockpit, making me doubly miserable.

During the past month, I had just about acclimated myself to the steam bath flight conditions in my OV-10. It reminded me of sitting inside a hot car with all the windows rolled up—or, worse yet, sitting inside a greenhouse. The design was intended to provide the FAC with great visibility, and North American Rockwell, the OV-10 manufacturer, had done a super job in that department—with the canopy rail at hip level and Plexiglas everywhere above that. But they had forgotten an air-conditioning system. The aeronautical engineers were thoughtful enough to install an air scoop, which allowed outside air to flow into the cockpit, but when the temperature routinely exceeded one hundred degrees, the ram air blowing in felt like it came from a blast furnace. Flight surgeons claimed that on a four-hour mission during the hottest months of the year, OV-10 pilots lost between three and five pounds, mostly due to dehydration. There were plenty of days I thought the estimate was too conservative.

I couldn't allow myself to get distracted by my discomfort and by the hot air blowing into the cockpit, because the Trail below demanded all the concentration I could give it. At first glance the roads and paths always looked the same. The twists and turns in the road network, the lush vegetation, the jungle-covered mountains and ridges—they never changed. The area over which we flew covered hundreds of square miles filled with detail that boggled the mind. Learning all that detail was an ongoing process, based on experience and exposure. It was like studying a snapshot, day after day. And that routine sameness, the very quality the bad guys had hoped would hide them from our twenty-four-hour-a-day search, eventually became an advantage. Constantly flying over the same terrain, we came to memorize every detail so that when even the smallest

particular appeared out of place, mental alarm bells
sounded. Clues jumped out like neon signs: a different
shade of dust on the foliage beside the Trail; freshly cut
trees; a set of tracks that wasn't there yesterday; a muddy
spot in a pool of water—anything that didn't exactly match
the mental snapshot. The hard part came in figuring out
where to start and how to let the mind's eye drink in the
whole scene and then pick up the changes. The process
wasn't unlike looking for the proverbial needle in the hay-
stack. Rarely was anything out of place. Sometimes we
would fly for days without ever seeing so much as a twig
pushed aside. On other days the targets we turned up were
so blatant and bold it would roll your socks down.

Binoculars welded into my eye sockets, I continued flying down the Trail at a leisurely pace, power levers positioned to give nine hundred foot-pounds of torque per
engine, producing 130 knots of airspeed. Glancing out the
front windscreen, I could see Chavane up in front of me.
For a few seconds, my thoughts drifted back to the late-
afternoon gunfight of a week earlier. That battle still
seemed unreal, like it had happened to someone else. My
right hand on the stick and feet on the rudder pedals both
received the signal from my brain before I consciously noticed that my aircraft was tracking directly for the saddleback ridge where I had let that gunner get the best of me.
Whether out of professional interest or morbid curiosity, I
had to take another look at the scene. If the gunner was
still there, I was determined to put a rocket down his
scrawny throat and blow his guts all over the ridge.

At the northern edge of Chavane's large meadow, a
well-used dirt road branched off the main Trail and wound
its way southeast toward the Vietnamese border. I had seen
that particular segment of road a few times before, never
giving it much attention since there was no cover on either
side for several kilometers. As I passed overhead, my mental alarm bells went off. At first I could make out only what
appeared to be a moving dust cloud, but a closer look with
the binoculars revealed four dudes dressed in green chugging

along on black motorcycles. I had never seen movement on the Trail before, much less people. Whatever they were up to, it had to be important to risk a run in broad daylight.

My heart pounding with excitement, I reefed the Bronco around in a high-G turn, the heavy burble letting me know we were right on the edge of an accelerated stall. When I rolled out, the line-up didn't look right, so I eased off the back pressure and continued with an aileron roll to the left to get the nose below the horizon and the wings relatively level. I still ended up tracking at a forty-five-degree angle to the road instead of flying directly down it as I wanted. By coming in at an angle, I introduced the lateral dimensions of right and left to the aiming solution. Had I taken a few more seconds to line up on the same axis as the road, I would have only had to worry about firing long or short.

As I continued the dive, the motorcycles realized I was after them and poured on the coals, making it tough to keep them in my gunsight. With what I hoped was the correct amount of lead, I popped off two willie petes and pulled up to reposition for a quick second shot. It was a good thing no one could hear me because I wailed in genuine pain as the heavy G forces changed my weight from 165 pounds to something just over 675 pounds, stretching and pulling my sunburned skin in ways only a Spanish Inquisition torturer could appreciate. Nursing myself and the aircraft over the top of a loop, I watched as the two rockets exploded ten meters short of the road and abeam the last cycle. Everyone kept right on going, but the explosions must have shaken number four's concentration. As he sped after the serpentine procession in front of him, he took the only curve in the road a little too fast and skidded out in a magnificent cloud of red dust. Instead of stopping to help, his buddies raced around the curve and disappeared into the first tree line they came to. I broke off my pass and pulled around in a level turn to get the perfect line on the fallen cyclist. As I started the roll-in, my target got up and pushed his machine about fifteen meters to a large, solitary tree just off the road at the very top of the curve.

From there the episode deteriorated into a scene from a
Laurel and Hardy movie. Regardless of the direction I came
in from, my quick thinking target deftly put himself and
his cycle on the opposite side of the large tree trunk. It was
like playing a grown-up version of peek-a-boo. I actually
began to respect that faceless, green-clad little man, scurrying ridiculously around the tree trunk. But after three
aborted passes, I'd had enough. I climbed to five thousand
feet and rolled into a vertical dive with the pipper superimposed on the top of the tree. I fired three rockets, then
sucked in the Gs, all the while yelping in agony and wondering if this guy was worth it and why I was doing this
to my sunburned body.

The first rocket hit short while the other two slammed
into the top branches, creating a shower of searing, white-
hot phosphorous. I circled slowly as the smoke cleared, half
hoping to see the NVA version of Evel Knievel running
for the trees. Nothing. There was no discernible movement.
The motorcycle lay at the base of the tree, but there was
no sign of Evel. I suspected he might have climbed into
the tree, and if that were the case, he was either hiding or
fried to a crisp. Either way, it really torqued my jaws that
the other three bad guys ran out on their buddy; to express
my disgust at their cowardice, I blasted the tree line where
they were hiding with a whole pod of willie petes. The
results were questionable, but the sight of the explosions
made me feel better.

From the large curve, I worked my way west, my interest piqued by the four motorcycles and where they might
have been coming from and going to. Any thoughts of continuing south to revisit the saddleback had long since van-
ished. The open segment of trail below me obviously
deserved more detailed scrutiny than I had given it. I
combed every inch of it, but nothing out of the ordinary
struck me until I returned to the fork on the main trail.
Precisely at the V where the roads split, I spotted the most
curious glass structure imaginable, so out of place that it
had to be a joke. What I saw made me start laughing until

I remembered the flak trap from the earlier training mission. Cautiously, but still smiling broadly, I made one low pass, then asked Hillsboro to send a fast-mover my way to confirm the strange target.

About an hour later, an F-100 fast FAC checked in with me. "Covey 221, this is Misty. Understand you've got a mystery target for me to look at. What's the form?"

A Misty FAC was the perfect guy to help me. They were famous throughout Southeast Asia as the crazy fighter jocks who flew modified FAC missions at low altitudes in high-threat areas.

Somewhat tentatively, I keyed the mike button. "Misty, Covey 221. I'm gonna talk you into this structure because I don't want to prejudice the case by telling you what I think it is. Right now I'm orbiting directly over Chavane. Have you got a tally on me?"

Misty replied, "I'm approaching the area now. Rock your wings so I can get a tally on you."

My sunburn made it too painful to jerk the airplane around more than necessary, so reaching up above my head, I hit the smoke generator toggle switch, a handy little gadget that pumped oil into the left engine exhaust, creating a trail of white smoke just like the Thunderbirds used. Within seconds Misty had a visual on me.

"Okay, Misty. See that stretch of road on the north edge of Chavane? Follow it west about three klicks to where it intersects the main north-south trail. That intersection forms a V pointing roughly west. Look right into the V, not more than ten feet off the road, and tell me what you see. I'll stay at fifty-five hundred over Chavane."

Misty arced around to the east, then rolled in to begin his low-level run along the road. As the F-100 streaked by the target, the swept-wing fighter appeared to be low enough to drop the landing gear for a touch-and-go. The pilot gave new meaning to the concept of flying down in the weeds.

Misty executed a hard pull up to the north without saying a word. Since I knew he'd seen the target, it was impossible to keep my curiosity in check. "Misty, Covey 221. You saw it, didn't you? I saw the same thing, so just blurt it right out."

A long pause filled the air before Misty answered me. "Covey, nobody's gonna believe this except you and me. I got a real good look at your target. Either I'm stone blind or that thing is an honest-to-god Bell telephone booth. The door was wide open, and I'll bet there was change in the coin return. Is that what you thought it was?"

"That's affirmative. You don't suppose the truck drivers call back home to Hanoi to talk to their wives on it, do you?"

Misty mulled my question over for a few seconds, then answered, "If they do, I hope a strange man answers or else the bastards get a busy signal."

Back at Da Nang during my debriefing, the intel officer was beside himself with glee. Never mind trucks, motorcycles, or guns—he wanted to know about the phone booth. He quizzed me for thirty minutes about size, markings, colors, visible wires, and exact map coordinates. As the debriefing wore on, I started to get a little impatient, but it was hard to get upset with the intel types for being as curious as I had been. The phone booth caper proved to be a good change of pace for all of us.

Two days and three VC rocket attacks later, the head Covey left word that he wanted to see me. Standing in the open door, I could see Lieutenant Colonel Ed Cullivan sitting at his desk, poring over a stack of paperwork. A fighter jock from way back, the good colonel had a ready smile and a gleam in his eye that told the world he had a genuine zest for living. Ed was of medium height with a slender build and had a head of black hair laced with gray, giving him a classic Cary Grant salt-and-pepper look. Much to the chagrin of all us young studs, the Da Nang nurses considered Ed the ultimate heartthrob. But more important, Ed Cullivan was a first-rate combat leader who knew how to get the most out of his young pilots without smothering them with too much supervision and needless bureaucratic rules.

Colonel Cullivan looked up from his work and motioned me into the small office which he shared with his operations officer. "Tom," he asked, "have you ever heard of the X-Ray mission?" Before I could answer, he continued. "I want you to take a crack at it. You're still a little green, but you seem to have a knack for flying yourself out of tight spots, and that's what this mission calls for. I want you to get together with Mike McGerty. He'll be in charge of your checkout."

A few hours later, Mike filled me in on the X-Ray mission. Roughly once a month, each of the four Coveys involved took turns staging out of Ubon, Thailand, for three days. The drill involved picking up a Laotian back-seater known as the X-Ray. These back-seaters were villagers who had been recruited and trained by the CIA. When one of the X-Rays got wind of or personally saw a lucrative Pathet Lao or NVA target in his area, he would pass the word and arrange for a clandestine pickup by Air America, the CIA's private airline. The Coveys were never privy to the details, but just before our launch, the X-Ray showed up, ready to fly and eager to point out enemy troop concentrations, hidden supplies, and communication centers.

On my checkout ride on June 9, McGerty and I flew to Ubon to touch base with the intelligence officers who knew about the X-Ray program. After an hour of double-talk from them, we jumped back in the airplane for a leisurely look at our assigned area.

The area of operations, or AO, included the southern third of the Laotian panhandle, called Military Region IV. Laos was divided into four military regions: regions I and II were in the north, while III and IV were located in the panhandle. MR-I received most of the attention because it encompassed the area where the CIA ran its covert military operation. Unlike the interdiction campaign along the Trail in southern Laos, the northern operation, known as "Barrel Roll," primarily supported the ground activities of about five thousand CIA-trained Hmong tribesmen under the personal command of General Vang Pao. As leader of the Hmong army, Vang Pao and his forces tried valiantly to prevent the NVA from taking over Laos. One of the perennial battle grounds was the infamous Plain of Jars, so named because of hundreds of large stone burial urns located on this strategically situated plateau.

In the south, MR-IV was dominated geographically by the Bolovens Plateau, a huge piece of real estate sloping up from the Mekong River and east some seventy-five miles to the rugged cliffs overlooking the Xe Kong River near the Ho Chi Minh Trail. In between, the poorly led Royal Laotian Army responded sporadically to NVA and Pathet Lao efforts to infiltrate and occupy the entire plateau. Scattered throughout the Bolovens were a series of strongholds and dirt airstrips known as PS sites, which Americans had helped set up. As focal points for Air America and army activities, the PS sites acted as magnets, drawing repeated enemy attacks. As it turned out, most of our X-Ray missions were flown in support of Royal Laotian Army troops deployed around various airstrips.

After Mike and I crossed the Mekong, we set up a lazy orbit over Pakse, the largest town in MR-IV. Pakse possessed a rich history and was absolutely vital to the defense of the region. But the town's fascination for me had nothing to do with its native charm or location. Pakse served as regional headquarters for the Raven FACs, a small, elite group of U.S. Air Force pilots stationed in Laos who posed as civilian employees for various government agencies associated with the State Department. Stories about the wild exploits of the Ravens had been leaking out for several years, so much so that their "cover" was certainly not a well-kept secret. According to rumors and word of mouth, they flew in anything but military uniforms. My less-than-authoritative sources told me standard garb consisted of Levis, cowboy boots, T-shirts, and dark sunglasses—spurs were optional. I had heard that Ravens did their FACing in the venerable O-1 Bird Dog but also checked out in the T-28 fighter bomber operated by the Royal Laotian Air Force. Supposedly Ravens took only volunteers who had at least six months of combat FAC experience, and then they took only the best of the lot. It was said that a history of family insanity helped, since the Ravens sustained an extremely high casualty rate—about 50 percent. In spite of the risk, the most appealing aspect was that Ravens could call their own shots, without any hassle from higher up: Just get the job done, whatever it took. To me that sounded too good to be true, and as I banked around Pakse, I made up my mind to set my sights on becoming a Raven.

From Pakse we headed east along Route 23, circling occasionally so Mike could point out specific landmarks and trouble spots. We made a special effort to overfly each of the PS sites so I would become familiar with their location and general layout. Through breaks in the clouds, we caught glimpses of PS-39, with its partially paved runway and distinctive half-moon-shaped perimeter defense trench. Nearer the edge of the plateau, we had a good view of the desolate-looking PS-21, as well as PS-71, a triangular-shaped special forces "A" camp with a small dirt airstrip alongside. The busiest strip by far appeared to be PS-38, a three-thousand-foot-long runway carved out of red dirt. At least a dozen buildings cluttered each side of the runway near midfield. While we circled, two short-takeoff-and-landing (STOL) Air America Pilatus Porters landed.

Finally we turned north for a short flight up to Saravane, the second-largest town in MR-IV. Saravane was on the western edge of the normal Covey AO, so I had seen it several times before. The situation there was particularly hot because NVA regulars virtually surrounded the town. Most people expected it to fall to the enemy at any moment, and the airfield had already changed hands several times in as many days. One of our FACs reported seeing a 37mm gun sitting right in front of the flight operations building.

As we circled over the besieged town, Mike took the controls of the OV-10. He lowered the gear and flaps and turned on a base leg to the beat-up red-dirt runway. Until just before we touched, I figured Mike would do a low approach, but to my disbelief, he flared nicely and plunked us down onto the rough surface. Immediately he cobbed the power, and after a few bounces, we were airborne again. As we accelerated, I grabbed the landing gear handle and raised it, since the lever in the back seat could be used only to lower the gear. I recall looking out the left side at small clusters of people standing beside the runway. They just stood there, as if frozen in time, almost oblivious to one of the greatest daredevil stunts since Medal of Honor recipient Bernie Fischer landed his A-1 in the A Shau Valley to rescue a downed pilot. I couldn't believe it. We had just executed a touch-and-go landing deep in Laos on a dirt airstrip about to be overrun by the whole North Vietnamese Army! I'm not sure what I expected from our unconcerned audience on either side of the runway, but a few cheers or a standing ovation would have been nice.

What I had just sat through was probably one of the most stupid, show-your-fanny acts imaginable, but up to that point, it was the most exhilarating event of my short combat career. My aimless chatter to my back-seater reflected my feelings. "Mike, you crazy doofus! That was great! It was wild. I can't believe you did that. Just look at those lumps of coal standing down there. They don't even appreciate what you just pulled off!"

Mike responded in measured tones. "It wasn't that big a deal. Nobody's impressed except you 'cause they've seen it a hundred times. Hell, half the Coveys have shot a touch-and-go at Saravane and the other half will. Just don't blab this around when we get home."

My euphoria began wearing off quickly at being told the stunt at Saravane was old hat. Still, the episode made for an interesting war story.

Cruising back over the Bolovens, I felt no sense of apprehension or foreboding as I did over the Ho Chi Minh Trail. The area was crawling with bad guys, but the scene below looked peaceful—just mile after mile of rolling hills covered with lush green rain forests. We would occasionally come across a sleepy village or a road leading off to nowhere, but for the most part the countryside seemed untouched. Without the threat of the triple-A guns that harassed us out on the Trail, we could enjoy the luxury of flying low enough to see detail without using binoculars.

After our day of exploring, Mike and I landed back at Da Nang late in the afternoon. We'd covered a lot of ground and seen all the PS sites, including that closeup look at the airfield at Saravane. As Mike debriefed the ride, I couldn't help feeling dissatisfied. The checkout had generated more serious questions than answers. I was genuinely excited about the prospect of working with troops in contact, yet everything about the X-Ray mission seemed so slipshod and piecemeal. Nobody bothered to describe the tactical situation, unit locations, troop dispositions, ground-fire threat, enemy order of battle, or any of the other details that seemed essential to understanding the "big picture." It seemed like the intel types and "spooks" over at Ubon wanted us to know only the barest details, and woe to anybody unpatriotic enough to ask a question. After thinking about X-Ray for a while, I concluded that the operation was more of a diversion for the pilots than a bona fide mission. Although the program had the potential for great adventure, it was really a FUBAR (fouled up beyond all recognition) affair with lots of room for unpredictable results. Later that same evening, a bunch of us were given a dramatic lesson in how FUBAR our own Covey mission could be.

The night started innocently enough. Six of us were sitting in the officers' club bar, playing "hi-lo" for drinks. The game was ridiculously simple. The instigator produced an MPC or dollar bill and silently picked two consecutive numbers from the bill's serial number. In turn each player guessed a number, the instigator advising whether the choice was above (high) or below (low) his secret number. Each guess generated a new high-low, quickly narrowing the range to just a few numbers. At some point an unlucky soul inadvertently "guessed" the secret number and had to buy a round of drinks for everyone at the table.

While we sat there playing, one of our new young lieu-tenants took off with an IP on his phase I night training mission. The IP flew his student to a strip on the beach called Marble Mountain for some touch-and-go landings. For some reason the control tower cleared the OV-10 for the landing, but never mentioned a trench that had been dug across the runway. The eager student touched down on the dark strip and pushed up the power for takeoff. At the last second, he saw the three-foot-high dirt mound and re-acted by jerking the Bronco into the air, avoiding what could have been a fiery crash. Unfortunately, the right main landing gear clipped the mound, bending back into a con-torted position.

With the right main hanging limply, there was no way to retract the landing gear. The IP had two choices: eject or try for a crash landing back at Da Nang. It was a tough choice. Ejection might have been easier, but the plane would be lost, and there were no absolute guarantees on the "nylon elevator." Landing required a precise maneuver involving touching down on the left wheel and holding that position for as long as possible, while hoping like hell the aircraft didn't ground-loop or cartwheel into a giant fireball. Pulling off such a feat in broad daylight was tough enough; to do it at night was extremely risky, requiring luck and superb stick-and-rudder skills.

After talking it over, the rookie flyer and the IP elected to land at Da Nang. With a beautiful bit of flying, they put the bird down on the left side of the runway and held the right wing up until just before it lost all lift. Then they gently lowered the right main onto the concrete. Predicta-bly, the gear collapsed, causing the OV-10 to veer sharply to the right and off the runway. The aircraft finally came to a halt some six hundred feet into the grassy surface be-tween the left and right runways. Both pilots hopped out unhurt, obviously ecstatic that the ordeal was over. Un-known to the two Coveys, though, the episode had a tragic ending.

When he heard about a pending emergency landing, an airman on the approach end barrier crew walked out to the edge of the runway to watch the drama firsthand. As the OV-10 left the runway and skidded through the darkness, the right wing hit the unsuspecting airman, killing him instantly. The pilots' momentary jubilation at surviving the crash turned to instant horror and grief. That he was totally blameless did not console the new Covey pilot. A good man had died needlessly, the victim of an incredible series of flukes and screwups. Ironically, damage to the aircraft was minimal.

In the week following my initial X-Ray ride, flying time grew scarce. The southwest monsoon, so-called because of the prevailing winds, generated the first sustained stretch of nasty weather over the Trail. With all the rain and low clouds, picking out trucks became virtually impossible. Most of the Covey missions were canceled because of the weather before they could even launch. The situation was particularly frustrating since the weather was great on the Vietnamese side of the mountains. In a cycle probably as old as time itself, the weather pattern would continue until October, when the wind shifted to the northeast, bringing rain to Vietnam and drying sunshine to Laos.

The weather-inflicted inactivity made for some interesting studies in human nature. The officers' club bar seemed to do a better business than normal, and tempers tended to grow shorter in direct proportion to time since the last flight. Watching the grounded Coveys was like watching a group of highly trained athletes poised to play the big game, only to be told of another rain delay. It was tough to stay psyched up. When we did get airborne, there were either no targets or no fighters available. Our intel officer told us that the NVA used the weather to their advantage, moving heavy concentrations of men and supplies down the Ho Chi Minh Trail under the protective cloud cover. Within weeks the Trail would become a quagmire of mud, slowing the flow dramatically. In the meantime the North Vietnamese logistics network would continue to operate, in spite of our sophisticated technology. Over multiple scotch-and-waters, we concluded that the NVA were literally and figuratively thumbing their noses at us.

Finally, on June 18, the weather broke. I packed some underwear and a clean flight suit and launched to Ubon to fly my first X-Ray mission. En route, I was pleasantly surprised by the relatively good weather over the Bolovens—lots of holes in the clouds, big enough to work fighters through.

After landing at Ubon and bedding down my aircraft for the night, I wandered over to the officers' club bar, stopping long enough to cash a check. Armed with a handful of U.S. dollars and a cold beer, I studied the layout. Physically the building wasn't much larger than the Da Nang Officers Open Mess, aptly referred to by its initials, "DOOM," but the similarity ended there. Even in midafternoon the Ubon Officers Club seemed busy, with about half the dining tables filled and a good-sized crowd at the bar. The dining room looked bright and cheerful, just like any nice club back in the States, and the little Thai waitresses were cute as buttons and quite friendly. By comparison, the DOOM resembled a big old barn, usually deserted unless a USO show blew into town. Our Vietnamese waitresses were as surly as they were ugly and seemed to take great delight in waiting until we selected something from the limited menu before cackling, "No hab."

Looking around the bar, I felt conspicuous in my faded green flight suit. Virtually all the other pilots in the place wore custom-made work suits, resembling flight suits but neatly tailored in assorted colors—dark green, gray, black, and several shades of blue. Evidently each squadron had its own version. I felt like a hillbilly in the big city.

Eventually, I hooked up with several buddies who introduced me to their friends, and we ended up passing a pleasant evening sipping Sing Ha beer and trading war stories about our experiences in Thailand and Vietnam. Most of the people gathered around the table were young fighter jocks assigned to the 8th Tactical Fighter Wing, known throughout the Air Force as the "Wolfpack." To a man they all sang the same tune, bemoaning their fate as F-4 GIBs, "guys in back." Because of a shortage of navigators, the young pilots found themselves flying in the back seat as copilots and weapons system operators behind more experienced front-seaters. Much to my surprise, many of them seemed genuinely envious of my adventures and responsibilities as a FAC.

At fifteen minutes before midnight, I ordered a half a dozen bottles of champagne, made everybody swear not to drink them until I returned, then skipped out the side door to a nearby hooch where I was bunking. At precisely midnight I returned to the noisy table, only this time I was wearing my clean flight suit—with brand new captain's bars. When I announced that the lieutenants at the table had better show a little more respect, they unceremoniously hosed me down with my own champagne.

By half past nine the next morning, I had completed the preflight and was killing time waiting for my X-Ray. At ten o'clock a white Toyota pickup glided to a stop beside me and deposited a small Oriental man carrying a helmet and a brown paper bag. The little man walked up to me, carefully set his helmet and bag on the ground, then put both hands together as if to pray. He bowed slightly at the waist, placing his hands directly in front of his face in the traditional Thai greeting known as the *wai*. Somewhat awkwardly I returned the greeting. He smiled broadly at my bungling effort, then grabbed my hand and shook it. With a heavy, lilting accent he addressed me: "Sah wah dee, Kup. My Thai name Prasert. Today you be pilot, I be X-Ray. How you say your name?" We went through several tortuous attempts at Yarborough before he settled on "Captain Tom." It had a nice ring to it.

Prasert stood about five feet six inches tall, typically slender with jet black hair and deep brown eyes with no discernible pupils. He wore gray slacks, a white open-collar short-sleeve shirt, and jungle boots. He had a pair of Air Force flying gloves stuffed in his back pocket. Prasert told me he was Thai by birth but had lived around Paksong, Laos, for most of his adult life. I kept hoping he would get around to discussing our mission because I had no clear idea of what we were supposed to do. Instead, we just stood there eyeing each other warily, wondering if the other was competent and what this day would bring.

Trying not to seem completely ignorant, I said light-heartedly, "Nice weather today. Hope you've got some good targets for us."

As if to signal he was ready to go, Prasert picked up his helmet and brown bag, then answered, "Plenty targets. I show you supplies we bomb. Maybe first we go talk to PS sites." It wasn't much of a clue, but at least it was something.

Clutching his brown bag tightly, Prasert deftly climbed into the back seat while I helped him strap in. I reviewed the radio wafer switch and a few emergency procedures, then climbed into the front seat. As I ran through the checklist, it occurred to me that only God, Buddha, and Prasert had any idea what was going on—and none of them was talking to me.

After engine start we taxied out toward the arming area. My curiosity finally getting the best of me, I asked Prasert what was in the brown bag. He answered innocently, "*Kin cow*—rice, my lunch." I smiled to myself at his simple explanation. What a letdown. I had been convinced he had something weird in that bag, maybe a shrunken head or some other exotic charm.

After the arming crew pulled the last of the safety pins, the tower cleared me onto Runway 05. With a quick peek at final to make sure the coast was clear, I pulled into position on the upwind side of the runway. Through the windscreen I surveyed the full nine thousand feet of concrete in front of me, focusing on a spot about three thousand feet away where theoretically we should break ground and become airborne. In the few seconds before takeoff clearance, I took a close look at the runway around me. Heavy black skid marks from hundreds of F-4 landings coated the surface. Although I couldn't see it from my position, the other end of the runway shared the same black color. By contrast the seven thousand feet of runway in between appeared at least three shades lighter.

Even before the tower controller could finish saying my call sign, I pumped the brakes and pushed both power levers forward. As the Bronco strained at full power, I quickly checked the engine instruments to confirm they were in the green. Through my helmet earphones I heard, "Covey 221, squawk zero-three-zero-zero normal. Contact Ubon Departure when airborne. Wind calm, cleared for takeoff."

"Covey 221, rolling."

At brake release we lurched forward and accelerated slowly. The OV-10's counter-rotating props virtually eliminated the torque that normally pulled an aircraft one way or another, and the two large rudders made directional control easy even at very low speeds. At just over one hundred knots, I eased in aft stick and we were airborne with a thunk, as the main gear struts bottomed out at lift-off.

Climbing eastbound out of Ubon, Prasert and I headed for the Mekong River, the border between Thailand and Laos. Peace on one side, war on the other. Passing overhead at Pakse, we looked down into the half-mile-wide river, floating debris clearly visible in the churning reddish brown water. Some of those floating logs and branches probably started their journey at the Mekong's origin high in the mountains of China.

From Pakse, Prasert asked me to fly over each of the PS sites, beginning with PS-39. En route, the weather turned reasonably good with scattered to broken low scud hanging over most of the Bolovens Plateau. Through breaks in the clouds, we could see large patches of green jungle.

At PS-39 Prasert took charge of the FM radio and contacted the small secret airfield. A friendly American voice answered, and within seconds the conversation deteriorated into an old-home-week chat. Prasert addressed the voice on the ground as "Dunc," whom I assumed to be either an Air America pilot or some sort of CIA operative. Dunc and

Prasert exchanged greetings and asked about each other's
family, friends, and health for at least five minutes. At the
first lull in the conversation, I butted in. "Dunc, this is
Covey 221. Sorry to interrupt, but what's your tactical situation? Is there anything we can do to help you out?"

Responding in a somewhat icy tone, Dunc answered,
"Negative, Covey. Everything's under control here. There's
a Raven in the area looking after us. You might try the
boys over at PS-38. Things are pretty active down there.
Now can you put Prasert back on?"

Miffed by the snub, I replied, "Sorry, Dunc. We're on
a tight schedule. We'll swing by later to see how you're
doing." Rather than answer directly, Dunc simply clicked
his mike button twice, and that was the end of it. Or so I
thought.

As we continued to cruise east, Prasert had little to say,
obviously pouting over the episode at PS-39. I felt bad
about spoiling the party; he and Dunc were clearly old
friends and had probably been through a lot together. On
the other hand, I felt like wringing his neck for using me
as his personal limo driver. The airborne social call was
new to me and seemed particularly out of place in view of
the war raging around us, but the visits evidently meant a
lot to Prasert, so I cautiously offered him a compromise.
We agreed to check each site to determine the situation,
then press on if they didn't need our help. In return I promised to fly back over the sites and, gas permitting, let Prasert
shoot the bull to his heart's content.

After brief conversations with Art and Bill at PS-21 and
PS-71 respectively, we checked in with Dev at PS-38. For
the first time that day I gained a little insight into the ground
situation. Dev told us that their "Sierra was weak." Pathet
Lao troops had dug in roughly four klicks east of the field
and an 82mm mortar position directly off the end of the
runway was really getting on their nerves. Whenever a Porter or a Huey tried to land, the mortar usually opened up.
The incoming rounds rarely hit the buildings or the people,
but more than a few explosions cratered the runway, the

lifeline for the whole setup. Dev expected a full-scale assault in the next few days and didn't sound optimistic about the Royal Laotian Army's ability to repulse the attack. On that happy note Dev signed off, asking us to swing by in an hour when a Porter was due to land. He hoped having a FAC overhead would make the mortar crew think twice before firing.

I hated to leave the area. If Dev was right, a good fight was brewing, and selfish as it seemed, I wanted to be part of it. After a month of flying over the Trail, I felt confident in my ability to handle air strikes, but troops on the ground raised the stakes considerably. It's what I had dreamed about and been trained for. As Prasert and I flew off to the west, a tinge of guilt colored my thoughts. I badly wanted to work troops in contact, a classic TIC. I couldn't exactly bring myself to wish a fight on Dev or the defending troops, but if a firefight came, I desperately wanted to be there to help—and perhaps to make a difference.

Just west of Paksong, my back-seater guided me to a small village several miles south of Route 23. When we first flew over the cluster of about thirty hooches, we saw a number of people milling around. On our second orbit, the place looked deserted. I could only guess that they knew what was coming.

Approximately a thousand meters south of the village, a narrow tree line formed the boundary between two large, open fields. Prasert told me that Pathet Lao troops had stacked a cache of supplies at the T intersection where the tree line joined a section of jungle. Although I saw nothing suspicious through the binoculars, there was no reason to doubt Prasert's claim. After all, it was his home turf, and pointing out the bad guys was what he was paid to do. After plotting out the coordinates on my map, I got on the horn to Hillsboro, using the code words on which I'd been briefed.

"Hillsboro, Covey 221. I've got a Statehouse-nominated, X-Ray-validated target for you, over." Since the normal scarcity of fighters had conditioned me not to expect a pos-

itive response to short-notice requests for air, it came as a
surprise when the code words apparently set some high-
level wheels in motion. Within seconds Hillsboro offered
to help. The controller answered, "Copy your X-Ray-
validated target. Statehouse confirms. Can you use some
fast-movers? I've got a set of Fox Fours in Cherry Anchor
about to come off the tanker. Gimme a rendezvous, and
they're yours."

I passed on a rendezvous off channel 72, the secret
TACAN station located on the Bolovens Plateau, then began figuring out run-in headings, pull-offs, and the dozens
of other details that are part of an air strike when civilians
or friendlies are a factor. With Prasert's help I picked out
a rugged-looking ridge line in case of an emergency bailout
and then settled back to wait for the fighters. As we droned
around, I agonized about the broken cloud deck at three
thousand feet. There were plenty of holes for the F-4s to
work through—it would simply be a matter of luck. One
minute the tree line was clearly visible, the next a gray
puffy obscured it. I couldn't decide whether to duck underneath the stuff or to stay on top so all of us could see
each other.

A few minutes later my fighters checked in with lots of
gas and wall-to-wall MK-82s. They picked up the highway
and the village with no problem but couldn't get a clear
view of the target. Several wide orbits later, a sucker hole
opened up, so I rolled in to mark the storage cache. Diving
through the hole, I pressed in fairly low and got off a good
rocket. Unfortunately, by the time Lead maneuvered around
for an east-to-west restricted run-in to keep from overflying
the village, the hole closed. We settled into a game of cloud
tag. There was nothing we could do except fly the pattern
a few more times and wait for the next opening. When it
finally came, the fighters had "no joy" on the smoke from
my first willie pete, so I rolled in a second time.

A split second before I fired, with the T intersection
lined up perfectly in my gunsight, the tree line erupted in
a huge explosion and fireball. At only two thousand feet
slant range from the target and closing fast, the only course

of action available to me was to honk back on the stick and try to pull clear of the blast pattern in front of me. The heavy G forces immediately tunneled my vision and blurred my eyesight as the blood drained from my head into the lower extremities. My mind raced. What had caused that explosion? Had my fighters dropped their bombs without clearance? Did my earlier rocket ignite whatever was hidden in the trees?

Although momentarily blind, I could still hear and feel the aircraft struggling. We were about to stall. Concentrate! Get control of the airplane, then worry about the target.

As I eased off the back pressure, my visual cues returned almost instantly. We were in a near-vertical climb directly over the billowing smoke of the blast. Before she stalled, I let the nose fall through the horizon and carefully banked us away from the immediate area. A quick glance at the instrument panel confirmed two good engines. When I looked back outside, my heart jumped into my mouth as the windscreen filled with the bottom of another aircraft, only about fifty feet away.

We barely had flying airspeed, so fancy maneuvering was out of the question. With more of a survival reaction than a conscious thought, I slammed the control stick full forward. This time the negative Gs forced me violently up against the seat belt, and without having to look back, I heard Prasert's helmet bounce off the rear canopy. Along with some of my maps and a couple of long-lost grease pens, a surprisingly large cloud of dust and debris from the cockpit floor floated up in front of my face. While simultaneously straining to see through the dust and pull myself back down into the seat, I watched helplessly as we covered the remaining few feet to the other airplane.

There was no sense of panic, no paralyzing fear, only the realization that Prasert and I were milliseconds away from dying in a fiery midair collision. There wasn't even time to flinch. In a split second, we flashed under the belly of the other bird and into the clear—without a scratch!

With the control stick back to neutral and using the air-

speed we'd gained in the unloading maneuver, I pulled us
hard to the right, hoping to catch a glimpse of the intruder.
Ninety degrees through the tight turn, we spotted him—a
lone Royal Laotian Air Force T-28 climbing back to altitude. Slipping to the inside of the T-28's turn in order to
cut him off, I finally had a chance to say something to my
back-seater.

"Prasert, are you okay?"

In a bit of philosophical understatement accentuated by
a somewhat shaky voice he replied, "Okay, okay. We come
too close." The man definitely had a lyrical way of cutting
to the heart of the matter.

No sooner had Prasert answered me than we both
jumped as a second string of bombs detonated off our left
wing tip. A second T-28 climbed straight ahead to our altitude, then started a lazy turn to join up with his leader,
who plugged along about a mile in front of us.

Leaning forward slightly, I switched to the emergency
Guard transmitter and attempted to contact the Laotian pilots. "Laotian T-28s operating just south of Route 23 in the
vicinity of Paksong. This is Covey 221 on Guard. If you
read me, come up on UHF frequency 282.0." Nothing. Not
a peep out of them.

Prasert's voice, considerably calmer this time, came in
over the intercom with a suggestion: "Maybe they hear better if I talk in Lao." Before I could digest the illogic of his
suggestion, he rattled off a long string of strange-sounding
words, all totally unintelligible to me, somewhat musical
with a distinct pattern of rising and falling tones. Almost
immediately a high-pitched voice answered in another long
stream of tonal words and phrases. After several more exchanges, Prasert translated for me.

"T-28 pilot say he fly low along the highway when he
see your rocket. When you fly back above clouds and nothing happen, he drop bombs on your smoke. Pilot say he
think maybe kill beaucoup NVA."

As the translation sank in, I still couldn't believe it. A
FUBAR situation if ever there was one. Without thinking,

I mumbled into the intercom, "Irrefutable logic in a complete vacuum."

Innocently, Prasert asked, "What you say?" He had no idea what I was talking about, yet it wasn't his fault he couldn't handle a few abstract English words. I didn't know three words in Lao, much less the subtleties of a foreign language. Consumed with equal shares of guilt, embarrassment, and frustration, I mentally kicked myself for getting boxed in, for not knowing the language, and for not being able to handle a simple air strike.

Whatever had been hidden in the trees, the uninvited T-28s had done a good job of blowing away the hiding place. Prasert and I saw a number of small boxes and lots of shredded straw and paper strewn around several of the bomb craters—not exactly the find of the century but provocative enough to warrant calling in the orbiting fast-movers. Carefully, I worked each F-4 in multiple passes on the target, always mindful of the possibility that the free-spirited Laotian Air Force might show up without warning. My fighters blasted the jungle cache with devastating precision, but we only turned up more boxes and straw. There wasn't a fire or secondary explosion to be had.

It was time to head back toward PS-38, so we turned eastward, leaving the village and the bomb craters and the boxes and the T-28s behind, physically and mentally. To ease the tension, I leveled off just above a ragged cloud deck that stretched for miles and looked like a sea of spun cotton. Because of the steadily rising heat, small whiffs had begun to build into columns. We darted in and out like a slalom skier running the gates at Squaw Valley. On a good downhill slope, a skier might hit 60 miles an hour—no comparison to our three-dimensional slalom at 240 miles per hour.

Next, I aimed the OV-10 at the very top of a growing cloud column, the object being to slice through the top two or three feet of the swirling mass. A few of the larger columns boiled up at a rate of climb in excess of several hundred feet a minute, so looking out through the lighted reticle

of the gunsight offered an interesting exercise in stick and
rudder coordination. As we closed in on our cloud target,
there was a momentary sensation of speed followed by a
reflex tightening of the stomach muscles just before "impact." It was great fun trying to pull off a perfectly timed
collision, with just the slightest tickle as we flashed through
the cloud top. After several more demonstrations, I even let
Prasert try his hand at it. His basic eye-to-hand coordination
was good, though I suspected he really didn't understand
or appreciate the game. He never seemed to get the hang
of it.

Once at PS-38, with Dev's concurrence, I set up an orbit
off the south end of the airstrip in the general vicinity of
the worrisome mortar position. We gave the area a good
going over and identified several likely spots, but there was
no way to be sure unless the guy loaded the tube and fired.

I heard the Air America Porter call on Dev's frequency,
indicating he was about five minutes out. To be on the safe
side, I armed up the right outboard rocket pod, ready to
roll in should the mortar crew give away their position by
opening fire.

Prasert saw the Porter first, then we both watched as the
strange-looking, single-engine, silver-and-blue aircraft set
up on a modified straight-in from the north, holding an
incredibly slow fifty-knot final approach speed. While still
about a hundred feet in the air, the pilot yelled into the
radio, "Somebody cover us! We're taking heavy fire!"

Obviously "somebody" was me, and my first thought
focused on the 82mm mortar. As I scanned the ground below in a furious search, I had absolutely no indication our
boy had fired. It had to be a different threat. In the confusion, everybody tried talking at once. Dev and I keyed our
mikes simultaneously to ask where—at precisely the same
instant the Porter pilot tried to tell us. In the resulting garbled transmission, we cut each other out. Before anybody
could retransmit, the little Air America bird touched down
on the red-dirt strip apparently no worse for the experience.

A long silence followed. We watched as the Porter tax-

ied to midfield and shut down; the pilot and one passenger
nonchalantly climbed out. Finally, Dev's easygoing voice
filled the earphones in my helmet. He passed on the pilot's
estimate of where the ground fire had come from. He cautioned me, however, that friendly troops were also in that
immediate area. Dev must have sensed my frustration, because he signed off with a somewhat hollow pep talk.

"Thanks for your help, Covey. We really appreciate you
keeping that 82 off our backs. Swing by tomorrow and
maybe we can have a go at the guys who shot at our
Porter."

In my mind the day had been a complete wipeout, at
best one of those days when everything you touch turns to
dog doo-doo. Disgusted and disappointed, I pointed the
Bronco westward, climbed back to altitude, trimmed her up
for hands-off flight, and then rested both my arms on the
canopy rails. From my actions Prasert probably guessed we
were heading home, but he asked the question anyway.

Without thinking I answered, "Yeah, let's go home. Too
much of a good thing will rot your teeth." As soon as the
words were out of my mouth I cringed, knowing full well
he wouldn't understand.

His voice heavy with concern, Prasert asked, "Captain
Tom have toothache?" I smiled in spite of myself, feeling
a little like George Burns talking to Gracie Allen.

"Yeah, a bad toothache," I responded, figuring the path
of least resistance would be easier on both of us.

Back at Ubon, Prasert and I agreed on a rendezvous time
for the next day and said good-bye; then the white Toyota
pickup whisked him away. Hot and sweaty, in a foul mood
to match, I trudged the mile from the flight line to the
hooch.

That night I tossed and turned, running instant replays
of the day's mission in my mind. As I mentally reviewed
the balance sheet, I totaled more screwups than "atta boys."
I kept thinking: Maybe it's me, maybe I'm just not taking
control of the situation. In my short combat career, I
seemed to have been mixed up in one weird event after

another—the fake truck, the check ride target, the 23mm hit, the phone booth caper—and now a near midair and the indecisive performance at PS-38. It all boiled down to being able to anticipate the unexpected, something I wasn't sure could be learned. I finally drifted off into a fitful sleep, my last conscious thoughts wondering whether I would ever learn.

On my second full day as a U.S. Air Force captain, I felt better about everything in general. For one thing I was twice as experienced as I had been the day before. Even the weather cooperated, producing a brilliant blue sky with only a few white puffies hanging at the six-thousand-foot level.

Prasert and I got airborne on schedule and flew directly to PS-38. Dev sounded genuinely glad that we were there, explaining that Pathet Lao troops had launched several heavy probes during the night. The Laotian defenders had managed to hold their own, but sustained several casualties. Dev speculated that they were nervous and scared, possibly on the verge of folding. If the Laotian Army bugged out, there was nothing between the bad guys and the airstrip.

After talking to Dev, the next step was to make direct contact with the ground commander. Prasert finally got him up on Fox Mike. In a nerve-wracking conversation punctuated by frequent translations for my benefit, my backseater fed me the map coordinates for both the friendlies and the bad guys. The ground commander's position roughly correlated to the word picture Prasert translated; the Pathet Lao coordinates plotted out five miles to the east, an obvious mistake in light of the continuing exchange of sporadic small-arms fire. I had to be sure of the positions, especially since the ground commander wasn't. The worst thing imaginable would be to run an air strike involving a "short round," the term used to describe the accidental bombing or shelling of friendly troops. As the FAC, I bore the responsibility.

At my insistence, Prasert instructed the friendlies to mark their position with colored smoke, just the way they'd taught us to do back at FAC U. The voice on the other end of the radio refused, claiming the smoke would reveal their hiding place—a good point. The ground commander did agree to help us by spreading a bright-colored cloth panel on the ground. We quickly identified three orange panels and could even see troops waving as we flew overhead. Getting a fix on the enemy position was tougher.

To hear the ground commander tell it, the bad guys were storming the walls, yet his voice sounded remarkably calm—too calm. In spite of his pleas to "drop bomb right now," I kept badgering him for more accurate information. First we made him reconfirm the map coordinates, which he insisted were correct. Next I had Prasert ask him for a compass bearing and an estimated distance to the nearest enemy position. By his calculation the position was northeast at fifty meters. When we pressed him about the distance, he waffled, changing it first to two hundred and then to three hundred meters. As a last resort, we asked if he could lob a couple of mortar rounds on the target and talk us in from there. Much to my relief, he said yes and told us to stand by.

Fifteen minutes later the commander announced he was ready. Making sure we stayed well away from his line of fire, I orbited at two thousand feet, a good altitude for taking in the whole scene. As I focused on the target, I assumed the mortar crew would use a white phosphorous round, similar to my willie pete rockets. When nothing showed up after several minutes, it was clear they had used something else or had fired into a completely different quadrant.

With sweat dripping into my eyes, feeling frustrated by the tedious translation process, I irritably asked for another round. This time we saw it, a dirty gray explosion much smaller than I had expected, about four hundred meters from the friendlies. When the ground commander confirmed the mortar round was on target, I felt ready to put the wheels in motion for an air strike.

Just as on the previous day, Hillsboro responded instantly to my request to hit an X-Ray-validated target, only this time the answer put me in a good news–bad news dilemma. Hillsboro's good news was that fighters were immediately available; the bad news, at least to me, was that they were Royal Laotian Air Force T-28s. If yesterday's performance was any indication, I could look forward to having my hands full. Actually, the old single-engine recip trainer, modified to carry guns and bombs, had a good reputation as an accurate dive bomber, but the thought of controlling non-English-speaking pilots and of relying on Prasert's comprehension and translation abilities left me in a cold sweat.

Four stub-winged T-28s appeared over PS-38 at four thousand feet, circling warily for five minutes before we finally established radio contact. From what I could gather, Lead and Three carried 250-pound general-purpose bombs while Two and Four packed high-explosive rockets. All four pilots listened politely as Prasert translated my instructions, and then it was time to put up or shut up. I warned the friendlies to take cover and then rolled in for the mark.

All the way down the chute, Prasert carried on a running dialogue with the ground commander. As we pulled off, I knew we had to be near the target when Prasert informed me excitedly, "Commander tell us to be careful. Many NVA shoot everything at you."

Looking down at my white smoke, I figured that if we could just get Lead's ordnance in the ballpark, the other flight members would dump their stuff on his. If Lead missed badly, especially in the direction of the Royal Laotian troops, I shuddered to think what might happen. Driving that thought from my mind, I set up a tight figure-eight pattern over the friendlies with the long axis parallel to the north-south run-in heading assigned to the fighters. As Lead rolled in, I broke hard to the right in a 180-degree level turn, ending up on a parallel course between him and the friendly position. When I felt certain his line-up was good, I cleared him in hot. As Lead pulled off, I reversed the process with a hard turn back to the left. Once established in the figure-eight pattern, it was possible to keep it up indefinitely, always turning into the fighters and always keeping them in sight.

Much to my relief, Lead's bombs literally blew my smoke away—a perfect bull's-eye. When I directed Two's rockets into an adjacent clump of trees, nothing happened. Instead, everybody went around the pattern until Lead rolled in for a second run. When Lead finished, Two joined in with several consecutive rocket runs, followed by Three's dive-bomb passes. As I waited for number Four to do his solo act, Lead said something on the radio and the whole gaggle rejoined, then flew off to the west without so much as a "Good-bye," "Thanks," or "See you around." They didn't even acknowledge when I tried to pass along their BDA.

With the departure of the T-28s, I felt mentally exhausted. On the one hand, we had accomplished the job under less-than-ideal conditions, and for that I was thankful. On the other hand, I couldn't seem to shake a nagging doubt about who had been in control of the air strike. My first close-air-support mission wasn't nearly as satisfying as I had imagined it would be.

On the way back to Ubon, we checked in with Art, Bill, and Dunc at the other PS sites. Prasert chattered away merrily, telling his old friends how we had just saved PS-38 from the entire North Vietnamese Army. In truth, we didn't find a single thing on the bomb damage assessment, much less any sign of the NVA. Not that the lack of tangible damage made the air strike a failure. On the contrary, the bombs and rockets probably gave a very positive psychological lift to the Royal Laotian Army. Hopefully, the bombs had just the opposite effect on the bad guys.

After landing back at Ubon, Prasert and I said good-bye for what turned out to be the last time. In the end he had been invaluable to me, and over the past two days of flying together, I had developed a fondness and respect for the wiry little X-Ray. As he disappeared down the road in the white Toyota pickup, I helped the crew chief refuel my aircraft for the return flight to Rocket City and to the Coveys' secret war over the Ho Chi Minh Trail.

July

PRAIRIE FIRE

Over the past two months, everybody had preached the same sermon: "Thou shalt never fly below fifteen hundred feet; always stay above the small-arms-effective range—you'll live longer." Yet in total disregard of that most sacred of FAC commandments, here we were skimming along the Ho Chi Minh Trail at treetop level in an O-2.

There was no denying how much more detail was visible from down low. I could actually see the texture of the trees and small ridges and hills under them. Staring out the right window of the Oscar Deuce, I fully expected to see bad guys blazing away at us from behind every bush. But the only human to be seen was the Prairie Fire pilot sitting in the left seat, grinning at my obvious discomfort. Feeling more than a little boxed in, I kept thinking to myself, "What a squirrelly way to start the month of July." Other confusing thoughts bounced around in my head as I recalled the strange events of June 28, just three days earlier.

I should have suspected something when Captain Frank "Fuzzy" Furr, commander of the supersecret Covey Prairie Fire flight, headed straight for me as I walked through Covey Operations. The Prairie Fire types rarely associated with the rest of us; they even had their own mission briefing room in the intel shop, a top secret place we could not enter. Judging from Frank's expression, I had a sneaking suspicion he had something more than idle chatter on his mind.

Fuzzy Furr was a short, stocky man, built like a fireplug but solid as a rock. The front of his half-unzipped flight suit revealed a gray T-shirt with a picture of an OV-10 and the slogan "Fly the friendly skies of Laos." As he walked up, he looked around the room as if to make sure we were alone, then grabbed me by the arm and pulled me off into a corner.

In very measured tones, he said, "Tom, all of us have talked it over, and we want you to come into Prairie Fire." That was it. No buildup, no hard sell, no explanation, just the equivalent of "Uncle Fuzzy wants you." It reminded me of a fraternity rush, yet from the look in Fuzzy's eyes, it was clear he had serious business on his mind. There was a brief, awkward pause while I waited for him to add something to his original statement. When he didn't speak up, I did.

"Fuzzy, I'm not sure what to say. I don't even know what you guys do. Could you give me an idea what I'd be getting myself into?"

Smiling, he said, "Sorry. I can't tell you anything except that it's the most exciting FAC mission going. If you sign up, we'll tell you the whole nine yards. I can promise you'll love it."

Since my first question had led nowhere, I hit him with a second one. "Why me? I thought you guys only took people with six months of experience flying the Trail. I've barely got two months'."

"It's simple," he answered. "You're a little older, you're one of the few Coveys who's ever worked a TIC, and you've been shot at and hit—and handled it well. We just think you'll fit in."

Trying to digest Fuzzy's words, I wondered why being shot at and hit was important to him. I also remembered the old adage about never volunteering for anything.

"Listen, Fuzzy. I just can't see diving into this, especially since you won't even tell me the square root of fox alpha about it. Besides, in another couple of months, I should upgrade to IP, and that's something I really want, sort of a personal goal. Can you see my point?"

"Sure, I hear you," Frank said, seemingly not in the least put off by my answer. "But maybe we can work something out. After a couple of months with us, I'll talk to the boss and see if he'll authorize an instructor slot in Prairie Fire. By then you'd be ready to take over as training officer anyway. This'll work great."

I could see the wheels in Fuzzy's mind turning. He figured he had it all sewn up. His face lit up with a smile, then he grabbed my arm again. "You think it over, and I'll talk to you again tomorrow afternoon. Prairie Fire is the best job there is, no shit. And we really do want you with us." As Fuzzy walked away, he looked back at me over his shoulder and said, somewhat melodramatically, "Don't mention this conversation to anyone, okay?"

That night I fidgeted around my room, trying to concentrate on a volume of the Squadron Officer School correspondence course, but I kept thinking about Prairie Fire. Fuzzy had said it was the most exciting FAC mission going. I knew the Prairie Fire troops got twice as much flying time as the other Coveys, so how could it be a bad deal? Yet there was something just as compelling in the argument that the only pilot I'd ever known who had died in combat bought it on a Prairie Fire mission. Still, that could happen to anyone on any given mission, so I tried not to blow that aspect out of proportion. As I continued to stare at the text in front of me, the words could have been Greek for the amount of comprehension that soaked in. Instead, I kept hearing, seeing, pondering Fuzzy's words to me: "The best FAC mission going . . . you'll love it . . . we want you in Prairie Fire . . . we think you'll fit in."

It wasn't much to go on. Frank had alluded to TICs and to getting shot at, probably a hint that the job entailed lots of action involving troops on the ground. My only other clue centered on the mysterious "no bomb line" grids on our big wall map in the intel shop. Those boxes seemed to change daily, but they always showed up along the most heavily defended areas on the Trail or the DMZ. The rumor mill had it that Prairie Fire pilots controlled some kind of secret war inside those NBL grids. Since there were no U.S. or ARVN troops assigned that deep in enemy territory, I

couldn't imagine who or what was fighting there. Before
the night was over, I had almost convinced myself that a
Prairie Fire FAC and a Raven FAC had to be one and the
same thing. The lure was irresistible. Besides, Fuzzy and
the other Prairie Fire types seemed like normal guys—aside
from their penchant for secrecy.

By the next morning, I'd made up my mind. That afternoon when Fuzzy came walking toward me, I didn't have
to say a word. Grabbing my hand and shaking it, he smiled
and said, "I knew you were hooked from the very beginning. Welcome to the club."

Some club. Watching the Trail rush by under the wing
of our O-2, I still didn't know what it meant to be a member. At our destination it would be explained, but until we
arrived, wild speculation would blot out most other
thoughts.

In spite of my preoccupation, one visual cue did catch
my attention, however. As we flew farther north, the jungle
and foliage beside the Trail opened up, revealing wall-to-
wall bomb craters. Along the main segments, hardly a tree
remained standing. The whole area had really taken a beating. The sheer tonnage of bombs dropped out there was
beyond any reckoning, and it was a wonder anything or
anybody had survived. But survive they had, as evidenced
by the steady stream of enemy troops and supplies moving
down the Trail each night.

At the triborder area where Laos and North and South
Vietnam joined, my pilot hung a right and headed for
Quang Tri Air Base, a busy field built along the beach just
a few miles south of the DMZ. As part of my tour, we flew
east along the DMZ, following the Song Ben Hai River to
the point where it emptied into the South China Sea. There
on the north bank of the river, a tall pole sported a huge,
red ceremonial flag—the North Vietnamese flag!

Flying over the North generated all sorts of ominous
thoughts, and for me the sensation of looking south at that
flag was like taking a left turn into the twilight zone. It was
one thing to fly combat missions in South Vietnam or Laos;

flying over North Vietnam put a whole new spin on things and made the pulse speed up. For some reason I remembered a training film we'd seen in Jungle Survival School, a supposedly factual portrayal of the experiences of an F-105 jock shot down over the North. *Here There Are Tigers*, the film's title, made reference to ancient maps that warned travelers to stay clear of the region because of tigers and other predatory animals. As I looked down at the flagpole two thousand feet below me, the hair on the back of my neck stood up, telling me the tigers might have changed but the ancient warning was still worth heeding.

Several minutes later we landed at Quang Tri and taxied to Barky Operations, headquarters for the FACs who supported the U.S. Army's First Brigade of the Fifth Mechanized Division. As I climbed out of the O-2, I could see a sinister-looking black jeep waiting for us. An army staff sergeant in fatigues and a Special Forces green beret nodded and motioned for me to climb into the back seat. He and the O-2 jock talked quietly as we bounced off down the dusty, rut-filled road.

Five miles west of the airfield, we approached a large, heavily fortified perimeter with a barricade gate. Two guards, each with a CAR-15 slung over his shoulder, raised the barricade and waved us through. Although they were clearly Oriental, the guards didn't resemble any of the Vietnamese I'd become accustomed to seeing around Da Nang. These men were taller and more fair-skinned, almost Chinese in appearance.

Several hundred yards in front of us stood a cluster of five one-story frame buildings, three on the left side of an open yard and two on the right. The buildings were long shotgun affairs with no windows. The upper half of each wall appeared to be a top-hinged panel that could be propped open to let air in. Behind the left set of buildings, an assortment of UH-1 Hueys and AH-1 Cobra gunships were parked in a large, cleared field.

Our jeep chugged to a stop in front of the second building on the left. Again without speaking, the SF sergeant motioned me in with a gesture that reminded me of an usher in a fancy theater. Once inside, I found the room totally unremarkable. The sparsely furnished office contained two desks, a few chairs, and a fairly sophisticated bank of radio equipment. The two Americans in the office stood up when we entered. An all-American looking young captain, reminiscent of the "Jack Armstrong" radio character, walked over and extended a huge right hand in greeting. He introduced himself as Jerry Stratton, commander of Mobile Launch Team 2—MLT-2 for short. Then he introduced his first sergeant, Kim Budrow, a pleasant-looking senior NCO who had an air of complete calm about him. As with all first sergeants, most folks called him "Top."

With the amenities out of the way, Jerry asked me, "How much do you know?"

"Nothing," I admitted. "Fuzzy Furr said someone at Quang Tri would fill me in. I'm assuming that's you."

"I'm your man," Jerry answered. "Grab a cup of coffee and let's go next door. It'll be easier using the maps."

Once in the next room, we settled into chairs in front of several acetate-covered wall maps, mostly 1:50,000 scale. The intricate assortment of grease pencil markings and color codes on the map meant absolutely nothing to me; most of the marks appeared to be concentrated in the DMZ and in a section of Laos due west of Quang Tri.

Much to my relief, Jerry started the briefing using the broadest possible verbal brush to paint the picture for me. He explained that Prairie Fire was the code name for a highly sensitive joint-service project whose mission was to gather intelligence by putting small, long-range reconnaissance patrols on the ground in Laos, Cambodia, and the DMZ. From the Vietnamese border, the Prairie Fire area of operations extended thirty-three kilometers into Laos and the same distance north.

According to Jerry Stratton, the organization I was about to join actually traced part of its linage as far back as the Office of Strategic Services, the famous OSS of World War II, whose small teams infiltrated behind enemy lines to or-

ganize resistance movements, gather intelligence, or carry
out sabotage. Years later, when President John F. Kennedy
came into office, he rapidly became a covert action enthu-
siast, envisioning the OSS successor, the Central Intelligence Agency, as a means for conducting stepped-up
unconventional warfare operations in a Cold War hot spot
known as Vietnam. Therefore, during the early 1960s, the
CIA, with the Kennedy administration's blessing, launched
a number of agent teams into North Vietnam—with poor
results. Primarily because of that disappointing effort, President Lyndon Johnson, in January 1964, turned the ultrasecret mission over to the military.

Warming up to his briefing, Jerry Stratton told me that
Military Assistance Command, Studies and Observation
Group (MACSOG), was formed to create a secret organization to carry out covert action against North Vietnam.
Jerry chuckled as he pointed out that the Studies and Observation Group, SOG, was about as thin a cover as had
ever been devised. Instead of the academics and scientists
the name suggested, the personnel were actually Green Berets borrowed from the 5th Special Forces Group. And the
various MACSOG commanders read like an Army who's
who of legends in the special operations world: Clyde Rus-
sell, Donald "Headhunter" Blackburn, Jack Singlaub, Arthur "Bull" Simons, Steve Cavanaugh, and John "Skip"
Sadler. The organization also included members of the U.S.
Navy's elite SEAL Team One. Virtually all of these highly
trained troops participated in one of MACSOG's four core
operational missions: Agent Networks and Deception, Covert Maritime Operations, "Black" Psychological Warfare,
and Covert Operations Against the Ho Chi Minh Trail.

Known as OP 34, the branch responsible for agent networks faced an incredibly difficult challenge. Their job was
to insert long-term indigenous agent teams into North Vietnam via airdrop or across the beach. Each team focused on
intelligence collection and on the cultivation of sympathetic
civilian contacts. The teams' secondary mission involved
psychological warfare and sabotage. Unfortunately, OP 34

teams fared no better than earlier CIA teams; most were killed, captured, or co-opted as double agents by Hanoi.

The Maritime Operations Group, OP 37, participated in a number of covert projects against North Vietnam, including cross-beach seaborne raids, the capture of North Vietnamese officials, bombardment of shore targets from special fast patrol craft known as "Nasty boats," the insertion of agents, and the interdiction of North Vietnamese craft moving supplies south by sea. The mission also included delivery of various psychological warfare materials, such as propaganda leaflets and radios, into North Vietnam. Much like OP 34, maritime operations produced a mixed bag of results. Expectations and reality did not mesh; the pinprick operations never achieved anywhere near the desired impact on Hanoi.

The third core mission, "black" (covert) psychological warfare, operated under the code name OP 39. Using a complex hodgepodge of deception, misdirection, and dirty tricks, OP 39 attempted to convince the Hanoi leadership that they had a serious internal security problem. One of the most ingenious methods employed was an elaborate fabricated resistance organization known as the "Sacred Sword of the Patriots League." The subterfuge included fake SSPL cells supposedly operating from locations throughout North Vietnam, bogus membership cards, leaflet drops, and a clandestine radio known as the Voice of the SSPL. To keep the North Vietnamese off balance, OP 39 also circulated counterfeit money, forged incriminating or embarrassing documents, and even booby-trapped ammunition used by regular NVA units.

By far the largest effort within SOG, and one of the most dangerous, was OP 35, involving the insertion of American-led covert reconnaissance teams against the Ho Chi Minh Trail in Laos. The teams, routinely commanded by Special Forces personnel, performed a variety of missions deep within enemy territory: bomb damage assessment of B-52 strikes; wire tapping; sabotaging logistics supply lines; directing air strikes against lucrative targets of opportunity; counting trucks moving down the Trail; and, on occasion, snatching NVA prisoners. The political sensitivity surrounding these hairy missions stemmed from the 1962 Geneva Accords, which declared Laos to be "neutral." As a result, all foreign forces were to leave. They all did—except the North Vietnamese. In total disregard of the international agreement, NVA strength along the Trail rose to 30,000 support troops, 60,000 security troops, and over 10,000 antiaircraft guns. Clearly a major network for infiltration, the Trail could transport 20,000 NVA soldiers a month from the North into South Vietnam.

Further complicating the situation, the reputation of one of America's elder statesmen was at stake. Negotiating for the United States, W. Averell Harriman had played a key role in brokering the neutrality of Laos, and he was hellbent on forcing strict U.S. compliance. Harriman's primary concern, shared by Ambassador William Sullivan in Vientiane, was the distinct possibility that a Green Beret on one of SOG's covert recon teams would be captured and put on public display, thus exposing American duplicity, not to mention our flagrant violation of the Geneva Accords. Faced with a delicate balancing act of measuring the legal, political, and ethical ramifications attached to honoring the Geneva Accords against the critical requirement to find out what Hanoi was up to in Laos, President Johnson reluctantly approved SOG covert missions into Laos. Originally code named "Shining Brass," SOG's cross-border missions became Operation "Prairie Fire" in 1967. That same year covert operations were extended into Cambodia; they were code named "Daniel Boone." Through it all the United States government staunchly denied that any American military personnel were on the ground in Laos.

The covert nature of the Prairie Fire mission, coupled with heavy losses among SOG reconnaissance teams, created monumental political problems requiring elaborate secrecy—and government deniability. Consequently, SOG missions were among the most highly classified of the war and therefore came under intense high-level scrutiny. The

approval process also evolved into a bureaucratic nightmare. At a minimum of thirty days in advance, SOG sub-
mitted a planned mission up the chain of command: first
stop was MACV, followed by a stop at Pacific Command
in Hawaii. Next came the Joint Chiefs of Staff and the
Office of the Secretary of Defense for review and approval.
From there SOG's planned mission went to the State Department, the CIA, and finally to the White House for au-
thorization. Much to the disgruntlement of MACSOG, at
any point in the process a mission could be altered or re-
jected. The whole setup was right out of a James Bond
story.

With the background portion completed, Jerry went on
to tell me that SOG further divided the organization into
three geographic operational regions: South, Central, and
North. Command and Control South, CCS, operated out of
Ban Me Thuot and focused on missions into Central Cambodia. Command and Control Central, CCC, based at Kontum, ran recon teams into northern Cambodia and southern
Laos. The area where I'd be working was known as Command and Control North, or CCN, with its headquarters at
Da Nang. CCN reconnaissance teams, called RTs, worked
all cross-border operations from Chu Lai north to the DMZ.
Within CCN several mobile launch teams operated, including Jerry Stratton's MLT-2.

At the tactical level, CCN assigned targets to a specific
recon team, then shipped the team off to the MLT for the
actual mission. Depending on the assignment, an RT could
range in size from five to twelve men, including two or
three Green Berets. It was the diversity of the rest of the
team that captured my attention. Many of the indigenous
troops were Nung tribesmen who had immigrated to Vietnam from southern China. That tidbit of information answered my question about the two guards I had seen on
first entering the MLT-2 compound. The teams also included Montagnard tribesmen, members of Vietnam's largest ethnic minority. Organized along tribal lines similar to
American Indians, the Jarai, Rhade, Sedang, and Bru each

had its own culture. The Montagnards were natural jungle fighters, and, coincidentally, there was no love lost between the tribes and the Vietnamese. But the best part was that a genuine rapport, respect, and even love had developed between the Special Forces and the Montagnards. They formed a unique brotherhood of warriors, willing to sacrifice and even die for each other.

One of the most intriguing parts of Jerry Stratton's briefing was a "show and tell" on the weapons carried by RTs. Individualism and personal preference were apparently a large part of the equation. While some team members carried the standard M16 rifles, others opted for the CAR-15. Still others, preferring foreign weapons for deniability purposes, chose the AK-47, the M3 "Grease Gun," the Swedish K submachine gun with silencer, or even a shotgun. Some teams increased their firepower by sporting an M79 grenade launcher. And most teams routinely carried Claymore mines and the M14 "toe popper" mine. When I asked about use of the AK-47, Jerry caught me completely off guard when he confessed that some teams actually dressed in NVA uniforms, necessitating the Soviet weapon to carry out the charade. Shocked that we would even consider having our own teams wear the bad guy's uniform, I couldn't stop wondering how I was supposed to tell them apart in the heat of battle. Things were definitely tending toward the weird.

Getting the teams safely in and out of enemy territory presented one of the biggest problems, and that's where I came in. My job was to be airborne commander of the "package," the name given to the helicopter and fixed-wing assets needed for the mission. Usually the package consisted of four UH-1 Huey "Slicks" carrying the team, two AH-1 Cobra helicopter gunships, and two Air Force A-1 Skyraiders for close air support. In really hot areas, we would order up a set of fast-movers, usually F-4s, to suppress flak and to act as a MiG cap.

In theory, I was supposed to neutralize the landing zone for the insert, cover the team while they were on the ground, then run the extract. Jerry was quick to point out that the operations never quite worked smoothly. Invariably the small teams engaged in firefights at point-blank range, requiring an experienced FAC to direct ordnance from the A-1s and Cobras well inside minimum safe distances, referred to as "danger close." A slow-thinking or panicky FAC could get himself, or the team, killed instantly.

As he talked, Jerry squinted and stared deep into my eyes, apparently searching for the qualities and attributes required of a Prairie Fire FAC. His gaze became so intense that I finally had to look away. His visual third degree shook me up. At that moment I honestly didn't know if I could hack it. I just knew I wanted to try.

Jerry finished by emphasizing that most of the time the team extracts became classic search-and-rescue operations, or SARs, with all the attendant difficulties and dangers. To be effective, I would have to fly right on the treetops. Prairie Fire FACs observed no minimum altitudes—my OV-10 would be fair game for any bad guy with a gun or a slingshot. When I asked why we used four Hueys when one or two could carry the entire team, Jerry looked at me pensively, then said, "The others are spares. We tend to lose a lot of choppers, and one of your jobs will be to rescue those downed crews." Then, as if to signal the briefing was over, Jerry proudly tossed me my own MACSOG shoulder patch showing a surrealistic human skull wearing a green beret, with fire flickering out of each eye socket and blood dripping out a corner of the mouth.

After the briefing, I could understand why Fuzzy Furr was so enthusiastic about the Prairie Fire mission. It had all the ingredients for one hell of an adventure: high drama, intrigue, danger, Special Forces, clandestine operations. We were talking real-life "Terry and the Pirates." If the flying was one-tenth as exciting as I expected it would be, I knew I had found a home. My earlier dream of becoming a Raven FAC faded completely.

On the flight back to Da Nang, I had a lot to think about, but my O-2 pilot took up where we had left off. He eased us down to just a few feet off the beach and pushed the throttles up for what amounted to a speed dash in the O-2 of 125 knots. The super-heated midafternoon air provided just enough turbulence to keep the ride challenging. Just as I was beginning to feel comfortable, the engines let loose with several heart-stopping sputters. I shot a quick glance at the pilot, thinking to myself that at such a low altitude his only choice was to crash-land on the smooth beach fifty feet below us. As if to confirm my suspicions, he muttered a single "Damn!" Simultaneously his right hand shot out and turned a couple of levers. A lifetime later—actually only a few seconds of real time—the engines caught and wound back up to speed.

Grinning a little sheepishly, my pilot confessed, "I forgot to switch fuel tanks."

A few minutes later, as my pulse settled down, we spotted a large ship several miles offshore. My pilot pointed us in that direction and dropped down even lower over the water. Coming up from the rear, very close to her starboard side, the pilot observed, "It's that German hospital ship, the *Helgoland*. Watch this."

I figured he planned to buzz the unsuspecting ship. Instead, he leveled off deck high, then pulled the nose up and executed a perfect aileron roll to the right. As we rolled inverted, the sight of all that water only a couple of wingspans below pushed my pulse rate back into overdrive. The placard on the instrument panel read, "Aerobatics Prohibited in This Aircraft," but the crazy Prairie Fire pilot easily disproved that notion by rolling us back to wings-level, exactly deck high, directly abeam the ship's bow. Smiling broadly, the pilot gave me a thumbs up and announced, "Piece of cake."

On July 3 two experienced Prairie Fire pilots, Bob Meadows, and Gary Pavlu, piled me into a jeep and drove me over to CCN headquarters near Marble Mountain, just south of China Beach. After only a few days in Prairie Fire, I instinctively liked these two veterans of the program. Each was completely different from the other, which encouraged my hope that stereotypes weren't the rule in our supersecret operation. Bob Meadows was a short, prematurely balding young man with a take-charge, almost cocky attitude. In contrast, Gary Pavlu was tall, slender, with a laid-back, easygoing manner. He had an interesting habit of calling everyone "Slick." Both Bob and Gary had reputations for being fearless and totally composed in the heat of battle. Watching both men, I developed a monumental case of hero worship.

The heavily guarded compound at CCN resembled MLT-2 at Quang Tri, except it was much larger. Bob and Gary introduced me around the command section, had my picture taken, and gave me a tour of the facilities. A cursory look revealed that the place was indeed heavily fortified, a direct result of large night attack in 1968 on the CCN compound when 16 Green Berets died at the hands of a one-hundred-man NVA sapper company, undeniable testimony to how badly the North Vietnamese wanted to stop or disrupt SOG operations. After viewing the guarded perimeter, we ended up at the all-ranks club, a small but well-stocked bar and recreation hooch. Several SF NCOs joined us for ice-cold beer served by a Vietnamese waitress. In short order the conversation turned to recent missions. At one point, one of the NCOs showed me the strangest ID card I'd ever seen. In addition to his name and picture, the following words appeared:

MILITARY ASSISTANCE COMMAND VIETNAM
STUDIES AND OBSERVATION GROUP
APO SAN FRANCISCO 96307

The other half of the card contained the following explanation:

_____

SPECIAL IDENTIFICATION AND PASS
The person who is identified by this document is acting

under the direct orders of the President of the United States!
DO NOT DETAIN OR QUESTION HIM!
He is authorized to wear civilian clothing, carry unusual
weapons, transport and possess prohibited items including
U.S. currency, pass into restricted areas, and requisition
equipment of all types, including weapons and vehicles.
IF HE IS KILLED OR INJURED, DO NOT REMOVE THIS DOCU-
MENT FROM HIM. ALERT YOUR COMMANDING OFFICER IM-
MEDIATELY.

I thought the ID card was the closest thing to a license to
steal that I had ever seen and said so, but the conversation
drifted to other topics. Eventually I commented about the
number of mercenaries we'd seen around the compound,
many of whom wore surgical bandages over what I assumed to be wounds received in combat. Everyone at the
table laughed, then the SF troops filled me in.

"In the first place," the NCO corrected me, "we don't
call 'em mercenaries. We call 'em 'little people' or 'indig'—short for indigenous troops. A few indig might have
been hit on a recent mission, but most of 'em did it to each
other. See, we taught 'em how to play poker, and they take
it real serious, especially on payday. At the end of the
month, they get into marathon card games, somebody ac-
cuses somebody else of cheating, and before you know it,
it's like Dodge City around here. Firefights all over the
place."

Everybody at the table laughed again. I wasn't sure
whether to believe the guy or not, but based on other weird
things I'd heard about and seen at CCN, there was probably
as much truth as exaggeration to his story. As we sat there
relaxing and drinking beer, someone eased into a new story,
this one involving Gary Pavlu and one of the MLT-2
troops, Staff Sergeant James L. "Marty" Martin. About a
month earlier Gary and Marty had been west of Quang Tri
in Laos putting an air strike with A-1 Skyraiders. In the
middle of it, Gary's O-2 lost power on its rear engine. En-

gine instruments indicated zero RPM, rising manifold pressure, and zero fuel pressure. It was a tough spot to be in, not only because he was so deep in enemy territory, but also because in theory the O-2 couldn't fly on only the front engine. When the rear engine would not restart, Gary had his hands full.

Unable to maintain level flight, Gary jettisoned his rocket pods and began an ominous descent toward Khe Sanh, just across the Vietnamese border. Finally, at about eight hundred feet above the ground, he coaxed the Oscar Deuce into level flight at about seventy knots of indicated airspeed. Too low to bail out, the two SOG aviators had a choice of trying to land on Khe Sanh's unsecured and heavily damaged runway, or of fighting the weather toward home field twenty miles east. With heavy rain and low scud blocking their easterly flight path, they decided to set up an orbit over Khe Sanh while one of the A-1s flew ahead to scout for a clear route to Quang Tri. With the second A-1 holding overhead and a SOG UH-1 Huey orbiting in case Gary had to crash land in bad-guy country, everyone waited. After twenty minutes of flying in an airplane that couldn't be flown on a single engine, Gary and Marty were relieved to hear that the weather had lifted slightly. They hedgehopped at low level through the rain squalls and finally executed a perfect single-engine landing at Quang Tri. To hear Gary Pavlu tell it, it was all in a day's work. As I saw it, Gary and Marty had pulled off an incredible feat of flying.

When Gary, Bob, and I returned to Covey Operations late that afternoon, there was a call from MLT-2. Kim Budrow told us that the entire area was on red alert, indicating that some type of attack was imminent. Earlier that morning NVA sappers had planted a water mine against a boat ferry near Dong Ha. The explosion killed forty Vietnamese civilians.

The next day, the Fourth of July, passed without any particular observance of the holiday. For the Coveys it was business as usual, but the date took on special meaning for

me. After a little over two months with Roomie, I finally
had the opportunity to switch rooms. In a bit of random
luck, Roomie was transferred to another FAC unit, and I
moved to the other end of the hall, into a room with an old
friend, Captain Evan Quiros. Evan and I had first met as
freshmen in college, our paths crossing later at several other
places, including Cannon and Hurlburt. Evan came from a
family of prominent ranchers in Laredo, Texas, and because
his name has a distinctly Latin flavor, I teased Evan un-
mercifully about being a "blond-haired, blue-eyed Mexican." His wife, Mary, was one of the sweetest, prettiest
ladies you'd ever want to meet, and Evan was totally devoted to her and to their children.

Over the next week, I flew every day, with Fuzzy Furr
and Bob Meadows taking turns teaching me the tricks of
the Prairie Fire trade. At first we concentrated on low-level
techniques and on learning the prominent landmarks
throughout the AO. Next, we watched while one of the
other Prairie Fire pilots ran actual inserts or extracts. Surprisingly, they all went like clockwork. Instead of the melee
I had expected, I reaped the benefit of watching several
textbook missions, complete with running commentary by
my instructor. I found it fascinating to observe an actual
combat operation as a student without being directly involved in it.

During those first missions, the sequence of events followed the script verbatim. The pilot running the show
teamed up with one of a small number of experienced SF
NCOs known as "Covey riders." Together, they flew every
mission. The pilot controlled the airborne assets while the
Covey rider helped with map reading and radios, talked to
the team on the ground, and interpreted the tactical situation
for his pilot and for the MLT listening on the same radio
frequency.

After a final look at the preselected landing zone, or LZ,
the Covey rider gave the go-ahead for helicopter assets to
launch. Simultaneously, the FAC contacted and set up a
rendezvous with his A-1 Skyraiders, Korean War–vintage

prop fighters capable of carrying huge loads of ordnance and fuel. Using the call sign "Spad," the slow-moving Air Force A-1s were perfect for the Prairie Fire mission, able to thread a needle with their bombs, orbit forever, and absorb incredible amounts of punishment. As an added bennie, the Coveys lived in the same building with the A-1 jocks, thus developing excellent rapport with these outstanding pilots.

When everybody reached the rendezvous, usually some ten klicks away from the target area, the FAC led the package to the LZ. Contrary to normal procedures, Prairie Fire FACs didn't use willie petes to mark the LZ because the exploding white phosphorous could easily set the whole place on fire and leave a smoke signal that could be seen for miles. Instead, the FAC rolled in for a shallow dive on the target, all the while giving the helicopters a running verbal update on what he saw. In addition to the verbal description, the long, low run-in to the target served the additional purpose of drawing ground fire from any bad guys in the immediate area. The pilots called it "trolling."

With all eyes glued on him, the FAC would continue to treetop level and, when directly over the LZ, would call out, "Mark, mark," then pull up sharply to a loose orbit over the area. Once the choppers confirmed a positive identification on the LZ, the operation shifted into the next phase.

Before committing the vulnerable Hueys, the FAC turned the Cobra gunships loose on the LZ to neutralize the area. Instead of using conventional ordnance, the Cobras fired fléchette rockets directly into the LZ and surrounding trec lines. Each fléchette round contained thousands of one-inch steel darts resembling nails, each capable of penetrating several inches of solid wood. At approximately the halfway point on its flight to the target, the rocket warhead exploded in a cloud of reddish smoke, releasing a shower of "nails" traveling at a tremendous velocity. The actual impact was barely visible from above, with only some dust and splintered wood swirling through the air; no chance of risky fire or telltale smoke. When a Cobra pilot squeezed off a fléchette rocket at approximately three thousand feet slant range, the resulting destruction could cover the area of a football field with one fléchette per square inch.

After "nailing" the LZ, the FAC would clear the lead Huey Slick for the approach, trailed by one of the Cobras to provide suppressing fire if needed. For the orbiting FAC, the trick involved orchestrating everyone's flight path so that the Slicks maintained optimum spacing and were always covered on final approach by a Cobra, ready to bring its guns to bear at the first sign of trouble. Assuming all went well, the Slick touched down briefly, deposited the first half of the team, then pulled off to a prearranged safe orbit area. As Lead lifted off, Slick Two would touch down with the rest of the team.

At that point the insert was far from over. The plan usually called for some old-fashioned sleight of hand. The package would move to another LZ and repeat the whole show at least two more times, for a total of two dummy inserts and one real one. The choice of which was the actual insert in the drama was purely random. To add to the authenticity of the deception, the teams often employed a firefight simulator known as the "Nightingale" device. During one of the dummy inserts, the team lit the fuse and tossed the three-by-four foot device onto the LZ. Using a combination of cherry bombs and M-80 firecrackers, the Nightingale cooked off in what sounded like actual automatic weapons fire. The phony firefight lasted about thirty minutes, giving the team plenty of time to move to the real LZ; hopefully, the sound attracted any NVA troops away from the actual insert and to the Nightingale.

The extract always involved more complications and variables than the insert, since there could be absolutely no ordnance dropped into the area until the FAC pinpointed the team's position, a nerve-wracking process requiring plenty of low, slow trolling over the hostile terrain. Once he found his team, the FAC called in the Spads and Cobras to blast anything that moved or looked the least bit suspicious.*

After watching two inserts and one extract, I felt ready to try it myself. With an experienced Covey rider in my back seat, and under the watchful eye of Bob Meadows circling above the show, I successfully managed to pull one team on July 8 and insert another one the next afternoon. As with the missions I had observed earlier, mine went off without a hitch.

The following morning, July 10, the charm wore off. The plan called for an insert on top of a prominent ridge called Co Roc, located just across the Laotian border about fifteen klicks southwest of Khe Sanh. Several years earlier NVA artillery firing from Co Roc's heights had pounded besieged U.S. Marines at Khe Sanh. Enemy activity along the ridge still made people nervous, so MACSOG was assigned to check out the situation.

Co Roc's sheer eastern cliffs made for an impressive sight from the air. The steep walls rose some twelve hundred feet above the muddy Se Pone River. The scene reminded me of a miniature version of half the Grand Canyon. Scrub jungle covered the top of the five-mile-long ridge whose axis was oriented roughly north to south. At the southern end of the amoeba-shaped formation, the terrain sloped gently down to the west for several miles before it flattened out into a large plain containing a major segment of the Trail.

For the morning mission, I found myself teamed up with a brand new Covey rider, Sergeant First Class Charlie Gray.

---

*To avoid confusing the reader, the various components of the package are identified throughout the book by a generic nickname—i.e., Spad, Slick, Cobra—rather than by actual tactical call sign. In Prairie Fire, each component used a different two-letter identifier. For instance, on a given day the call signs might be as follows: MLT: "Alpha Delta;" Team: "Mike Kilo;" Huey Slicks: "Tango Zulu;" Cobras: "Lima Oscar;" FAC: "Sierra Mike;" For security reasons, the call signs changed daily.

As a couple of rookies, we were to observe the operation and to act as backup to Bob Meadows, who was running the insert. Based on my brief Prairie Fire experiences, I expected to watch another milk run.

On this occasion two dummy inserts preceded the real one. They went off with no difficulty, so I positioned us up-sun at an altitude of thirty-five hundred feet, well above the package but two thousand feet below the orbiting A-1s. Sergeant Gray and I watched as the Cobras nailed the LZ, both of us wondering out loud how anybody could live through that deadly hail of killer fléchettes.

Next, Slick Lead started his descent to the target, setting himself up on a south-to-north run-in. At approximately fifty feet in the air, just as he started increasing the angle of attack to go into a hover, the Huey shook violently as a B-40 rocket snaked out of the tree line at his ten o'clock position and exploded in the rotor assembly.

Sergeant Gray and I watched in horror as the Huey pilot fought to regain control of his crippled bird. Immediately, the radio filled with excited yells. Slick Lead shouted, "We're hit, we're hit bad! She's pulling hard to the left!"

From the Covey, "Lead, go for the clear area to the west. Stay with it! We'll cover you all the way. Cobra Two, get on him, get on him, goddamn it!"

Trailing a thin stream of black smoke, Slick Lead managed to roll out on a westerly heading, all the while descending at about the same rate as the terrain sloped down. Without even realizing it, I found myself diving toward the struggling Huey, as if by getting closer I could somehow help. Through my helmet earphones I heard voices shouting, "Stay with it! Just a little farther! You've got it made, just keep her flying a few more seconds!" The shouting voices were Charlie Gray's and my own.

After clearing a final tree line, the chopper appeared to hover momentarily, then flip on its side and fall the remaining twenty-five feet to the ground. The bird bounced once, breaking in half as it crashed back to earth. At impact, the Huey disappeared in a huge, mushroom-shaped fireball.

Somewhere, someone keyed a mike and said, "Sweet Jesus!"

Several seconds of ominous quiet followed before Bob Meadows came up on frequency. "Okay, everybody snap out of it. Let's set up a tight orbit while I go down and see if there are any survivors."

Not thinking anyone could live through that inferno, out of habit I reached for my binoculars to get a closer look at the fire-engulfed wreckage. After focusing, I was amazed to see figures moving around the burning Huey. Within a matter of seconds, Slick Three, carrying the medic—or *bac si*, the Vietnamese word for doctor—swooped in to pick up five dazed survivors who had miraculously been thrown clear on impact. The pilot and copilot, probably still in the twisted, burning wreck, were unaccounted for.

Late that afternoon, Charlie Gray and I returned to the crash site with a full package, including a special recovery team code-named "Bright Light." The insert went unopposed, allowing the larger Bright Light team the luxury of setting up a perimeter defense while the remaining team members sifted through the burned-out wreckage. As we suspected, they found the dead pilots still strapped in their seats.

Once the Bright Light team secured the bodies and reboarded, I sent the helicopter package back to Quang Tri. It was time to give the long-suffering A-1s their chance. Under the rules of engagement, at sunset we had the option of using any unexpended ordnance the Spads had left over. I knew just where I wanted them to drop their stuff. In the last rays of light, the white smoke from my willie pete billowed out of the tree line that had been the hiding place for the bad guy with the B-40 rocket. All of us felt the same way, and there was no need for a lot of conversation.

"Okay, gents, set 'em up, push 'em up, and hit my smoke. Give me a pass with the nape for starters."

Coming in low out of the west, the two lumbering A-1s dumped their canisters of napalm onto the top of Co Roc. Then they came back around and blasted the area with high-explosive rockets and for good measure raked the jungle with mini-gun fire. In the dim light from the burning nape, it was hard to tell if we had hit anything, but the raging fires and explosions were a kind of catharsis for all of us, a release of the tension we had been feeling since the crash.

Charlie Gray and I flew back to Quang Tri in silence and touched down on the dimly lit runway and taxied to Barky Ops. Following a quick debriefing at MLT-2, I returned to the airfield to climb into my OV-10 for the fifth time that day. As I slipped on my parachute harness over my survival vest, one of the Barky crew chiefs walked up and tapped me on the shoulder.

"Sir, I think there's something you ought to see." I followed him to the right wing tip, where he focused the beam of his flashlight for me. "Looks like an AK-47 round," he said. "Went in through the wing tip and came out over here on the right aileron. No real damage, but you were lucky."

Immediately I thought about Bennie, my old crew chief back at Da Nang who had also commented on my luck after the 23mm round did a number on our airplane. As with that earlier incident, I didn't have the faintest idea when the AK round had found its mark. I tried to reconstruct the four sorties I had flown that day, but they all blurred together. The only clear picture I had was of the chopper breaking in half and of the mushroom-shaped fireball. It had been a long day, never to be forgotten.

That night back at Da Nang, I tumbled into my bunk, physically and emotionally drained. That stupor-like feeling was rapidly becoming the rule rather than the exception. With my daily trips to Quang Tri, the main compound at Da Nang became just a place to sleep. At night I would land on Runway 17 Left and more often than not stumble back to my room, turn the air conditioner on high, and climb into bed. The multi-sortie sixteen-hour days left me limp as a rag. Through bleary eyes I began to see my fellow Prairie Fire pilots in a new light. They weren't so much antisocial or secretive as they were dog-tired. The pace, particularly my heavy training schedule, was a real bear, and I looked forward to getting on the regular rotation—or at least to getting used to the grind, whichever came first.

As tired as we were, there always seemed to be time for at least one good meal a day, and in that department we had no problem. The main compound dining hall had to be one of the best-kept secrets of the war. Anyone from colonel to airman basic could eat three great meals a day there, all for practically nothing: breakfast, twenty-five cents; lunch, sixty-five cents; dinner, fifty-five cents. My favorite was breakfast. The cooks turned out eggs and omelettes cooked to order, pancakes, waffles, sausage, bacon, toast, fruit, sweet rolls, and plain old cold cereal. Anyone who complained about that food had to be crazy.

Of course, with Murphy's Law fully operational, we all had a sneaking hunch that our dining hall was too good to be true. Sure enough, toward the end of the month, the VC came through with a particularly heavy 122mm rocket attack, right into our backyard. Most nights the incoming rockets landed on the west side of Da Nang Air Base or sailed completely over us into the city. But on that particular night the bad guys really found the range on the main compound. It was bad enough that one rocket blew the front off our small post office; the real insult came when another rocket exploded just behind the dining hall, riddling the refrigeration unit and freezer with several dozen shrapnel holes. The Combat Support Group chose that occasion to shut down the dining hall for a complete remodeling, lasting about six months. There was another dining hall two miles down the road at Gunfighter Village, but it wasn't the same; it wasn't convenient; and most of all, it wasn't ours.

According to my personal log, I flew each day between the twelfth and the twenty-third of July, for a total of twenty-two sorties. On most of those days my Covey rider was Jim "Marty" Martin, a multiple-tour veteran of Southeast Asia and one of the most experienced back-seaters in the program. Like most of the SOG troops, Marty went by his personal code name, "Satan." Unlike his code name suggested, however, Marty had a friendly face and a kindly manner and, although he wasn't much older than the pilots he babysat, the gray touches in his hair and his vast experience made him seem more mature to us.

Satan had one peculiar habit I could never quite get used to. Whenever we were flying, he would address me in the third person and only as "Sir." If Marty saw something he thought should be brought to my attention, he'd announce on the intercom, "If Sir will look out the left side at ten o'clock low, he'll notice . . ." Or he might say, "If Sir will listen up on the Fox Mike radio, he'll hear that the launch site is calling for a status report." Throughout the months we flew together, he never switched tenses.

Satan more than made up for that minor quirk with his instant grasp of hot tactical ground situations. When he talked to team leaders, he seemed to have a sixth sense and an uncanny ability to interpret their predicament by listening to their inflections and tone of voice. He could read a man's fear level by hearing him talk on the radio.

Satan had another habit that was equally odd but highly appreciated. During the really hairy extracts, he would easily pick up on the tension I felt. At just the right moment, he'd key the intercom and very softly begin singing "The Ballad of the Green Beret":

Fighting soldiers from the sky,
Fearless men who jump and die.
One hundred men will test today,
But only three win the Green Beret.

Every time Marty started his singing, the tension broke like a crack of thunder. No matter how bad the situation, I would always stop and smile when I heard those lyrics, loosen my grip on the control stick, and relax. To this day I'm convinced Satan's sixth sense helped me keep my cool and fly better. Without my being aware of it, he probably saved my neck on any number of occasions.

On the morning of July 23, Satan and I teamed up to run an insert at the extreme western limit of the Prairie Fire AO. We inserted the team near a steep karst rock formation a few miles north of Route 9, a key infiltration route from Laos into South Vietnam. Right away I got on the horn to Hillsboro, passing along the prearranged code words to let them know the team had been inserted and that the no-bombing rule applied to a six-kilometer square box around the team's position. Only a Prairie Fire FAC could expend ordnance inside that NBL.

"Hillsboro, Covey 221, over."

"Covey 221, Hillsboro. Go ahead."

"Rog, Hillsboro. We just played the Gray Cloud ball game. The area's hot as of 1025 Hotel."

With the administrative business out of the way, Marty and I cruised around the area on a listening watch, just in case the RT ran into trouble and came up on the radio. During our excursion we overflew the Khe Sanh area, with Satan giving a history lesson. He showed me the old Lang Vei Special Forces Camp where, in early February 1968, enemy tanks attacked along Route 9. As Satan pointed out the overgrown perimeter of Lang Vei and the still-visible hulks of several burned-out Soviet PT76 tanks, I studied the scene with the same kind of detachment one might have on a visit to any famous Civil War battlefield in the States. For me, the names Khe Sanh and Lang Vei conjured up vivid images of great, surging battles where heroics and sacrifice were the order of the day. But looking down at the ordinary dirt road, the dilapidated camp, and the deserted airstrip, I felt somehow cheated that the scene below me didn't measure up to my larger-than-life expectations.

Several miles northwest of Khe Sanh, Satan pointed out a small burned patch of ground, almost completely insignificant except for the pieces of debris scattered about. As we circled, Satan explained that the scar on the ground was actually a recent crash site, the impact point where Rick Meacham and his Covey rider had died two months earlier. We circled in silence, then Marty summed up the whole war, more poignantly than any poet or philosopher ever could have. To no one in particular, he mumbled softly, "This whole area is good country, prime real estate, bought and paid for with American lives." I took a pencil and scribbled Satan's words on my clipboard, then banked sharply around to the east and headed back to Quang Tri.

Back at MLT-2, we sat around killing time. After lunch I had stretched out on an empty bunk to read a magazine, only to fall asleep in the afternoon heat. Waking with a start, I opened my eyes to find Kim Budrow shaking my shoulder. As I swung my legs onto the hooch floor, Top filled me in. "We just picked up a call from the radio relay. The team's in contact, but they figure they can hold on with some air support. You and Satan are gonna take a couple of Cobras out to see what the problem is."

Within minutes we were strapped in, cranked, and taxiing. Even with only a half-full centerline fuel tank, the Bronco would need every inch of Quang Tri's three-thousand-foot runway to get airborne. The outside air temp registered a typical one hundred degrees, so I back-taxied into the overrun for an extra hundred feet. At brake release we seemed to crawl forward, eating up runway without much corresponding increase on the airspeed indicator. To compensate for the strong right crosswind off the ocean, I held a healthy dose of right aileron into the wind and a little left rudder to keep us tracking straight down the sixty-foot-wide runway. After an eternity, we reached minimum safe single-engine flying speed, and I yanked us into the air just as we ran out of concrete.

Following our rendezvous with our Cobras at Khe Sanh, we pressed out along Route 9 toward the team. When we arrived overhead, the team leader, known as the "One-Zero," told us they were taking some harassing fire from a small enemy patrol trying to climb the steep north face of the karst. The One-Zero felt his position was secure, but a little insurance would make him feel better. He asked us to hose the north face just to be on the safe side, so I fired a couple of willie petes for reference and, using corrections from the team, the Cobras blasted the brittle limestone rocks with mini-guns and high-explosive rockets. On the first few passes, we took a moderate amount of small arms fire, but by the fourth pass, the only firing was ours.

Since we had plenty of bullets and fuel left, I pulled the Cobras off to the east and set up an orbit, just in case the One-Zero needed our services again. After two trips around the flagpole, the mission began to take on a completely different complexion when Cobra Lead notified me he was in trouble.

In a calm voice, he announced, "Boss, this doesn't look good. I think we picked up a few lead souvenirs back there. We're getting some surges and heavy engine vibrations. Let's take up an RTB."

Shortly after we started back to base, it was obvious Cobra Lead had throttled back trying to take the strain off his malfunctioning engine. He held a shallow descent, but all of us recognized that he would run out of altitude before we could get out of bad-guy country. As he passed through a thin broken layer of puffy clouds at twelve hundred feet, the engine gave out. It couldn't have happened at a worse location. We were directly over the 1032 ford, a major intersection where Route 9 crossed the primary north–south segment of the Ho Chi Minh Trail. Even a rookie like me knew the place was crawling with NVA regulars.

Cobra Lead dropped like a rock, still heading east and trying to stretch his glide in a maneuver the helicopter jocks called auto rotation—roughly similar to a dead-stick landing in a fixed-wing bird. Lead managed to cross Route 1032 before turning south into the wind toward a large clearing five hundred meters south of Route 9. Cobra Two and I followed him right down to the deck, where at the last possible moment, Lead honked back on his controls to break the descent, then settled into a safe but bone-jarring landing. The Cobra bounced a few times before skidding to a halt.

Right away I started feeling the panic and pressure begin to grab just below my rib cage. An acid, burning sensation seemed to move slowly up from my guts, through my chest, and then into my throat. It was up to me to get those two pilots out. But how? As I took a gulp of water to neutralize the burn in my throat, I heard Marty's rendition of "The Ballad of the Green Beret" come drifting over the intercom. A quick look in the mirror at his calm face told me instantly that the man had faith in me. I winked at his reflection and said, "Hang on, Marty, and keep singing."

To keep us close, I slammed the stick against my right leg, pulling us around in a steep four-G turn at weed-top level. When the downed Cobra came back into our field of vision, we saw the two pilots out of their chopper, running full speed toward a small gully about a hundred meters to their east. Before we could tell whether they made it, a hail of tracers flashed by us, evidently fired from some scrub bushes on the southwest corner of the large open field. As several more volleys streaked around us, I felt like a duck in a carnival shooting gallery, but I held the high-G turn for all I was worth. At what I guessed to be the right point, I unloaded the Gs and rolled us out, heading directly for the bad guys, hoping the head-on run would present the smallest possible target under the circumstances. We passed over their heads at about ten feet before I zoomed the Bronco into a climbing, jinking turn back to the east. No tracers followed us, prompting Satan to comment sarcastically, "I think Sir's low pass scared them."

From our altitude of one thousand feet, we had a reasonably clear view of the whole area. Cobra Two flew a tight orbit several hundred feet below us, ready to roll in on anyone moving. We caught a glimpse of the downed crewmen huddled against the red-dirt embankment nearest the chopper. In spite of my repeated radio calls to them, neither had yet come up on the survival radio each carried. They seemed intent on watching the tall elephant grass immediately in front of them. From our vantage point, the grass swayed gently in the breeze, easily masking any movement by enemy troops who might be crawling around in it.

In those first hectic minutes, most of my conscious

thoughts focused on how to rescue the downed fliers. Through training and conditioning, my instincts told me to contact Hillsboro and lay on a full-blown SAR using Air Force "Jolly Green" rescue helicopters. Under the pressure of the moment, I totally forgot our clandestine operation and our self-contained ability to handle the situation with SOG assets. Instead, I called Hillsboro repeatedly, desperately trying to get anybody on the radio. When we couldn't raise them, I even began climbing to a higher altitude, hoping to improve radio reception.

Reviewing the bidding, I broke into a cold sweat thinking about the one-hour-plus reaction time of the Jolly Greens, assuming Hillsboro had even heard my urgent call. I kept asking myself, could we cover these guys that long? Did I have enough gas? Was it a mistake not to fill my centerline tank? Would Cobra Two have enough ammo to keep the bad guys pinned down? Before I had time to whip myself into a complete frenzy, the ground situation heated up, forcing me to do something other than worry and fret.

Cobra Two picked out two separate enemy patrols about four hundred meters west of the gully, both converging in that direction. As he strafed the closest bunch, I felt myself snap out of the fog and indecision that had been clouding my judgment. For some reason, the sight of the bullets kicking up the dirt acted like a tonic. At that moment I realized the idea of using the Jolly Greens had been a bad one. Time was critical, and necessity really was the mother of invention.

I yelled to Satan, "Call the launch site and tell them to scramble every Slick and Cobra they've got." Then I asked Cobra Two, "If things get really bad, can you guys lift them out, even if it's only for a short distance?"

"We can do it," he answered, "but you'll have to give us some covering fire. Stand by while we fire off the rest of our rockets. There'll be more room on the skids after we jettison the empty pods."

I couldn't be sure how much time we had, and it was very unsettling not being in radio contact with the two pilots in the gully. To make matters worse, I wasn't at all sure about how effective my covering fire would be. Willie pete rockets were certainly deadly, but I would have given anything to have the four M-60 machine guns the OV-10 normally carried. Months earlier, in a very controversial decision, Seventh Air Force removed the guns from the Bronco, claiming FACs relied on their own ordnance too often, flew too low on strafing runs, and generally took too many chances when armed with machine guns. It would have been sweet revenge to have the responsible staff weenie along in my back seat for a firsthand look at the real world.

I calculated that the reinforcement helicopters would need about twenty minutes to get to us. If we could just keep a lid on things till then, we might get through this. The situation was far from rosy, but at least we had a plan.

While Cobra Two sprayed HE rockets around the large field, I pulled out my binoculars and focused on the gully. Our boys crouched just below the rim, out of the direct line of fire. But as I watched, a steady barrage of bullets kicked up dust along the crest. We were definitely out of time.

Cobra Two and I got our signals straight. He followed me down the chute while I pickled off several willie petes to keep everyone's head down. I reefed us around in a hard turn and fired two more rockets into the area adjacent to the Cobra's intended touchdown point. The white smoke billowed out, only to be caught by a gust of wind and blown directly across the helicopter's flight path. Suddenly, the Cobra disappeared, engulfed in blinding white smoke.

Seconds later Cobra Two cobbed the power and climbed away from the fiasco I had created. Before the angry pilot could say anything, I said apologetically, "Sorry about that. Let's set up again. I'll keep the rockets farther out this time." All I got in response was an indignant "click, click" from his transmitter.

On the second try, I moved a little farther west and came in right on the deck. With Satan calling out the Cobra's position for me, I put the pipper on a grove of small trees concealing one of the patrols. As we closed at practically zero dive angle, puffs of smoke dotted the length of the grove as everybody and his dog took his best shot. We were so low that my first rocket hit the ground with its motor still running, the rocket snaking wildly through the weeds like a big Chinese firecracker. The second rocket hit a glancing blow and ricocheted back into the air, sailing over the target and finally exploding several hundred meters away.

My radio blared, "We're almost in. Keep it up, Covey. You've got 'em all shooting at you!"

As we came back around for another run, the downed pilots bolted from the gully just as Cobra Two touched down. It seemed to take them forever to cover the twenty-five yards to their waiting salvation and, as they ran, I continued to pop off a steady stream of willie petes. By then, smoke obscured most of the field and tracers filled the sky, but fortunately, most of them were wild shots, probably directed at our engine sound.

When we bottomed out on that last rocket pass, Marty and I witnessed an incredible sight. In the waiting Cobra, both pilots had their right-side canopies open, merrily blazing away with handguns. Besides having huge brass *cajones*, the two helicopter pilots had to be certifiably insane!

A split second after the running pilots had jumped on the skids, Cobra Two lifted off and began hedgehopping to the east as fast as they could fly. Satan and I hosed the area one last time, then took out after the Cobra. In the slow climb back to altitude, we flew alongside the gunship-turned-troop-carrier. Perched on each skid, the rescued fliers were all smiles and waves. I felt elated too, like a kid on the last day of school before summer vacation. To celebrate, we did multiple barrel rolls around Cobra Two.

Late that afternoon, Satan and I returned to the crash site with a new load of rockets and a new mission. The downed Cobra contained classified equipment and documents, and our job was to blow it away. I briefed the orbiting Sky-raiders and cleared them in hot. Spad Lead demolished the chopper on his first pass, and the wingman blasted it a second time to make sure. We naped and strafed the large field for good measure, but with no apparent results. For BDA I gave the Spads one AH-1G Cobra destroyed.

Marty and I were tired but still on an adrenaline high, so as the sun set, we took one last swing over the karst hiding our team. After I gunned the engines to get his attention, the One-Zero gave us a coded "team okay" over the radio. They were secure in a night defensive position, so we headed back to the barn. Climbing through thirty-five hundred feet, my VHF radio came back to life.

"Covey 221, Hillsboro. How do you read, over? We've been trying to talk to you for the past two hours. If you copy, say the nature of your problem."

I couldn't bring myself to tell the controller the whole story. "That's okay, Hillsboro. The problem went away. We're RTB to channel 103. Catch you tomorrow."

August

RESCUE AT ROUTE 966

The dog days of August at Da Nang gave new meaning to the concept of high summer. Not only did we fight Charlie, the grunts' nickname for the VC, but everybody suffered under the sweltering heat. On those incredibly clear, hot days of 1970, the temperature creeped up to over one hundred degrees on a regular basis, with the humidity not far behind. Far offshore in the South China Sea, we all watched the daily buildup of storm clouds, hoping they would drift our way with some cooling rain. But in a monsoon climate, it was feast or famine. In another two months, we would give a month's pay for just one day of dry weather.

In early August we said good-bye to Fuzzy Furr, our very capable leader and affable friend. Fuzzy's new job was taking him to a staff assignment at the 504th TASG at Cam Ranh Bay. We hated to see him go, but during our one-year tours, new guys arriving and good friends leaving was the natural order of things.

The job of Prairie Fire boss fell to Mike McGerty, my old teacher from the Ubon X-Ray mission. Now Mike would become the FNG, and his education and training would take center stage. To facilitate McGerty's training, Bob Meadows, our training officer, shifted me south of Da Nang to a temporary MLT operating out of Chu Lai. McGerty would receive his training in the more active northern areas of the Prairie Fire AO, just as I had.

Shortly after I made the shift to Chu Lai, a terrible aircraft accident jerked us all up short, forcing us to reflect on the brutal, fickle nature of war. One of our A-1 jocks, returning from a mission, experienced engine failure en route from Chu Lai to Da Nang. As the big Spad lost altitude, the pilot went through all the emergency procedures in a desperate effort to restart the huge twenty-seven-hundred-horsepower recip engine. In retrospect, he probably should have bailed out earlier, but all of us felt a strong desire to save our aircraft if possible. When the pilot finally realized that further efforts were futile, he activated the Yankee ejection mechanism, a system in which a powerful rocket attached to the pilot's parachute harness literally snatched him out of his seat and clear of the aircraft. For whatever unfair force was at work, for whatever cosmic circumstance had to be satisfied, the rocket did not fire. The pilot was already too low to bail out over the side, and had no choice but to ride the Skyraider in.

No one could determine exactly what happened in those last few moments. Just a few feet above the trees, the Spad apparently went out of control, cartwheeling into the ground with a shattering explosion. The pilot died instantly. None of us talked about it much, but there seemed to be an unspoken feeling that if fate had willed our friend to die, he had been cheated—he should have been allowed to die in combat instead of in a stupid aircraft accident.

The intensity of operations at Chu Lai quickly forced the A-1 crash to the back of my mind. SOG's cross-border effort from Chu Lai was short but intense, partially dictated by the mission but also shaped by meager resources and the rapidly approaching wet season. I personally had my hands full getting used to the new AO and to a different group of people. One of the necessary, but dull, administrative chores involved assembling and arranging the twenty-five pounds of extra maps required to work the new area. Throughout that early breaking-in period, we always seemed to be pressed for time or behind schedule.

In spite of the pace, the Chu Lai missions gave me a chance to see a couple of old friends flying as Helix FACs for the Americal Division. On my first visit I was astounded. The Helix FACs lived in pleasant, four-man hooches practically on the beach. To me it had all the makings of a really plush setup—comfortable hooches located in a shady grove, a beautiful beach just on the other side of a small embankment, and the South China Sea for a backdrop. The setting made our own China Beach look tacky by comparison. It was easy to see why most Helix FACs hated to come to Da Nang.

Living so far from family, it was a special treat to see a friend from "back in the world," so I made a point of searching out Helix 16, Captain Carl D'Benedetto. Carl and I had been to school together and were later stationed together at Cannon AFB and at Hurlburt. My wife and I were good friends with Carl and his wife, and the four of us shared lots of good times. Carl's dark good looks and friendly personality made him popular with everyone.

When I ran into Carl, we had only a few minutes to talk. He was understandably confused about a Covey FAC flying missions out of Chu Lai, and I felt odd and more than a little underhanded at being unable to tell him the whole story, but he took my feeble explanation in stride and didn't press me. Instead, Carl gave me the good news that we'd soon be neighbors at Da Nang, that he had been selected to be one of the 20th TASS Stan/Eval pilots, and that we would be seeing a lot more of each other.

On the morning of August 10, I made the fifty-five-mile flight south to Chu Lai. I hated the takeoffs and landings on their runway. The airfield was set up much like that at Da Nang, with two long, parallel runways. A Marine fighter outfit used the conventional concrete runway on the west side of the complex. Everybody else, including the Helix FACs, used the east runway, a temporary affair made of pierced steel planking, or PSP. Bouncing over the PSP felt like driving over a washboard. On takeoff roll or landing, my instrument panel vibrated so violently that it was impossible to read the individual gauges. My eyes suffered a similar fate, fluttering up and down with each bounce. At the midrange speeds, I worried that my airplane and my eyes would be the victims of simple harmonic motion, vibrating to the point of tearing themselves apart.

Charlie Gray and I teamed up to run the mission, the insertion of a road watch team just across the border into an isolated area that was being heavily infiltrated by the North Vietnamese. Charlie seemed a little skittish about the operation for a couple of reasons. First, the Chu Lai AO was new to him also, so neither of us was very familiar with the region or the landmarks. Second, Charlie shared my nervousness about working with the untried helicopter assets from the Americal Division. I knew by reputation they were good, but we were used to working with the troops from the 101st Screaming Eagles stationed at Phu Bai. Finally, Charlie's real feelings about being a Covey rider began to show. I never knew his motives for getting into the program, but I began to sense that he didn't like to fly, and that he didn't have that much confidence in the hotshot fighter pilots to whom he was forced to entrust his life.

After the bouncing takeoff out of Chu Lai, we leveled off at two thousand feet above the terrain for the flight to the Laotian border. From our vantage point, all we could see was one steep mountain ridge after another. Each long ridge, running roughly north to south, was completely covered by an incredible variety of lush vegetation. On our westerly flight path, the scene reminded me of an endless series of huge, emerald green ocean waves surging onto a beach. In several of the valleys between the highest ridge lines, we could make out patches of dense early-morning fog, giving an eerie effect to the panorama below us. In spite of the rugged beauty, the terrain seemed somehow sinister, like a dark alley in a tough neighborhood late at night. Nobody would stop you from entering the alley, but you instinctively knew you'd have to fight your way out— and the thugs hidden in the shadows invariably carried razor-sharp switchblades, chains, and brass knuckles. It was their turf, and they fought dirty. As Charlie and I looked down at the jungle, we both sensed we would probably end this day fighting our way out of some no-name Laotian valley—an old-fashioned, dirty rumble—all because we had to find out who or what lay hidden at the end of that dark alley.

Thirty minutes before the package arrived, we located the LZ, a small clearing nestled in the crotch of two small intersecting ridges. The only approach to the football-sized field was from the west. The swaying yellow-green elephant grass gave the illusion that the LZ was flat, but if our maps were correct, the field sloped up at least fifteen degrees. With the steep hill directly in front of us and another one to our immediate right, there wasn't a lot of room to maneuver. We knew it would be risky getting the helicopters into that partial box canyon, but once on the ground, the team would have a great view of Route 966 just five hundred meters to the west.

At 0900 we linked up with the package and led them to the target area. As I flew in to mark the LZ verbally for the waiting Cobras, it felt strange to dive lower than the target and then fly uphill to get there. After calling "Mark, mark," with the hill looming right in front of us, I sucked the stick back into my lap to start an upward vector climb, then stood the protesting Bronco on her left wing tip in a hard, rolling G turn to the north. From the back seat, Charlie complained loudly, "Christ, that was close!" A quick peek at Charlie in the mirror revealed that his eyes were the size of saucers.

We continued to bank around to our left, eventually setting up an orbit directly over the LZ and just a few hundred feet above the tops of the two hills. After clearing the gunships in hot, we watched from our vantage point while the Cobras worked the area over with a hail of fléchettes. We could also see our Slicks orbiting about a mile to the east, impatient to get in and out.

The moment of truth arrived. It certainly wasn't the time for a Knute Rockne pep talk, but I felt compelled to let the Americal pilots know what I expected of them. "Listen up, gents. The approach and pull-off to the north are tricky, so be on your toes. There seems to be an unpredictable wind swirling around near the crotch joining the two hills. Be alert for prop wash. Slick door gunners, when you're in the hover, watch the slopes above you. The bad guys could easily be firing down on you. We've got to have a good, tight pattern, so Cobras, keep it tucked in and your guns ready to bear. Everybody arm 'em up and let's do it."

There was no radio chatter as Slick Lead flew down final with his Cobra escort. A thousand feet above me I could see the sunlight reflected off the canopies of the circling A-1s. At least a dozen pairs of friendly eyes focused on the LZ as the Huey eased into the tall grass and let his precious cargo of six team members jump out the left troop door.

All of us saw it at the same instant. Before the Huey got ten feet off the ground, the air filled with small arms and machine-gun fire. The Slick belched several clouds of black smoke from its exhaust, then began to serpentine, first to the right, then back to the left. Two seconds later, the chopper dropped out of the sky and smacked into the ground with a shattering force. The Huey flopped over on its left side and simply lay there like a dead fish.

There was no fire or explosion. At first I thought the chopper had fallen on the team, but Charlie spotted them scurrying up the hill for the cover of a nearby tree line. Quickly, I thought through the key elements of the predicament we faced: one downed chopper and crew, one small team wandering around the woods, bad guys firing at us from two sides, and a tricky approach into the LZ. On the plus side, I had the assets in place to do the job: good weather and lots of gas. There was nothing left to do but get on with the rescue, yet I couldn't help wondering where all the NVA had come from. How was it that they just happened to be positioned in force around that particular LZ?

I wasn't sure how Charlie was holding up in the back seat, so as calmly as possible, I said, "Charlie, see if you can raise the team on Fox Mike. Find out what they see and hear and tell them to dig in as close to the LZ as possible. I'm gonna work over the south face with the Spads, then we'll go for an extract."

I ventured a quick look at Charlie's face in the mirror. He appeared stern but composed. He was back in his element and answered crisply, "Roger that. Here's where we earn our combat pay."

While Charlie tried to raise the team, I briefed the Spads. "Okay, Spad Lead, here's the drill. I need a couple of passes from you guys against that southern hill. Let's start off with HE rockets and strafe. I'd like you to plan your runs north to south with a pull-off to the west. Keep a sharp look out 'cause the Cobras will be just below you on a perpendicular flight path suppressing fire on the other hill."

Next, I turned my attention to the Hueys. "Slick Two, as the Spads come off their second pass, I'll give you the signal and then you need to touch down on the northeast corner of the LZ. You scarf up the team. Cobra Lead will cover you. Slick Three, land as close to the crash as possible. Have the *bac si* and door gunner do a fast check for survivors. Cobra Two will cover you. If either of you takes fire, abort the run."

I armed two rocket pods and rolled into a curvilinear pass on the south face, spacing four willie petes along the length of its slope. Racking us around in a tight 270-degree right turn, we gave the eastern hill the same treatment. There was just time for one final set of instructions. "Spads, hit anywhere between my smokes on the south hill. Cobras, hit anywhere between my smokes on the east hill. You're cleared in hot."

I climbed a couple of thousand feet and set up an orbit slightly west of the LZ. A thousand feet below, the Slicks milled around waiting for their turn. Just when I thought we had it wired, one of the Hueys yelled over the radio, "Covey, break left! Somebody's shooting big stuff at you!"

Without waiting to confirm it, I cobbed the power, stomped hard left rudder, and slammed the stick to the left. Down we went in a series of tight aileron rolls. For a split second during each revolution, I could see the string of

23mm airbursts following us. Then, as fast as it started, it stopped. As we leveled off on the trees and circled back into position, I realized I hadn't been paying attention and had drifted out over the Trail. The gun was down there somewhere, more of a nuisance than a real threat, so we avoided the issue by keeping our orbit directly over the LZ.

As Charlie and I choreographed and watched the attack, the big A-1s and the Cobras began their intricate weave, spraying the jungle slopes with high-explosive rockets and 7.62mm mini-gun fire. As the Spads pulled off their last pass, the Slicks were in perfect position on short final with the Cobras coming off their runs and back around to cover. For added insurance, I had the Spads drop M-47 smoke bombs along the south hill, hoping the thick white smoke would give the vulnerable Hueys some masking cover as they ran the gauntlet of fire into the LZ.

So far, so good. The Slicks touched down in the tall grass and seemed to sit there for an eternity. I saw two figures leap out of Slick Three, run to the crashed chopper, and climb up on its side. I shot a quick glance toward the tree line, hoping to see our team, but my attention was diverted when a long stream of tracers came pouring out of the jungle about halfway up the hill. Before I had time to say anything, Cobra Lead rolled in and hosed the area, silencing that threat at least temporarily.

When I looked back at the LZ, both Slicks had lifted off, straining for altitude and airspeed, while I directed the Cobras in covering fire against the two hills. At the first break in the action I asked Charlie, "Did you ever see the team?"

He answered, "I never saw them. I don't think they got out. Something must have happened."

We knew the chopper pilots had their hands full, but I couldn't wait. "Slick Two, Covey 221. Say status of the team. Over."

Somewhat irritably, I thought, the pilot responded, "Stand by, Covey." About thirty seconds later, he keyed his mike again. "We've got five on board, smiling and laughing!"

Elated at that news but wondering about the sixth team member, I checked in with the other Huey. "Three, were there any survivors?"

"Rog, Covey. We got the two pilots and the door gunner. But the crew chief is dead, trapped under the wreckage, along with one of the indig team members. We couldn't get them out of the wreck."

On that sad note, I rounded up the package and pointed them toward Chu Lai. Charlie and I remained over the crash site for fifteen more minutes, making sure we had all the landmarks memorized, because we both knew we would be back later with a stronger team in an all-out effort to recover the bodies of Army Specialist John Crowley and the indig team member. We hated to go off and leave them, fearful that the enemy troops might tamper with the wreckage while we were gone. More out of frustration than conviction, I fired off all my remaining rockets into the trees around the LZ. Maybe the sound of the explosions would make the bad guys think twice before coming out of hiding to investigate the downed Huey. With any luck we'd be refueled, rearmed, and back on the scene before they got organized.

Back at Chu Lai, it took the rest of the afternoon to get the twelve-man Bright Light team down from Da Nang. Bright Light was actually the code name for a top secret program designed to rescue POWs, evadees, and downed aircrews when a normal search and rescue effort was not feasible. Brainchild of one of the Air Force's most experienced special operations officers, Colonel Harry "Heinie" Aderholt, the Bright Light program was the action arm of a secret cover agency within MACV called the Joint Personnel Recovery Center, or JPRC. SOG always kept several Bright Light teams on strip alert for a week at a time. Missions ranged from tracking and rescuing downed pilots evading capture in North Vietnam to raids on suspected POW camps in an attempt to rescue the prisoners. Bright

Light teams had rescued almost five hundred ARVN prisoners in daring raids; unfortunately they never liberated a single living American POW. These same teams were often called upon to risk their lives to recover the bodies of SOG members or aircrew members who had died in North Vietnam, Laos, or Cambodia. Such was the mission our Bright Light team would perform at the LZ overlooking Route 966.

While we were waiting, Charlie and I flew one more sortie across the fence, trying to determine if NVA units were moving to reinforce the area around the fight of earlier that morning. During their brief time on the ground, our team thought they might have heard motorized equipment moving out on the Trail. Charlie and I combed every inch of that section of Route 966, but all we got for our trouble was a good hosing from yet another 23mm gun.

After refueling again, we finally got the package airborne at 1630. This time I kept the chopper force orbiting while the Spads saturated both hills with CBU-25, rockets, and strafe. When they finished, I let the Cobras nail the whole area for good measure.

Covered by the Cobras, Slick Lead eased into the LZ unopposed and deposited the first half of the Bright Light team. As he lifted off, the Huey shuddered under the heavy force of multiple machine-gun hits as automatic-weapons fire poured out of two pockets halfway up the southern hill. I had a sick feeling in the pit of my stomach as I began talking to my package.

"Slick Lead, take up a heading of 045 if you can and say your condition."

"Covey, we're all okay but the transmission sounds like it could come apart any second now. I've got the RPM beeped up about as much as she'll take. We'll never make it all the way back to Chu Lai."

After a long swig from my water bottle, I answered him. "I got a good copy, Lead. I'll send Cobra Two and Slick Four with you in case you have to set her down. Your best bet is Kham Duc, northeast for thirteen miles. Break, break.

Cobra Two, give us an update on Lead's status every few minutes."

As the mini-package headed for Kham Duc, Charlie laid some more bad news on me. "Are you listening up on Fox Mike Two?" he asked. "The One-Zero says they're taking small-arms fire from that south hill. He'll try to stay put if you can turn off the heat."

Despite all our efforts, the hill was obviously still crawling with bad guys. It was time to pull out all the stops. Switching over to the UHF radio, I told the Spads, "Let's burn 'em out. Give me the napalm along that south face. You're cleared in hot, but for God's sake, don't drop short."

The nape would do the trick, but One-Zeroes generally didn't like us to use the stuff. The residual fires were unpredictable, often moving toward the team and flushing them out of otherwise good hiding places.

While the A-1s splashed the target, Charlie and I talked over the situation between conversations with the team. They could still hear lots of ground fire, but it was all directed at us. By the time the Spads finished, the team reported all quiet. I felt uncomfortable committing the rest of the Bright Light team without the spare Huey, but we had to recover those bodies while there was a lull, and there wasn't time to wait for the rest of my package to make it back to our location.

Once more we double-teamed the targets, with Cobra Lead suppressing to the east and the Spads beating up on the southern hill. In all the confusion, Slick Two started his run into the LZ. On short final he aborted, riddled by AK-47 fire. Badly shot up but with nobody hurt, the UH-1 limped out of the area and headed back to Chu Lai.

With half my package shot to hell and nothing to show for it, we decided to call off the recovery. We had clearly stumbled into a hornet's nest, a lot bigger than we could handle in the one hour of daylight remaining. Charlie estimated we were up against battalion strength and that the cagey NVA regulars were using the crash and our team as bait. It made sense. During those long hours while we were away, the bad guys had apparently moved half of North Vietnam into prepared positions around the crash. They probably let the team onto the ground before opening up, knowing full well we wouldn't give up until we had our troops back.

In light of what had already happened, it was embarrassing to ask the last Huey to try for a pickup, but there was no choice. When I asked Slick Three if he would give it a try, he answered, "No sweat, Covey. Just give me lots of cover." I could have hugged the crazy fool.

We were all short of gas and ammo, so this one had to count. As the Slick made his run, the Spads and the remaining Cobra strafed both hills, now almost totally covered in deep afternoon shadows. In the twilight, tracer ammunition crisscrossed the sky. I dropped full flaps and flew formation with the Huey all the way down final, hoping the sight of the low-flying OV-10 would keep a few heads down. It didn't work. Before we made it over the LZ, Slick Three pulled up sharply and broke hard to the north, his gunner slumped half out the door in a lifeless heap.

I thought to myself, what a hell of a mess. No gas, no choppers, no daylight, and our team down there counting on us to get them out. As I was about to ask Charlie to call back to Chu Lai for another Huey, the One-Zero began whispering on his radio. I had never heard that sound on a radio before, but it could only mean the worst kind of trouble. Sergeant First Class Tony Coelho's heavy breathing and muffled words sent chills down my spine.

"They're coming in for the kill," he hissed. "Heavy movement twenty meters to our northeast. For reference, they should be about fifty meters due east of the crash site. Put some hurt on them!"

As I listened to that pathetic whisper, my mind seemed to shut down and I couldn't figure out what to do. The only relevant thought I had concerned my FAC training back at Hurlburt. For some reason all I could grab hold of was a classroom lecture about minimum safe distance for dropping various types of ordnance. I honestly couldn't remember anything that could be delivered around friendly troops inside one hundred meters. Without thinking about what I was saying, I finally blurted out, "I can't take the responsibility for dropping stuff that close to your position. You'll have to move and give us some room to work."

The team leader's response felt like somebody had punched me in the stomach. In firm but quiet tones, he retorted, "Son, forget your goddamn rule book and get on with it. I'd rather take my chances with you killing me than let the VC get us. Put it in danger close."

A man that eloquent had to be saved. I took another gulp from my water bottle before I answered. "Get your heads down. I'm in from the west, and when my rockets hit, you bug out north as fast as you can run. The Spads will be in fifteen seconds behind me."

As we came down the chute, both hills lit up with small-arms fire. Fortunately, I was so preoccupied with lining up the target in my gunsight that there was no time to worry about it. From a shallow dive angle, I squeezed off two willie petes before racking us into the tightest G turn I could pull without stalling. The Bronco buffeted all the way through the turn, but she kept climbing and flying like the thoroughbred she was. At the 180-degree point in our turn, the One-Zero sang out, "You're right on! You're right on! Fire for effect!"

With the heavy G forces giving my voice a funny, wavering sound, I grunted out to the Spads, "Hit my smoke." As we continued the circle, they blasted the area with HE rockets and strafe. In the growing darkness, the explosions made for a spectacular light show. The team wasn't answering Charlie's request for a correction, so I could only hope they were moving. To keep the pressure on, the Spads made one more pass, then advised they were below bingo fuel and heading home. To complicate matters, my remaining Cobra started home also. Now it was up to Charlie and me, and we only had a few more minutes before we would have to leave.

It was almost completely dark. The sun had set behind the higher mountains to our west; in a few more minutes, we wouldn't be able to see anything. To complicate the situation further, a small patch of ground fog had developed along a streambed just off the LZ, in exactly the direction our team had moved. As Charlie and I circled forlornly over the scene, the muzzle flashes down below, now plainly visible in the growing darkness, confirmed our worst suspicions. As we counted at least 130 separate flashes, we knew we could never get the team out, at least not that night.

It was a long five minutes before the One-Zero reestablished radio contact. As Tony talked and simultaneously gasped for breath, I could hear steady exchanges of gunfire over the radio. "We're off the north edge of the LZ and about one hundred meters down the slope in the first big tree line. Chuck is right on the crest in the elephant grass firing down on us. They're in the open, so blast 'em!"

Since my rockets were the only game in town, I rolled in to do as the man said—blast 'em. I only had the vaguest notion of where the team was, but there was no time to sort it out. I put the pipper on the edge of the LZ and fired one willie pete. I couldn't see the impact, but as we pulled off the run, the One-Zero shouted, "You're long. Tell the Spads to go about one hundred meters short of your smoke."

As I maneuvered for the second pass, I said to my backseater, "Charlie, tell him there aren't any Spads. Tell him to keep the corrections coming."

The second rocket was better. The One-Zero yelled encouragement. "Bull's-eye. They're screaming up there! Keep pounding that area!"

Just as I was wondering how best to use my last two rockets, the UHF radio crackled. "Covey 221, Spad 03 and 04 are back with you. We've been monitoring your freq and came back to help out. We can give you two twenty-mike-mike passes each, but then we've got to get out of here." The voice on the radio was that of Spad Lead, Lieutenant Tom Stump. Along with his wingman, Captain Ed Gullion, they had to be running on fumes. But like every-

body involved with SOG, these courageous A-1 jocks
would take any risk to help a team out of a tight spot.

Charlie Gray passed on the good news to the One-Zero,
but he let the other shoe drop with it. Trying to sound as
optimistic as possible, he explained, "There's no way we
can pull you out tonight. If the Spads beat up that crest just
above you, do you think you can move into a solid night-
defensive position and hold on till morning?"

After thinking it over for a few seconds, Tony Coelho
answered, "We can hear 'em up there, and they're hurt and
disorganized. If you break the contact for me, we'll be here
at first light waiting for you."

I asked Charlie, "How in the hell can he be so calm
about spending the night in the middle of an NVA battalion?"

"He's one of our best One-Zeroes," Charlie replied. "As
I recall, he got a DSC about six months ago on a mission
similar to this one."

For the final time that night, I dove the OV-10 into all
those winking muzzle flashes. In what turned out to be a
piece of blind luck, my smoke hit twenty meters above the
team's position. The Spads did the rest, raking the edge of
the LZ with a deadly hail of cannon fire. When it was over
and the A-1s had departed for the second time, we climbed
to a safe altitude and contacted the team. In a whisper the
leader told us most firing had ceased and that he was on
the move. Charlie and I both promised him we'd be back
to pull him out at first light. Then we headed for Chu Lai,
almost out of gas and feeling totally dejected about having
to leave those poor devils out in the jungle.

We didn't have a lot of time to feel sorry for ourselves.
I was genuinely concerned about our fuel since we had only
three hundred pounds remaining, by far the lowest I had
flown with in my brief career. As we neared Chu Lai, the
pucker factor went up a little more when I couldn't raise
the tower and couldn't make out any runway lights. My
heart sank when a passing C-123 answered my radio calls,

informing us that Chu Lai was Condition Red—under attack—and that the field was closed.

I briefly considered landing on the blacked-out runway, but instead turned north on a direct line to Da Nang. Several minutes later, just as I contacted Da Nang Approach Control and explained our minimum fuel situation, the fuel-low caution light blinked on, indicating something less than 220 pounds remaining. Approach Control wasn't thrilled when I asked for a straight-in visual approach against traffic, but they finally agreed and handed us over to Da Nang tower for a landing on Runway 35 Right.

When we touched down, I sneaked a peek at the fuel gauge. In the dark cockpit, the needle fluctuated on the very bottom of the graduated scale. It had been close.

After taxiing to the Covey revetments, I shut both engines down and took off my helmet while the props were still turning. As I sat there in an exhausted stupor, all I could hear was the whishing sound as the props wound down and the crackling and pinging noises as the engines cooled off. When everything had stopped, Charlie and I climbed stiffly out of our seats and onto the concrete ramp. As I stood there facing him under the bright flight-line lights, I hoped I didn't look as bad as he did. We had taken off fifteen hours earlier, flying four sorties and spending nine and one-half of those hours in the air. And we weren't through yet. Bob Meadows met us with a jeep and a beer and drove us directly to the Prairie Fire briefing room so we could plan the rescue for the next morning.

None of us slept much that night. When we launched the package at dawn, we went out loaded for bear, fully expecting the NVA to have reinforced throughout the night. The first clue to the contrary came when Charlie tried to make radio contact with the team. Every man in the package was on pins and needles waiting for the reply. At the sound of the One-Zero's voice in my earphones, I felt myself exhale loudly; I had literally been holding my breath since Charlie had first keyed his mike button.

The team was in good shape but needed a few minutes

to move up the slope to the edge of the LZ. They reported all quiet—no noise, no patrols, no sounds from the bad guys since just before midnight. They did, however, hear what they thought to be the sound of someone prying pieces of metal from the downed chopper. As a precaution, we surrounded them with a concentrated saturation bombing and strafing of the hills overlooking the LZ. Before committing the Cobras and Hueys, we blasted the area with four flights of fast movers carrying the traditional close air support load: high-drag 500-pound bombs called "snakeye," and canisters referred of napalm. Collectively, the deadly duo was simply referred to as "snake and nape."

Slick Lead made it down final and into a hover without incident. We held our breath again as the team scrambled out of the concealing tree line and into the open troop door of the Huey. As the UH-1 lifted off and turned to the north, the Cobras plastered the faces of both hills with rockets and mini-gun fire. Strangely, we never saw or heard a shot fired in return. With no apparent opposition from the NVA, we talked to the launch site about going back in to recover the bodies in the wrecked helicopter, but they made the decision to cancel the whole show. We never returned to the LZ overlooking Route 966.*

A few days later, the Spads were kind enough to invite me to one of their "hail and farewell" parties. It was just the sort of distraction we needed. Uniform of the day was the party suit, a garish copy of our flight suits tailored and fitted in an outlandish assortment of colors. The A-1 jocks wore either a black or an olive-drab suit. My Covey party suit, in royal blue, clearly upstaged anything there. Individualism was expressed in the various patches on the party

*On 24 August 1999, an investigative element from the Joint Task Force-Full Accounting, Camp Smith, HI, located the downed helicopter in Xekong Province, Laos. When the team rolled the Huey over, they found human remains. On 5 June 2000, the remains were positively identified as those of the helicopter crew chief, John E. Crowley.

suit—Yankee Air Pirate; Participant, Southeast Asia War Games; the Covey patch, depicting the world-famous beagle, Snoopy, dancing a jig over crisscrossing tracers; the Covey Prairie Fire patch, showing Snoopy astride a machine-gun-firing doghouse, diving into a wall of red flames. As accessories, I wore the traditional Covey scarf, black with yellow polka dots, and a brass chain and medallion with the letters WAR.

As I entered the private room of the DOOM club, the scene appeared tame enough. A U-shaped banquet table dominated the room. In the far corner, most of the Spads and invited guests congregated around a small bar. Predictably, the conversation focused on flying and recent adventures or war stories. The setting reminded me of the dozens of other fighter pilot bashes I had attended over the past few years.

Then the tenor of the evening began to change. The head Spad invited all of us to order the drink of our choice from the bar. Someone produced a large stainless steel pot into which everybody dutifully poured his drink—beer, scotch, bourbon, vodka, gin, Bloody Mary, crème de menthe, brandy. After a quick stir, each of us dipped his glass into the vat. When everybody had a brimming glass full of "Spad Sauce," the head Spad lifted his glass in a toast, "To the Spads," to which all of us responded by chugging the nasty, potent, olive-drab concoction. From there, the party rapidly went downhill.

Shortly after we sat down to dinner, one of the Spads tossed a dinner roll across the room at some unsuspecting soul, to the rousing cheers of his buddies who shouted the warning "Incoming!" Periodically throughout the meal, volleys of rolls arched back and forth across the tables.

Following dinner, some enterprising Spad grabbed the remnants from a sour cream bowl and drew a large bull's-eye on the back of the closed door. Next, he handed me the bowl of "ammo" and instructed me to sling a handful of the stuff at our target. From wherever the "mark" splattered, I issued corrections to the Spads who stood at the far end of the room and tossed their drink glasses at the target. In no time we had broken every glass in the place. The party took a definite downturn when the irate club manager refused to bring in another tray of glasses.

As a fitting cap to the evening, the head Spad shouted, "Anybody who can't tap-dance on the table is queer!" To a man, all thirty of us in the room leaped on the U-shaped tables and proceeded to do individual impressions of Gene Kelly. Under the heavy weight, the tables collapsed, sending pilots, dishes, and leftovers crashing to the floor in a twisted, broken heap. With good cause, the club manager unceremoniously booted us out. Our understanding flight surgeon patched up the bruises and stitched up the cuts, then shuffled us all off to bed, battered but relaxed after letting off the dangerous head of steam that had been building.

In the days that followed the bash with the Spads, we returned to the Prairie Fire mission ready to tackle whatever came our way. For me, operations took a decided turn toward the routine. For the remainder of August, most of my flights involved escorting supply helicopters to a remote mountaintop due west of Da Nang and just across the border into Laos.

The object of our supply effort was "Sugarloaf," a SOG radio relay site perched precariously on top of a seventy-two-hundred-foot mountain. From its commanding heights, the highly trained commo troops stationed there could intercept most line-of-sight radio transmissions from SOG teams operating in the Chu Lai AO, then pass them on to the MLT or to CCN headquarters at Da Nang. Technically, the plan was a good one. Realistically, the technicians on the mountaintop fought a never-ending battle against isolation, boredom, limited supplies, and determined assaults by NVA units in the area who wanted nothing more than to wipe out the flagrant little camp operating in their backyard.

Small enemy patrols harassed the relay site regularly, but they never had the strength to mount a frontal attack against the mountaintop perimeter. Instead, the bad guys decided to disrupt the vital supply line by shooting up our supply-laden choppers as they tried to land on the postage-stamp-sized LZ. My job was to direct the fire of supporting Cobras, hopefully pinning down the enemy troops long enough for our choppers to slip in and out unharmed.

On a normal day, we would fly several round trips escorting huge CH-54 Skycranes with large cargo nets full of supplies suspended under their weird-looking fuselages. The combination of high heat, high-pressure altitude, and heavy loads strained their big engines to the limit and cut the Skycranes' maneuverability to practically nil. Without the help of the Cobra gunships, the big birds were sitting ducks as they lumbered into the relay site with their precious cargo.

Our tactics of spraying suspected positions with rockets and machine-gun fire were generally effective, although results were arguable. For starters, the relay site would brief me on enemy activity during the preceding night. Usually the commander passed on his best guess about directions and distance to sounds, movement, or actual fire received. "Pretty quiet last night. We did hear somebody stomping around just before dawn. Sounded like the noise was on a bearing of 130 degrees, maybe two hundred meters out."

Based on the relay site's estimate, the Covey rider and I would survey the area, pick out the most likely spots, then fire a couple of willie petes into the target. Keying on our smoke, the Cobras worked the areas over while the CH-54 made its run onto the mountaintop. For all we knew, the sounds we attacked could have been some animal rooting around in the tangle of vegetation, but this was no time to be cautious—anything or anybody moving up the side of the mountain was considered the enemy. Besides, the relay site could hear the bad guys shooting at us on every resupply sortie, so we knew the threat and the danger were real.

These missions seemed easy compared to inserting a team on the Ho Chi Minh Trail. Since there was never any doubt about where the friendlies were, controlling air strikes was a snap. Most of us began to regard the daily resupply missions as milk runs. We knew the NVA fired at us, but we tended to dismiss the danger as minimal. Of course, it was always possible to get hit when the bad guys emptied clip after clip in our direction; but fortunately, the sky is a big place, and most of us felt that if we were to get blasted, it would be the result of a lucky shot—what pilots called the "golden BB."

On August 22 I had a welcome break from the routine resupply missions. South Vietnam was a veritable cross-roads for Air Force flyers, and I should not have been sur-prised to run across yet another buddy from the world, but I was nevertheless pleased to see my roommate from pilot training, Captain Norm Komich, show up at Da Nang. The best part was that Norm had been assigned as a Jolly Green helicopter pilot living on the ground floor of the Covey hooch. Norm was the kind of tonic we all needed. He had a great sense of humor and was one of the most naturally upbeat people any of us would ever meet. Norm took a lot of good-natured kidding over his very meticulous eating habits, stemming primarily from an unquenchable desire for "greens and grams of protein." Norm took the teasing gra-ciously because none of it was vicious—nobody dared to be nasty because he was a world-class body builder and former Mr. Massachusetts. His biceps were about the size of an average man's leg. Throughout his tour, Norm tried, in his heavy Boston accent, to convert us to better health through proper diet, rest, and no booze. He never suc-ceeded, but it was always fun letting him try.

Fortunately for me, I had friends to fall back on when the action heated up—old buddies like Evan Quiros, Carl D'Benedetto, and Norm Komich. On the morning of Au-gust 31, I slept in since I was on the afternoon resupply run to Sugarloaf. At about 10:30 that morning, Evan walked into our room, acting sort of stiff and tentative. I figured that something was bothering him and that he would get around to telling me in his own time. Finally, Evan took a deep breath and said, "I guess you didn't hear about

Mike McGerty. The word just came in a little while ago. He got shot down out around that mountain you guys are always flying to."

I felt myself recoil from Evan's news. At first I was angry with him. I'd been in the room all morning. How could I know about McGerty? Then I took a close look at Evan's face. It was drawn tight with tension. He probably felt as awkward about telling me as I felt about hearing it. None of us knew how to handle circumstances like that, much less how to express them. My reaction had been classic—shoot the messenger.

When I finally trusted my voice enough to speak, it sounded hollow to me, as it had when I had heard that Rick Meacham had been shot down. "Did he eject?" I asked.

Evan simply shook his head no, then added softly, "The back-seater didn't get out either."

We flew the afternoon resupply run as scheduled. After the last chopper dumped his load on the LZ, I circled down the northeast face of the mountain to the crash site. Through the heavy foliage, we could just make out the disintegrated mess that had once been an OV-10. The Bright Light team had already recovered the bodies of Captain Mike McGerty and Sergeant First Class Charlie Gray. Nobody could shed much light on what had happened. The relay site said Mike and Charlie were checking out some movement in a small ravine. The troops on the mountaintop heard a long burst of automatic-weapons fire, followed by a sputtering engine and a loud crash.

Flying back to Da Nang, I remembered that Mike had been in the Prairie Fire program for only three weeks. He had just been fully checked out a couple of days before. And Charlie Gray, veteran of God only knew how many scary missions on the ground, hated to fly with us. So we teamed the two of them up and sent them out to cut their teeth on resupply missions to the radio relay site—a regular milk run, laced with golden BBs.

September

I assumed we would have a hard time recruiting new pilots into Prairie Fire after the word got around about Mike McGerty's death. I couldn't have been more wrong. Mike's death uncorked a river of sentiment as well as volunteers, all wanting a chance to fly for Prairie Fire. Each had his own reasons—adventure, curiosity, revenge, even a desire to win a few medals. Whatever the reasons, the head Covey, Ed Cullivan, had the unenviable job of picking a new Prairie Fire boss. While he sorted through the applicants, we kept flying missions.

I had the early morning go on the fifth of September. At Covey Operations, the briefer brought me up to speed on the current and forecast weather. In what amounted to a preview of the coming monsoon season, the coast from Da Nang north was socked in with low scud and drizzle. The weatherman expected a gradual burnoff by late morning, but until then, everything along the coast was instrument flight rules (IFR).

Just before dawn, I finished preflighting and completed loading several crates of fresh vegetables and a bag of mail, referred to as "Pony Express," into the cargo bay of aircraft 661. Whenever possible, we tried to help out the MLTs by hauling a few goodies to them. When they had to rely on the normal supply system, the wait tended to stretch out.

Right after lift off, the horizon disappeared into a swirling gray mass of clouds. Totally engulfed in the thick soup, I had no choice but to concentrate on flying precise instruments. While the departure controller vectored me via radar to various altitudes and headings, I stayed glued on my instruments, fighting off a slightly claustrophobic feeling and the uncomfortable sensation that my OV-10 was in a diving right turn when my instruments indicated the Bronco to be climbing on a steady heading. An untold number of pilots had bought the farm over the years because of vertigo, an unreliable feeling deep in the inner ear. I had no intention of being one of them, so I fought the sensation and settled into the mental discipline needed to speed up my somewhat rusty instrument crosscheck.

Tracking outbound on the Da Nang TACAN 330-degree radial, I kept climbing, hoping to break out of the soup. Passing through five thousand feet, the inside of the clouds took on a lighter cast, and at six thousand feet I broke out into the bright morning sunshine. Regardless of my mood when starting out, flying instruments inside dirty gray clouds always seemed to depress me. But the pilot who doesn't get an instant thrill when he breaks out of the weather and into the dazzling sunshine set against an incredibly blue sky has yet to be born. Climbing into the clear was almost like a rebirth, a new lease on life. After a couple of quick aileron rolls in celebration, I leveled off at sixty-five hundred feet and headed for Quang Tri, thirty miles in front of me, hidden somewhere under all that weather I had just climbed through.

I had hoped to find a few breaks in the clouds for a VFR descent, but the deck was solid. When I contacted Hue Approach Control, the news was even grimmer. Quang Tri was reporting below aircraft approach minimums, with a three-hundred-foot ceiling and half-mile visibility due to rain and fog. To top it all off, Quang Tri's TACAN, channel 103, was off the air, leaving only a low-powered non-directional beacon for navigation and instrument approaches. Reluctantly, I set up a holding pattern over the beacon in hopes that the crud would burn off enough to put the field above minimums.

As I ginned around the holding pattern, I talked to First Sergeant Budrow at MLT-2. Top didn't sound particularly happy with my report. He respectfully but pointedly reminded me that we had teams on the ground who needed our attention and that I wasn't any use to the war effort in a holding pattern over Quang Tri. He was absolutely right, and the guilt gnawed at me with each successive trip around the imaginary racetrack. More than anything, I wanted to help Top, yet there seemed no legal way out of the weather-inflicted mess. The rules and regulations concerning instrument approaches had been pounded into my head from day one as a young student pilot back at Laughlin AFB, Texas. Our bible on flying instruments, *Air Force Manual 51-37*, defined the dos and don'ts; flying an instrument approach into a field known to be below minimums was definitely a no-no. From my perspective at that moment, the rules were absolute, with no provision for interpretation—or, God forbid, flagrant disregard. Fortunately, I was about to get another lesson in judgment.

The lesson developed slowly over the course of forty-five minutes in the holding pattern. The first ingredient involved a natural phenomenon. Far to my east, thunder bumpers had already started their ritual buildup over the South China Sea. As the cells gathered strength, they cut loose with an impressive display of lightning. The static discharges were no danger to me, but they did have an unnerving effect on my ADF navigation needle. With each lightning flash, the ADF needle spun around and pointed at the thunderstorms. At least fifteen seconds passed before the needle settled down and pointed at the beacon. For all practical purposes, the ADF would be unreliable for an instrument approach.

The second part of the lesson was just as unexpected as the lightning. As I listened to the five radios we monitored, I heard Batcat, an electronic warfare EC-121 aircraft, talk to MLT-2. Batcat reported heavy sensor movement in the vicinity of one of our teams. The movement could be anything from troops to trucks to water buffalo. Whatever the movement, it probably spelled trouble for the team.

When Batcat signed off, Top gave me a call. "Covey

221, did you copy that transmission from Batcat?" Top's voice was calm and unemotional as always, but the hidden message came through loud and clear.

I answered, "Rog, Top. I copied. Let me check with Approach Control and I'll get back to you."

Instead, I called directly to Quang Tri tower for a weather update. They confirmed the ceiling was still below minimums for an ADF approach, but visibility had improved enough to allow a few helicopters to take off under special VFR rules. A light bulb blinked on in my brain: Special VFR might be the answer. Under those rules, certain slower-moving aircraft could take off and land as long as they remained beneath the cloud layer. I'd never heard any of the Coveys talk about flying special VFR, so I wasn't sure whether it was legal or not. More than likely, it was a case of if you're not going to like the answer, don't ask the question.

My immediate problem was to somehow get below the weather. From the holding pattern, I moved a few miles east until certain I was over water. I ran through a quick descent check, reduced the power, and started down at 150 knots indicated airspeed. As the Bronco slid back into the thick clouds, I paid special attention to the chatter on the approach control frequency. The name of the game was to maneuver well clear of any IFR traffic moving up or down the coast. The real danger, slight as it was, came from other pilots like myself who were thrashing around in the clouds trying to beat the system.

During the descent, I decided to make five hundred feet my hard altitude. If there were no visual references by then, I'd climb back on top. I was flying a modified box pattern, holding each heading for about thirty seconds so as to remain fairly close to an imaginary geographic point over the water. With slight adjustments for the prevailing wind, I would stay in the ballpark.

I leveled off at five hundred feet, still inside the dark clouds. Rather than give up, I decided to fly around the box one last time. Nothing on the first two legs. As I droned northwest on the third leg, I caught a glimpse of whitecaps below me. The hole closed up almost immediately, but the lure was irresistible. On my attitude indicator, I set up a glide slope of three degrees nose low. A few seconds later, I coasted out the bottom of the clouds into a rainy gray drizzle just three hundred feet above the churning water. There wasn't much of a horizon, but off to my left I could just make out the dim outline of the beach.

From there it was uneventful. I crossed the beach searching for familiar landmarks until, finally, the city of Quang Tri loomed directly in front of me. It was easy to pick up the Highway One Bridge across the Cua Viet River; at the bridge I hung a right and followed the highway to the airfield, four miles northwest.

Once on the ground, the Barky crew chiefs refueled the aircraft while I waited for the Covey rider to show up. When Satan arrived, we strapped in and started up the engines. The weather still looked lousy, so it came as no surprise when the tower told us the field was still below minimums. Trying to sound as confident as possible, I countered with a request for a special VFR clearance. Much to my relief, tower cleared us for a special VFR departure, and we blasted off to check on our teams.

I followed the same drill three times that day. The experience definitely came in handy, because throughout the remainder of my tour, I flew special VFR on many occasions. Never again did I hold up the war effort while droning around in an instrument holding pattern.

Back at Da Nang, the Covey commander had made his choice for Prairie Fire boss. There had been some speculation about my getting the job, but with three months in grade as a captain, I was considered too junior. And the older Prairie Fire troops would finish their tours the following month, so they were nonstarters. It was no secret that Colonel Cullivan had been hit hard by the Meacham and McGerty losses. He desperately wanted somebody he could count on to control the free-spirited Prairie Fire pilots, perhaps someone with a little more seniority. He ended up

Low-level flying became an integral part of the Prairie Fire mission. Here an OV-10 Bronco attacks targets deep in Laos near the Ho Chi Minh Trail. (*U.S. Air Force photo*)

A fish-eye view from the back seat of the Bronco. With its great visibility, maneuverability, and armament, the OV-10 rapidly became the premier FAC aircraft of the war. (*U.S. Air Force photo*)

Once inserted on the ground in Laos, the small Special Forces–led recon teams needed all the help they could get. In this shot a Cobra gunship dives to attack NVA troops moving against a seven-man SOG team. (*U.S. Army photo*)

When no landing zone was available, our helicopters often rescued SOG personnel using ladders. Here, members of a reconnaissance team ride out on ladders after an emergency extraction from Laos. (*Courtesy of Richard Madore*)

The third member of the SOG airborne package, the incomparable A-1H Skyraider, wings north over Da Nang Bay en route to another Prairie Fire mission. The Spad's awesome load of weapons and long loiter time made it the perfect close-air-support bird. (*U.S. Air Force photo*)

Flying against the big guns in Laos proved to be nerve-wracking as well as hazardous. After being hit by ground fire, the F-4 Phantom in the foreground dumps fuel while returning to home base. (*U.S. Air Force photo*)

Three veterans of the Prairie Fire Program posing beside an Oscar Deuce. From left to right: Gary Pavlu, Jim "Satan" Martin, and Bob Meadows. (*Courtesy of Jim Martin*)

The venerable O-2 "Oscar Deuce" was one of the mainstays of the Prairie Fire operation. This O-2 is skimming in low over the South China Sea en route to a landing at Quang Tri. (*Courtesy of Jim Martin*)

To suppress antiaircraft guns along the Ho Chi Minh Trail, FACs generally called in the "fast-movers." In this instance, an F-105 Thud Loaded with five-hundred-pound bombs poses for a photo en route to the target. Note the Daisy Cutter fuse extender on the outboard right pylon. (*U.S. Air Force photo*)

A Prairie Fire party in progress at MLT-2, Quanq Tri. Standing from left to right: First Sergeant Bill Valentini; Covey Rider Jerry "Blister" Grant; Major Bob Denison, the Covey Prairie Fire commander. (*Courtesy of Evan Quiros*)

During the Vietnam War, Da Nang became a crossroads for Air Force fliers. My roommate from pilot training, Captain Norm Komich, turned up at Da Nang as a "Jolly Green" rescue helicopter pilot, flying the HH-53. The Jollies flew some of the hairiest missions of the war, penetrating deep into North Vietnam to rescue downed pilots. (*Courtesy of Norm Komich*)

Another good friend, Captain Carl D'Benedetto, was an FAC in the Americal Division at Chu Lai. After moving to Da Nang, Carl "evaluated" me on an unusual midtour check ride. (*Courtesy of Carl D'Benedetto*)

An F-100 Super Saber drops a pair of Mark 82 bombs in support of a SOG team operating deep in Laos. (*Courtesy of Tom Yarborough*)

To gain an advantage while running missions on the Ho Chi Minh Trail, some SOG teams disguised themselves to look like the enemy. RT Virginia is shown dressed in NVA uniforms and carrying AK-47s. (*Courtesy of Ron Knight*)

A photo of Tom Yarborough at Da Nang airbase, March 1971
(*Courtesy of Tom Yarborough*)

The Muff Divers' Lounge served as the focal point for most Covey FAC social activities. The permanent residents, resplendent in Covey party suits, are (from left to right): Captain Larry "Big Bippy" Thomas, the author, Captain Sonny Haynes. Relaxing in the foreground is our mascot Muff, the wonder dog.

picking a good man—his trailer mate, Major Bob Denison.

Bob was a hard-flying, hard-playing boss, with many of the same leadership qualities Ed Cullivan had. He had a knack for harnessing our youthful enthusiasm without squashing the independent streak that had attracted us to the Prairie Fire mission in the first place. Bob realized that, as young lieutenants and captains, his Prairie Fire troops took on more responsibility in a single mission than many pilots did during an entire tour. He would look the other way when we stretched the rules, but he was quick to come down hard if we took unwarranted risks.

Early in his checkout, Bob Denison had the opportunity to meet and fly with one of the truly remarkable characters from the Covey rider ranks. Code-named "Blister," Sergeant First Class Jerry Grant was a barrel-chested mountain of a man who had forgotten more about being a Covey rider than most men ever knew. Blister was loud and brash but, on a hot mission, he was efficient and fearless. Over the years, many recon teams and Prairie Fire pilots owed their lives to his fighting instincts.

For the most part, our time with Blister was limited to airborne missions. While we were flying, he'd expound on all manner of subjects. One of his favorite topics was the solid gold chain he always wore around his neck. The chain was huge and gaudy, somewhat like Blister himself. Each gold link was as big as the end of a man's little finger. The standard measurement for gold chains came from Thailand, where the weight was measured in half ounces, or *baht*. Most of us wore a two or three *baht* chain. Not Blister: His chain contained forty-four *baht* of solid gold.

When Blister and I flew together, he usually called me by the Vietnamese word for captain, *daiwe*. Invariably, the conversation turned to his *baht* chain.

"Hey, Blister. You wearing your chain today?"

"Roger that, *Daiwe*. I never take this baby off. I do *everything* with my chain on. You're really lucky to be flying with me, *Daiwe*. If we get shot down and captured, I'll buy our way out. Then you'll be sorry you made fun of my chain. It's like an insurance policy."

In a mock scolding tone I replied, "Blister, if we get captured, the bad guys aren't gonna ask you for that chain. They'll simply blow your head off and take the chain. How's that grab you?"

Blister would sputter and fume for a few seconds, then he'd answer, "You're entitled to your own opinion, *Daiwe*. But I still say the gold will come in handy."

A few nights later at the DOOM Club, Blister's gold chain did come in handy. On that particular night the club was full because a USO show was scheduled. For some unexplained reason, Blister showed up at the Covey hooch suffering from the effects of a whiskey front and wearing a sanitized Prairie Fire flight suit—no name, no patches, no rank. Instead of leaving him alone, we took him over to the jam-packed club and introduced him as "Colonel Grant." He carried off the charade without a hitch, and in five minutes everyone believed he really was a bird colonel.

Blister's new rank entitled him to a certain amount of preferential treatment, but the best was yet to come. When the Vietnamese waitresses spotted his gold chain, their eyes bugged right out of their heads. They escorted Blister to a reserved table next to the stage, and while everybody else had to wait twenty minutes to get a drink, Blister had every waitress in the place hanging all over him, begging to take his drink order. Scheming opportunists, we Prairie Fire pilots crowded around the celebrity table and had "Colonel" Grant order our drinks too.

Just before the show started, a couple of real Air Force colonels came over and introduced themselves. We politely stood up. Blister just sat there glaring contemptuously at the intruders. When Blister started talking, I saw my short career flash before my eyes.

In a surly tone, he demanded, "What do you men do for a living?" The two mumbled something about combat support group jobs. Blister was unimpressed. "Is that right? Well, I fly combat missions with these FACs sitting around

this table. They're probably the best and the bravest goddamn pilots you've got on this base. I hope I never hear
they're being mistreated, or I'd have to file an official protest. Then unofficially, I'll come back over with a few of
my Special Forces troops and we'll have to kick some ass.
Dig?" The two colonels mumbled something else before
beating a hasty retreat back into the crowd.

Armed with three drinks each and surrounded by all the
waitresses in the club, we sat back in our chairs as the USO
show started. Right away we were disappointed. The rumor
going around was that the show starred a couple of genuine
"round-eyes" from Australia. Instead, half a dozen Filipino
girls bolted onto the stage, singing and dancing the funky
chicken. It wasn't that the ladies weren't pretty. They were
exotic beauties with great faces and long, good-looking
legs. But like many Oriental women, they were petite and
slim, with no real shape. They were flat chested with no
hips. Pretty as they were, practically everybody in the room
would have killed for a substantial American blonde with
blue eyes and lots of curves.

Despite their disappointment, the assembled pilots, gentlemen that they were, decided to make the young ladies
feel welcome and appreciated. The shouts began slowly,
then built into a deafening roar: "Take it off! Show us your
boobs! On your knees, bitch!" The pretty young entertain-
ers never batted an eye. They had seen and heard it all
before, at camps and clubs from one end of Vietnam to the
other. My favorite was a sweet-looking young girl who had
the best singing voice of the group. Her rendition of "The
Shadow of Your Smile" would have been a real showstop-
per, except she pronounced the word as "schwadow," to the
hoots and great delight of the rowdy audience. I was feeling
sorry for her until the end of the song, when she stepped
off the stage onto the table next to ours and let some drunk
bury his face in her crotch.

The show ended on a predictable note. All the ladies
came on stage at once and led us in a sing-along version
of John Denver's popular hit "Country Roads." For a finale,

the ladies performed the mandatory anthem familiar to every GI who ever served in Vietnam: "We Got to Get Out of This Place."

The morning after the USO show, we piled "Colonel" Grant into an O-2 and sent him packing to Quang Tri, where they badly needed his help. It was clear to all of us that the level and intensity of our cross-border operations had picked up dramatically. We were hard-pressed to find enough warm bodies to keep up the pace. We seemed to be sending more and more teams across the fence, and those teams seemed to get themselves in trouble on a regular basis. Rarely did a team manage to stay on the ground for a full five-to-seven-day mission. By the middle of September, 50 percent of our teams were being blasted off the LZ within three hours of the insert.

To counter the success of the American-led teams, Hanoi had fielded a huge security force of over forty thousand dedicated troops to neutralize and destroy SOG teams. By 1970, most sites contiguous to the Trail and capable of receiving helicopters were under permanent observation by LZ watchers. When a SOG helicopter approached, the LZ watcher signaled the alarm and set the cat-and-mouse game in motion. A local NVA reaction force of one hundred men or more immediately moved toward the team's insertion point while professionally trained tracking teams, often with dogs, began the hunt. Not only did the counterrecon companies spread out and search carefully selected areas for the RTs, they also staked out nearby LZs to thwart the extraction of the team. Often, that meant concealed .51-caliber antiaircraft machine guns designed to ambush the rescuing helicopters and FACs. Although our teams used their radios sparingly, enemy troops also employed radio detection finding devices to track team positions to within yards of their actual location.

Statistically outnumbered some eight hundred to one, SOG team members still managed to accomplish their highly dangerous missions despite the huge numerical superiority of the NVA. It was primarily a matter of quality over quantity. SOG RTs epitomized stealth in the jungle, and they prided themselves on being able to move unseen and unheard right under the enemy's nose. If a firefight did erupt, however, the team instantly transformed itself into one of the most highly trained, lethal light infantry units in the world. Rather than cower, a One-Zero almost always struck the critical first blow, then had his team evade toward a predetermined defensive position or LZ. If the RT had to stay and fight it out, hopefully the supporting Covey FAC could bring in air strikes to help even the odds.

And of course the teams had some tricks of their own. To discourage and throw off the trackers, teams often left small M14 "toe popper" mines along the egress route. And to confuse the tracker dogs, SOG teams effectively employed CS tear gas powder shaken on the ground as they moved. To further confuse the enemy, some RTs wore enemy uniforms. Thus disguised, a Vietnamese-speaking member of the team might actually pass for an NVA soldier. Even if the outfit caused an enemy sentry to hesitate for only a few seconds, those critical seconds were probably his last on earth.

With so much at stake, it was a tough arena for training new Prairie Fire pilots, but there was no other choice. Bob Denison completed his checkout in record time, yet we were still behind the power curve. Within a matter of weeks, Bob Meadows and Gary Pavlu would finish their tours and head back to the world, leaving us at a loss for experienced pilots. Without realizing it, I suddenly found myself cast in a new and unfamiliar role, that of an old head. One day I was the new guy; the next, I was Prairie Fire's training officer, responsible for getting the new pilots combat ready. The time was flying by. Only a few days earlier, my father-in-law, Ken Wood, had finished his tour at Cam Ranh and gone back to the world.

One of my first jobs came as a shock. I knew Bob Denison had been scouting for new talent, but when he told me my roomie, Evan Quiros, was the choice, the news shook me up. For some reason, I didn't want Evan associated with

Prairie Fire. I knew he was a first-rate stick-and-rudder man, so that wasn't the problem. Sorting through my feelings, I narrowed down the reasons to two: First, in my mind the mission was too dangerous for such a dedicated family man; and second, for selfish reasons I didn't want to have to worry about Evan. It was okay to train guys I didn't know very well. It became a different ball game when the emotional attachment was more than casual. Initially, I planned to talk him out of it, but Evan was so enthusiastic about Prairie Fire that there was no denying him. In spite of my misgivings, I knew deep inside that Evan would be a natural in Prairie Fire.

On September 23, Evan and I flew together for the first time. He had already run a couple of inserts and extracts under Bob Meadows's watchful eyes, so he had a good feel for the mission. There were no teams on the ground that day and no plans to insert any, so we did a little freewheeling. After trolling up and down the DMZ several times, we ended up near Khe Sanh. I pointed out "Hickory," our radio relay site located on one of the mountain peaks just north of the abandoned Khe Sanh airstrip. The site also offered the perfect location for another highly classified operation, the National Security Agency's Polaris II radio intercept station. NSA and SOG operated a similar site in southern Laos, code-named "Leghorn."

More to himself than to anyone else, Evan said, "I think I'll go down and introduce myself." With that, he rolled us into 135 degrees of left bank and pulled the nose of our Bronco down into a perfect run-in heading for Hickory. We leveled off one-half mile out, at an identical altitude with the mountaintop. As we streaked over the sandbag fortifications at ten feet, Evan slammed the stick into his left thigh and aileron-rolled us down into the adjacent valley. His timing had been absolutely perfect. If he had been just one second earlier on the roll, we would have dinged a wing tip and earned ourselves a number on the weekly casualty list.

To prove it was no fluke, Evan arced back around to the

north and rolled in a second time. Evidently our first pass had attracted someone's attention, because as we closed in on Hickory we could see several troops standing on top of the bunkers waving at us. I had a horrible vision of our eight-foot props decapitating one of those poor waving fools, but mercifully, Evan offset just a little to the left so as to miss them. A split second before we buzzed over their heads, one of the troops pointed a pen-gun flare at us and fired it. Before we could react, the red-hot flare zipped between the right engine and our canopy, about three feet from our warm bodies.

Evan must have read my mind. Instead of continuing the air show, he jinked us down below the relay site's rim and away from the line of fire as fast as we could run.

I was irate. Switching the radio wafer switch over to Fox Mike, I gave the relay site a call. "Dammit it, Hickory. Your boys almost blew us out of the saddle with a pen-gun flare. Tell 'em to knock that crap off. We're on your side!"

The voice on the other end sounded far from sympathetic. "Listen up, Covey. I'm sick and tired of you hotshot flyboys scaring the fool out of us with your no-notice buzzing. If you'd like to come around for one more pass, I promise you we won't miss."

As much as I hated to admit it, the voice on the radio had a valid point. We had started it, and they had almost finished it. All of us had been pretty dumb. Rather than leave the whole thing hanging, I passed on a halfhearted apology to Hickory. Yet while I was talking, I noticed Evan had maneuvered around to almost the identical spot from which he had rolled in on the two earlier passes. I had a hunch he was about to roll their socks down with a third pass, so I gently came on the controls and said, "Let me have her for a second." Then I banked around to the north, away from Hickory, and toward the western DMZ.

After pointing out a couple of helicopter crash sites, I turned the controls back over to Evan. As we crossed into the northern half of the DMZ, I asked him, "Were you gonna take a third run at those dudes?"

With what sounded like pure impishness in his voice, he answered, "Who me? Come on, get serious."

I thought to myself, "I bet it would have been one hell of a great low pass."

For no particular reason, I decided to show Evan a new road being built by the North Vietnamese into the extreme western part of the DMZ. Because of the bombing halt, we weren't allowed to hit it, and without any harassment, the NVA road crews had managed to carve out a fairly sophisticated highway, dug into the side of several mountains. The southern terminal of the road ended not more than a kilometer inside North Vietnam.

From our two-thousand-foot altitude over the DMZ, we spotted the road easily. What was on the road watered our eyes. In broad daylight a convoy of six trucks inched southward along narrow cliffs. Under the rules of engagement, the trucks were technically safe from air attacks. It didn't make any sense. It also didn't take a genius to figure out that those trucks weren't hauling toys to the orphans.

Evan and I were thinking the same thought. We couldn't put an air strike in, but the rules didn't say anything about lobbing in a couple of marking rockets—just to shake things up a bit. Evan armed up one of the outboard pods, then pushed the power up to full military. Next, he set up a descending 270-degree turn to the left, finally rolling out in a shallow dive heading straight for the trucks, several miles out in front of us. With the OV-10 at full power and 240 knots, Evan pulled us up into a steep, 60-degree climb. Then he pushed the stick forward abruptly, zero "G"ing down to 45 degrees of climb. At what he guessed to be the perfect moment, Evan pickled off four willie petes.

It was easy to follow the four rockets streaking upward during the two seconds of rocket motor burn. At shutdown, the four-foot-long rockets went ballistic, captives of momentum and gravity. As they coasted down the back side of the arc, we lost sight of them. I had about given up on our willie petes as duds or unscorables when the first snowwhite smoke drifted up. It hit well short of the target, but in succession, number two split the remaining distance and three and four exploded right in the middle of the convoy.

Both of us let out a shout and started laughing. Any damage done by the rockets was questionable, but we would have given anything to see the looks on those smug drivers' faces. Chalk one up for the good guys. We certainly hadn't won the war, and we might even have violated the rules of engagement about expending ordnance in North Vietnam, but there was no denying that the encounter was a remarkable piece of flying and shooting by Evan.

Although each day of flying for SOG was its own reward, not to mention a nonstop adrenaline rush, the Prairie Fire pilots occasionally enjoyed having an afternoon off. Toward the end of the month we found an opportunity to do a little socializing with the other Coveys. The occasion was a steak cookout in the open area between our operations and intel buildings. In the late afternoon as we stood around drinking beer and talking about flying, I wondered out loud how we had acquired the steaks, a rare commodity around Da Nang. What I learned was a lesson in the art of scrounging. It seemed that one of our OV-10 jocks, Lieutenant Richard "Zot" Barrazotto, had acquired over the years a real knack for horse trading. That talent made him a natural as our squadron scrounger. In this case Zot managed to scrounge a dented 230-gallon Bronco external fuel tank from our maintenance troops. It wasn't exactly clear what he traded them, but the term "backroom deal" cropped up more than once in the conversation. Next, Zot traded the tank to the Marines, who intended to use it as part of a self-help water reservoir and shower stall near their tents. In return he got several cases of liquor. The liquor went to a 366th Tactical Fighter Wing mess sergeant who was happy to trade for several cases of USDA steaks. As a result, the Coveys thoroughly enjoyed the cookout, thanks in large part to an unofficial system of commodity trading that was part of the military culture in Vietnam.

A few days later, on the twenty-ninth of September, I flew another mission into the DMZ, but this time I went in fully armed. In a reversal of an earlier decision, Seventh Air Force headquarters in Saigon decided to reinstall the four M-60 machine guns on the OV-10. The intent was to give the FAC a limited attack capability. In most troops-in-contact situations, the first minutes of the fight were the most critical, so instead of waiting helplessly for the fighters to arrive, the OV-10 FACs could now deliver enough machine-gun fire to keep the bad guys' heads down. The low-level strafing runs were admittedly risky, but nothing compared to what those grunts on the ground had to endure. As often as not, our slow-firing M-60s provided just enough punch to break the contact.

The OV-10 jocks in the Prairie Fire business found the M-60s especially suited to our mission. When one of our teams got into a firefight in the middle of Laos, it usually started inside of twenty meters. At such close quarters, a well-aimed burst of machine-gun fire was the only option, short of dropping ordnance on top of our own teams. In addition, by delivering our own firepower, we no longer had to try to describe the target to orbiting Cobras or Spads. In the heat of battle, even after we had put down a smoke rocket for reference, we could never be 100 percent sure the other guy saw the target as we did. Our M-60 machine guns weren't the cure-all, but they did give us added capability when it was needed.

Satan and I had already flown two sorties that morning. At approximately 1500, we took off on a third sortie, due north into the DMZ. Our job was to act as high cover while one of the new O-2 Prairie Fire jocks ran his second solo team insert. If the situation went sour, we were there to help out or take over.

I set up a high orbit a mile east of the LZ, a barren hilltop two hundred meters south of the Song Ben Hai River. The terrain in that area was made up of low hills, ridges, and valleys. Repeated B-52 Arc Light strikes had left little vegetation. From the air the place resembled a moonscape, complete with thousands of craters scarring the surface. In contrast, just a few miles to the north, the countryside looked relatively green, with only a few bomb craters dotting the area.

As the Covey FAC rounded up his helicopters and headed into the LZ, Satan and I were nervous. We were running a partial package with only Slicks and Cobras. For some reason, we had no A-1 support that afternoon. Since the insert was planned for a relatively quiet section of the DMZ, the decision was made to press on. We didn't anticipate going up against any big triple-A guns, so the general belief was that the Cobras could handle the action without the usual help from the Spads.

The dummy insert went off without a hitch and, as Satan and I watched, our trainee appeared to have everything under control. When the operation shifted to the primary target, the situation heated up in spades. The Cobras nailed the LZ with a vengeance, followed closely by Slick Lead carrying half the team. When Lead touched down on the small hilltop, the four team members jumped clear and dashed across the LZ to the western slope of the hill. A split second later, two NVA soldiers popped out of camouflaged spider holes and riddled the vulnerable helicopter at point-blank range with AK-47 fire. Before the door gunner could respond to the threat, an AK-47 round found its mark, blowing his left eye out and killing him instantly. Slick Lead poured on the power and managed to limp out of range of the deadly fire, aided by his flying skills and by the covering dust storm his rotors whipped up on top of the hill.

Looking down on the scene, we could see the spider holes on the northwest sector of the hilltop, roughly one hundred feet from the team crouching just below the rim. The close proximity of the friendlies made for a sticky close-air-support situation. As I was about to offer some advice, my student took charge, shouting instructions and making the right decisions.

"Slick Two, break it off! Abort your run right now. Move back to the holding pattern. Cobra Lead, see those white rocks on the southeast corner of the LZ? Give me one mini-gun pass on a run-in line from those rocks to the two spider holes."

Though the pilot had made a good start, I couldn't resist adding to the instructions. "Cobra Lead, confirm you've got a tally on the team position and acknowledge mini-guns only."

He responded, "Roger on the team pos, and I copy mini-guns only. Am I cleared in?"

"You're cleared in hot," the FAC shouted. Then, forgetting to change his wafer switch to the proper radio, he added, "One-Zero, if you're on frequency, get your heads down. The Cobras are gonna plaster the LZ."

Hundreds of small geysers of dust from the impacting bullets swirled into the air around the spider holes. As Cobra Two rolled in to give the target the same treatment, Satan pointed out several larger explosions in the same area. At first I thought one of the Cobras might have accidentally fired an HE rocket, but then we spotted the source. One of the team members was standing bolt upright, firing M79 grenade rounds at the bad guys. He fired at least a half dozen of the 40mm shells before finally taking cover.

The heavier firepower produced an unexpected benefit. The exploding "blooper" rounds exposed an entire network of holes and tunnels dug into the northern rim of the hilltop. For all we knew, the whole area was linked by passages and tunnels. One thing became painfully clear: Putting the rest of the team on the ground was out of the question. Rescuing the stranded members took top priority.

In the Oscar Deuce with the fledgling Prairie Fire pilot, Jerry "Blister" Grant finally managed to get the One-Zero to come up on his PRC-25 radio. As cool as always, Blister exchanged information with the team, then advised them to move around to the south face of the hill and dig in. To cover the movement, the Cobras began continuous attacks against the enemy positions along the northern rim. After multiple strafe passes, the gunships pulled out all the stops by blasting the complex with rockets.

On one of the attacks, Cobra Lead spotted a group of

bad guys working their way south along the eastern slope of the hill. Caught in the open, the patrol scattered quickly under heavy mini-gun fire, leaving behind two dead or wounded comrades.

A few minutes later, the situation took a turn for the worse. Within a period of sixty seconds, Cobra Two reported oil pressure problems and Cobra Lead's fire control system went haywire. Under normal circumstances the Spads would have taken up the slack, but with no A-1s, we were out of luck. Our only immediate option was to have me cover one of the Hueys as he went in for a pickup. I automatically armed up the rockets, then remembered the machine guns. Since it had been so long, I was a little cloudy on exactly how to arm up the M-60s. Carefully, I placed the left-hand gun switch to ready. In that configuration, I'd be firing only the two guns located in the left sponson. Next, I flipped the master arm switch on, then squeezed the trigger. There was an audible "clunk" as the two guns charged themselves. After cycling the master arm switch off and back on, we were ready.

As Slick Three reached the halfway point on the east-to-west run-in to the LZ, I rolled in well behind him and to his right. When he was on very short final, I squeezed the trigger and poured long bursts into the spider holes along the northern edge of the target. My 550 rounds per minute from each gun kicked up quite a dust cloud. The tracer ammunition formed what appeared to be a continuous red line from the machine-gun muzzles to the hilltop. At impact, some of the tracers ricocheted back up into the air, seeming to float as they careened off at wild angles. We passed over the crest of the hill at about fifty feet and kept right on going. I cobbed full power as we climbed straight ahead, then pulled us through a modified chandelle to head us back the other way. On the reverse course, we were head-on with our chopper, which had just touched down. Once more I fired burst after burst into the target area, hoping that none of the ricochets was bouncing in the helicopter's direction.

By the time I had executed a second chandelle, I could see our chopper lifting off. As I closed in behind him, some movement on the east face of the hill caught my eye. Four bad guys had popped up out of nowhere and were attempting to drag off the two casualties from the earlier Cobra run. Easing the stick forward to get the OV-10 down even lower, we were just below the crest of the hill when I put the pipper on the feet of the enemy soldiers and pressed in close. At approximately eight hundred feet of slant range I opened up, pouring a long string of tracers right into them. My aim seemed to be confirmed when all four slumped to the ground. With the hill directly in front and above us, I sucked in the Gs as hard as I could pull. The Bronco practically swapped ends, shuddering and protesting as I asked her to do things she wasn't meant to. Through my tunneled vision, I could see that we would clear the crest by a matter of feet.

Relaxing the back pressure, I let the aircraft zoom into a steep climb. Over the intercom, I gloated to Satan, "Marty, could you see that strafe from the back seat? I nailed their hides!" Before he could answer, I rolled us into ninety degrees of bank to get another look at our target. The scene below wasn't what I had expected to see. Much to my embarrassment, all four bad guys were on their feet, running as hard as they could for whatever spider hole they'd been hiding in.

While I was wondering how I could have missed, with machine guns no less, our trainee had rounded up his package, including the rescued team, and started back to Quang Tri. As we followed the O-2 back into the traffic pattern, Satan tried to console me. Attempting to sound positive, but laughing all the same, Satan announced, "I thought we had them too. Sir's aim was right on the money. It's the damnedest thing I've ever seen—dead guys running around like that, not even realizing they'd been shot."

October

BATTLE DAMAGE

By the first of October, the pace of the air war in I Corps had definitely shifted into low gear; Mother Nature had accomplished what the Viet Cong and North Vietnamese couldn't. A killer typhoon out in the South China Sea had taken deadly aim at the Vietnam coast, and as a precaution most of the flying units had already evacuated to bases in Thailand where they would continue to fly combat missions over the Ho Chi Minh Trail. But at Da Nang the remaining pilots and ground crews moved around aimlessly in the uncharacteristic silence, waiting and wondering about the approaching storm. For them the ominous quiet on the flight line roared louder than any J-79 jet engine running up on the test cell.

In contrast to the life-and-death struggle going on in Laos, those of us who stayed behind to face the fury of the typhoon found ourselves overcome with boredom and restlessness, along with nagging anxiety, probably stemming from uncertainty about the storm and fear of the unknown. In the process, the pace of our action-filled young lives ground to a standstill. With the typhoon-induced slowdown came long, uninterrupted hours during which we contemplated events and people and also confronted our innermost thoughts—thoughts almost always wrapped up in a powerful preoccupation with combat missions over the Trail. With time to reflect, I began thinking about my job and groping for an explanation that would help me make sense of my role. To me, each Prairie Fire mission seemed to be a self-contained act within an endless drama. Each mission had its own beginning, middle, and end, but relevance to previous missions was lost in the production. Players tended to appear for a few acts, then disappear without fanfare or applause, to be replaced by other players in the same olive-drab costume. In a future act, I too would take my cue and exit the stage. The big question was would I exit standing up or feet first? So far, only about half of our Prairie Fire pilots had managed to live through the trial-by-fire.

When the first typhoon-force winds finally slammed into the coast, our pent-up tensions began to break in proportion to the increasing wind gusts. Outside on the streets of the main compound, the sheets of rain pulsed and danced in odd geometric patterns across the black asphalt. In our first ventures out into the stuff, ponchos flapping in the gale, we found that the only way to negotiate the stinging rain was to walk backwards. And the soggy experience of fighting the storm just for the privilege of a mediocre meal at the DOOM Club quickly lost its appeal. So like most self-respecting young pilots, we came up with a convenient if unconventional alternative: We camped in the Covey barracks, drank large quantities of Chivas Regal scotch, and subsisted on junk food or care packages from home.

Halfway through the first day of the storm, a small group of hard-core Coveys began congregating in a room belonging to Captain Sonny Haynes, an easygoing Texan who was one of the most popular members of the squadron as well as one of the best pilots. Nobody handled combat pressure better than Sonny. And since he also made a great host, more and more idle Coveys began crowding into Sonny's place, anxious to be a part of the round-the-clock typhoon party. Sonny's cohost, Captain Larry Thomas, lived in the room next door. A native of Commerce, Texas, Larry had a keen mind and an equally sharp wit. He took a lot of good-natured kidding over his somewhat portly shape and acquired the nickname "Big Bippy," borrowed from the popular television show *Laugh In*.

With crowd control becoming a problem, Sonny and

Larry sat down over a bottle of scotch, determined to find a solution. They did. They simply took a saw and a sledge-hammer and knocked a hole in the wall between their rooms. The two sets of bunk beds were shoved into the "sleeping room" while a sofa, chairs, and a refrigerator ended up in what was to be the "party room." The happy arrangement produced only one problem. The irate housing officer curtly informed the assembled drunks that rules were rules—two men to a room and no exceptions. Over another bottle of scotch, Sonny and Larry sat down to resolve this new dilemma.

The three of us had been classmates at fighter lead-in training at Cannon Air Force Base, so we'd been friends for over a year. When they asked me to save the day by moving in with them, I was both pleased and flattered. I felt guilty about moving out on Evan, but I truly missed associating with the other Coveys. I also thought that moving in might provide a good opportunity to break down some of the barriers between the Prairie Fire pilots and the mainstream Coveys.

Sometime during the course of the typhoon and associated parties, I packed up and moved in with Sonny and Big Bippy. The party room became such a big hit and obvious morale builder that the housing officer decided to look the other way and not enforce the occupancy rules, as long as the three of us consented to sharing the place with the rest of the Coveys. During that same period, we settled on a name for our twenty-four-hour-a-day party room. A crudely painted sign proclaimed: "The Muff Divers' Lounge— where the elite meet to eat."

The typhoon eventually ran its course, leaving us soggier and more philosophical than before. In the process of hud-dling together to ride out the storm, we Coveys had inad-vertently created a much-needed social release and hangout—a place to go and enjoy friends when not flying missions over the Ho Chi Minh Trail.

On the third of October, with the remnants of the ty-phoon pushing well inland, we got back into the war. It was time to start a new act. All of us felt restless from the inactivity, so on my first day back at Quang Tri following the typhoon, my Special Forces friends came up with a novel way to get the edge back. The SOG troops called it "coming out on strings," but I called it complete lunacy. In a weak moment, I somehow allowed the MLT-2 commander, Jerry Stratton, to talk me into being hoisted off the ground attached to a rope dangling out the door of a Huey Slick. Suspended underneath the hovering chopper, my sole connection to it was by way of a loop in the rope through a series of D rings on a harness I was wearing—something called a Stabo rig. Hanging there helpless and afraid to move, I began spinning and gyrating wildly in the downwash from the Huey's rotor blades. Cautiously, I extended my arms as Jerry had instructed me to; within seconds the spinning ceased. I was out on strings. Suspended about twenty-five feet below the chopper and one hundred feet above the ground, I initially kept my gaze fixed on the far horizon, but after the first circle around the large field behind the MLT-2 Ops buildings, I finally mustered the nerve to look around. The wind blast, the engine sounds, and the smells flooded my senses. What a complete change from the sensations inside the closed cockpit of my OV-10. The only experience I could think of to match it might be flying in an open-cockpit biplane. After another circle around the field, the Huey went into a hover and gently set me back on solid ground. With the aid of a couple of grinning NCOs, I separated from the string and walked over to Jerry.

"Not bad for an Air Force puke," he chided. Then, as he helped me out of the rig, he handed me a couple of D rings and said, "Put these on your parachute harness. It's not as good as a Stabo rig, but if you ever have to bail out, you can hook up to the string and we can lift you out."

I felt the gesture deeply, for Jerry's offer of the D rings involved more than any practical use they might have had. In my mind those rings represented acceptance. I had passed the test and become a full-fledged member of the SOG family. At that moment, on the afternoon of October

3, I mentally switched from being an FNG into the role of old head and accepted combat veteran.

As Jerry and I walked back across the field to the Ops hut, he explained a little more about extracting a team using the strings. In time-critical situations with no LZ available, coming out on strings might be a team's only option. If done correctly, three or four men could hook up and be lifted out at the same time. The Stabo rig left the team members' hands free, enabling them to fire their weapons and, as an added bonus, a wounded or unconscious troop could be extracted with no danger of slipping off the rope.

Jerry's explanation made it sound so simple. Yet in recalling my own brief initiation a few minutes earlier, I remembered how incredibly vulnerable I felt hanging out there in space, little more than a moving target with nothing but my flight suit shielding me from a potential hail of bullets. Doing it for fun was scary enough. Coming out on strings in actual combat had to generate paralyzing, debilitating fear. My hat was off to Jerry Stratton and his recon teams. They were pros in every positive sense of the word, and were definitely a special breed of warrior. These men knew how to fight, and when called for, they knew how to die.

In a graphic demonstration of all those qualities I so admired in the SOG troops, one of MLT-1's reconnaissance teams paid the ultimate price two days later. On the afternoon of October 5, my ex-roomie, Evan Quiros, was airborne, returning from Quang Tri after inserting one team and scouting a number of LZs for future missions. Flying over a solid cloud deck, Evan found himself facing a different kind of a storm, every bit as deadly as the recent typhoon, but a lot more personal. As he cruised south along the Laotian border near Route 922 and about ten miles west of the A Shau Valley, Evan monitored a transmission from the One-Zero of RT Fer-de-Lance, Staff Sergeant David "Babysan" Davidson. Already a legend within SOG, twenty-three-year-old Babysan advised that he had heavy enemy movement around his team, clearly a dangerous situation. With no chance of slipping in under the weather, Evan set up an orbit over the RT, hoping the sound of his circling OV-10 would keep the bad guys off balance long enough for the team to make a run for it. After exhausting most of his fuel, he had no choice but to return to Quang Tri for gas.

Launching out of Quang Tri at 1810, Evan returned to the team's general location. As he approached, Evan's blood ran ice-cold as he heard a voice whispering over the radio. In a hushed tone, the One-One, Sergeant Fred Gassman, asked Evan to mount an emergency extraction. What was left of the seven-man team was in heavy contact on three sides and low on ammo. Babysan had been hit and had fallen off a cliff.

Faced with heavy weather and darkness, Evan knew a rescue was out of the question. But to keep the team's spirits up, he told them to keep their heads down while he armed up his rockets. Counting on a big dose of luck, Evan began firing blindly through the low cloud deck, praying his rockets would explode close enough to break the contact without hitting the team. The first few salvos landed well north of the target area, exploding harmlessly in the thick jungle. Directions from Gassman based strictly on sound weren't effective either. Finally, the gutsy One-One realized the hit-or-miss tactic wouldn't work. In a perfectly calm voice he said to Evan, "Covey 220, we're out of ideas and time. Got any suggestions?"

At first Evan couldn't think of a positive answer to the hopeless question. Then he recalled that a few of the teams carried small portable radar beacons. Keying off that signal, sophisticated sensors aboard an AC-119 Stinger gunship could lay down a deadly wall of mini-gun fire, theoretically to within just a few yards of friendly troops. It was their only chance.

Evan told the trapped team, "I've ordered up a Stinger gunship. You've got to hang on another forty-five minutes. In the meantime, I want you to get your beacon set up."

His voice heavy with dejection, Gassman replied, "No

good. The One-Zero had the instrument on him. He's some-where down on the rocks below us."

Evan shouted, "Your only hope is to find that beacon. You've got to retrieve that beacon!"

After the truth of Evan's words sank in, the One-One answered, "I'll give it a try. Here goes nothing—wish me luck."

Evan continued to circle in the darkness for several long minutes, hoping beyond hope that the courageous Green Beret below would find the all-important radar beacon. When his radio receiver finally crackled, Evan's heart sank into his boots. In a quivering, weak voice, Fred Gassman said simply, "I've been hit—and in the worst way." There were several groans, then the radio went dead.

For the October 6 missions, we launched the entire Prai-rie Fire pilot force. During most of the morning, we searched at treetop level for the missing team, but there was no trace of RT Fer-de-Lance. With two OV-10s and two O-2s cruising around the same vicinity, we must have made tempting targets, but we couldn't get the bad guys to fire at us. Anxious to turn up any kind of clue, we let our minds play tricks on us. The slightest bit of static on the radio, a momentary fleck of reflected morning light, two rotted logs lying near a trail forming a natural "V"—we clung to the wildest kinds of possible evidence and jumped to the most amateurish conclusions. Throughout that morn-ing of false hopes and phony optimism, there were two negatives none of us would bring up: We couldn't find the team, and we couldn't bring ourselves to believe that there was no longer a team to be found.*

By midafternoon we called off the search and went back to business as usual—only the business went sour in a

---

*The remains of David Davidson and Fred Gassman have never been recovered. On several occasions the North Vietnamese released pic-tures of American POWs, and the Davidson family identified two that bore a remarkable resemblance to "Babysan." Hanoi continues to deny any knowledge of David Davidson or Fred Gassman.

hurry. In what turned out to be a strange bit of timing, I was leading a package out of Phu Bai as one of the other Coveys flew inbound with his package and freshly extracted team. The plan called for us to swap out the A-1s just east of the A Shau Valley. We were particularly careful working around the A Shau, a major infiltration route into Thua Thien Province and the old walled city of Hue. Ever since the Cambodian incursion in May, the place had been a hotbed of enemy activity. In July the fighting had become so intense that the 101st Screaming Eagles evacuated a key position in the A Shau called Fire Base Ripcord. Now, as Laos transitioned into the dry season, enemy infiltration down the Trail increased dramatically, and in the face of heavy NVA opposition, the ARVN First Division was about to be driven out of another A Shau hot spot, Fire Base O'Reilly.

As I tuned in the correct tactical radio frequency, it became clear the situation out over the A Shau was bad. The radio chatter indicated that someone in the inbound package was in trouble. Apparently the Spads had taken a lot of ground fire in support of the extraction, and a few of the rounds had found their mark.

Right away I recognized the A-1 pilot's voice as that of one of my friends from back at Da Nang. The stricken pilot, "John," was advising the FAC, "The cylinder head temp is off the charts, and she's starting to smoke. I'm gonna have to get out."

The Covey answered, "I copy, Spad Lead. If you can, stay with her until we cross the fence and clear the A Shau. That way we'll have a chopper waiting for you when your feet touch the ground."

In between radio calls, I told the other FAC, "Bob, I'm inbound to you and will be over the east wall in five minutes. We're fat on gas and ammo if you need us."

Switching to his FM radio, the package commander replied, "Keep pressing, Tom. But I don't think we've got five minutes."

Seconds after that transmission, John shouted, "Okay, I can't wait. I'm punching out."

A long pause followed; then the Spad wingman chimed in, "John, get out of it! Get out now!"

"I can't. The Yankee didn't work."

"Don't you have anything?"

In a low-pitched, angry-sounding voice, John replied, "I don't have a damn thing."

As I listened in horror to the drama taking place ten miles in front of me, I pushed up the throttles for more speed. My package would have to fend for itself. In a cool voice, the Prairie Fire FAC talked to the rapidly descending A-1. "Spad Lead, go for the pass between those two ridges directly in front of you. You've got a good glide going. Hold her steady on a heading of about 120 degrees. Looking good."

Then the FAC's voice jumped up about three octaves. "Lead, no! No, for Christ's sake. Back to your right! To your right!"

Somebody else came up on frequency. "He went in. Big fireball on the east wall. Negative 'chute."

Crossing the range of low hills forming the east wall of the A Shau Valley, I saw it. Bright orange-red flames consumed a football-field-sized area just below the rim of the small ridge. A pall of sooty black smoke floated straight up above the inferno. The package commander was still in control but obviously shaken by what he had witnessed. When we talked on the company FM radio, he sobbed, "If he'd just stayed on that heading. He had it made. Why didn't he listen? He just went into a left bank and held it. Tom, he wouldn't listen to me. Why didn't he listen?"

When my package arrived on the scene, I put them in an orbit just south of the crash site. Fifteen minutes later the other FAC rounded up his package and headed home, low on gas and demoralized. With his departure, I became the on-scene commander. In surveying the crash, I felt certain the pilot hadn't survived, so a rescue wasn't the issue. But I did want my troops to recover John's body. We called

back to the MLT and got permission to cancel the insert
and to use the team as necessary around the wreckage.

For the first order of business, the Cobras and I flew
several low passes around the area, trolling for ground fire;
there wasn't any. Next we directed Slick Three to lower
the medic to the ground near the crash. Most of the fire had
burned out, revealing the twisted wreckage of the big Skyraider. Hopefully, the *bac si* could poke around the site
under our protective cover.

As he sifted through the smoldering debris, the *bac si*
found part of John's helmet, badly shattered and burned.
Strangely, there was nothing else identifiable around what
had once been the cockpit. The real shock came when the
medic dislodged a section of the right wing, approximately
fifty feet from the fuselage. At first the charred body was
unrecognizable. All that remained was a torso, minus head
and limbs.

The fire had rendered everything at the crash site white-
hot, so any recovery would have to wait. I was also concerned about the *bac si*'s safety. Wandering around down
there alone, he'd make an easy target for any bad guys
attracted by the crash. I was also worried about any ordnance on board the Spad that could still cook off. Rather
than lose another good man, we ordered the medic out. He
did manage to recover the burned helmet.

My package flew back to Phu Bai while I remained over
the crash. I passed along the coordinates and the details to
King, call sign for the Air Force HC-130 aircraft responsible for coordinating all search-and-rescues for downed pilots. The controller aboard King accepted the sad news
stoically. I advised King of the recovery plan for the following day when the wreckage had cooled, then I signed
off and circled down for one last look at the crash. Searching the scene, I could think only about the anger in John's
last radio transmission. I tried to imagine the feelings he
experienced when the Yankee extraction system misfired.
This was the second time I had seen an A-1 pilot's ejection
system fail and cost a life.

Dropping down to just one hundred feet above the ground, I was struck by the irony of the situation. If John had been just fifty feet higher as he made the turn, he would have cleared the crest of the hill and had a shot at a forced landing in some fairly open terrain. Like the other Prairie Fire FAC, I found myself asking, "Why did he turn left? Why didn't he listen?"

We managed to recover John's remains the following day. There was barely time for a short memorial service before we suited up again for more missions; operational requirements mercifully left no time for extended grieving. A different Prairie Fire FAC took over in the A Shau Valley, and I moved back north to the MLT at Quang Tri.

On October 10, with thoughts of the missing team and the dead A-1 pilot still churning in my mind, I almost met the same fate. Marty Martin and I had already flown once that morning in marginal weather conditions scouting for LZs. When the sun finally came out around 1500, we launched a second time, heading for a particularly hot area west of Khe Sanh. Flying right on the trees, Satan and I plotted several likely spots for future inserts. Then, as we climbed back to the east, some movement on the Trail below caught our attention. Several hundred meters north of the intersection of Routes 9 and 92, we spotted at least a dozen figures on the road. A quick check with the binoculars confirmed a road crew hard at work patching ruts and craters. They seemed oblivious to our presence, so Satan and I decided to ruin their day. From an altitude of fifteen hundred feet, I rolled in on the enemy troops while simultaneously arming up my two outboard pods. Recently we had started flying with fourteen high-explosive rockets in our bag of tricks, in addition to our two pods of willie petes and two thousand rounds of machine-gun ammo. The scene below me seemed custom-made for an HE rocket attack.

Pressing in from the south, I was about to fire when a .51-caliber machine gun opened up from a concealed pit near the road crew. The stream of tracers raced up from our left at the same instant the two rockets roared out of my LAU-59 pods. As I sucked in the Gs to start a steep turn to the left, all hell broke loose. With a tremendously loud bang, the left canopy disintegrated into a thousand pieces of flying glass. Something red-hot streaked in front of my face and shattered the top of the canopy. Perhaps instinctively or perhaps out of fear, I had released the control stick and moved my right hand upward to shield my face. I winced in surprise as a dagger-shaped piece of canopy imbedded itself deep in my palm.

In the split second that followed, I seemed to view the hectic action in slow motion. Through my peripheral vision, I watched helplessly as the left canopy frame bowed into a contorted shape, then broke loose and flew up into the wind stream. For some crazy reason, I reached out of the cockpit to try to catch it, only to be thrown back violently by the air blast. Under the tremendous aerodynamic force, aggravated by our nose-low, ninety-degree left bank, the top hinges snapped like balsa wood. The metal frame sailed up and over my shattered canopy on a trajectory that sent it crashing into the right engine propeller. The gnarled three-blade Hamilton prop, badly bent and completely out of balance, began vibrating and shaking us to pieces. The OV-10 felt like she was about to tear herself apart.

At some point in the melee, I managed to get back on the controls. Somehow, I got us back to some semblance of level flight, just a few hundred feet above the trees. As we limped off to the west, the machine gun crew added insult to injury by hosing us until we were out of range. When the tracers stopped, I turned my attention to the problems over which I had some control. First, I tried reducing power on the vibrating right engine. It made no difference. It was clear I needed to shut the engine down. Before going through the emergency procedures for engine shutdown, I reached for my checklist out of habit. It was gone, along with all my maps and my binoculars. The wind stream had sucked them right out of the cockpit, and they were probably scattered all over the Laotian countryside. For some reason, the thought of all those maps fluttering down on the machine-gun crew struck me as ridiculously funny. They shoot lead bullets at me, I retaliate with a "map bomb."

I forced myself to get on with it. Reaching up to the left side of the glare shield, I paused a second, then punched the emergency-stores release switch, known as the "salvo button." As advertised, the heavy centerline fuel tank and all four rocket pods tumbled away from the aircraft. With the excess weight and drag gone, the Bronco seemed to leap forward. Then, with virtually the same motion, my left hand slipped down on the right condition lever and pulled it back into the feather and fuel cutoff position. Within seconds the wounded engine began spooling down, the vibrations decreasing in direct proportion to the turning prop.

In the thirty seconds or so since the nightmare had started, Marty and I had not been in communication with each other. Initially there hadn't been time. Complicating the situation, the wind blast in the cockpit was so incredibly loud that it drowned out my voice as I tried to shout into the boom microphone on my helmet. Finally, I lowered my seat to its bottom position, cupped my hands around the mike, and yelled, "Marty, are you okay? Can you read me?"

"Nothing serious back here. How's Sir?" Before I could answer, he followed up with, "Are we gonna make it back home?"

At that moment I honestly didn't know—but we were still flying, and that's what counted. Physically, we were both okay—peppered and nicked by hundreds of pieces of glass but otherwise in good shape. The Bronco was a different matter. As I nursed her through a slow climb, I took a minute to study the damage. In addition to the missing canopy and the shutdown engine, there was a large, basketball-sized hole in the leading edge of the wing just inboard of the right engine. It appeared that after chewing up the propeller, the canopy frame slammed into the leading edge, and from there it had probably glanced up and over the wing. With a sickening premonition, I knew where to look next. By twisting in my ejection seat and using the mirrors, I could sight back along the right boom to the tail. From the looks of things, the top two feet of the right vertical stabilizer had been sheared off. I wasn't sure what was holding the horizontal stabilizer in place.

As we made a wide turn back toward Quang Tri, I called the tower for a weather update. The news wasn't good. Since our takeoff, the winds off the ocean had shifted to a direct crosswind gusting to thirty knots, ten knots above the maximum allowable limit for the OV-10. As badly as I wanted to get us on the ground, Quang Tri's narrow sixty-foot-wide slab of concrete wasn't the answer.

The flight southeast to Da Nang's big runway turned out to be trickier than we had bargained for. Halfway there, a solid wall of cumulonimbus cells towered in front of us. Gingerly picking our way through the CBs, Satan and I were soaked as the rain pelted us. Wet and miserable, I forced myself to concentrate on coaxing the single-engine Bronco through the maze of buildups and squall lines blocking our path. Each bump and bounce reinforced my fears for the structural integrity of the crippled OV-10.

As we neared Da Nang, I started looking for holes in the clouds to descend through, since we were still cruising at forty-five hundred feet. After a few more minutes of thrashing around, I caught a glimpse of Da Nang Bay off our left wing tip. Carefully, we spiraled down through the hole, always turning into the good engine. Since nobody knew we were coming or what our condition was, I decided to give them a clue by turning the master control knob on the transponder to the emergency squawk code of 7700. Da Nang Approach Control picked up the electronic distress signal right away.

"Aircraft squawking emergency on the three-five-eight degree radial at five miles, contact Da Nang Approach on two-forty-three-zero or two-seventy-nine point five. If your transmitter is out, squawk ident."

"Approach, Covey 221. How copy, over."

"Covey 221, Approach. You're loud and clear. Go ahead."

"Rog, Approach. I've got battle damage and the right engine out. Two souls on board and lots of gas. I'd like to switch over to tower for a long straight-in approach with a delayed gear call. I've got a tally on the field."

"Covey 221, squawk standby and contact Da Nang tower, channel two. Good luck."

At one-half mile on final with 130 knots of airspeed, exactly 30 knots faster than normal OV-10 approach speed, I lowered the gear. Because of my uncertainty about the extent of damage and what effect it might have on aircraft handling at low speeds, I kept the airspeed high and the flaps up. On short final I centered the rudder trim and shoved in on the left rudder pedal to keep us close to a coordinated flight condition. As we crossed the threshold and settled into the ground effect, the extra speed caused us to float. Slowly, I eased the power back on the good engine and we touched down with a solid, friendly thunk. We were home!

A large crowd met us when we taxied in. Satan and I were thankful to see everyone, but apparently our welcoming committee felt the two of us looked worse than our beat-up airplane did. After letting me look over the damage on aircraft 645, someone finally stuffed me into a jeep and drove me to the hospital. But before we were separated, Satan and I managed to talk briefly. He told me that when the front canopy disintegrated and the aircraft had rolled into a nose low, 90-degree left bank, he thought I had been killed. At that point his hand was on the ejection D-ring and he was within two seconds of pulling it. Satan only hesitated when he felt me come back on the controls and begin to put us back to wings level.

After the medics at the Da Nang Hospital patched me up, I returned to the Muff Divers' Lounge only to run into some verbal flak that hurt me a lot worse than the glass shard that had penetrated my palm. For obvious reasons, the day's events had left my nerves a little raw, so when several mainstream Coveys, with a head start on the beers, began asking me about my latest adventure, their questions and comments struck me as being accusing in nature. I had suspected for some time that there was a prevalent feeling among the regular Coveys that if your airplane got hit by enemy ground fire, you must have done something wrong. The O-2 jock sitting across from me confirmed my suspicion.

In what seemed to me to be a sneering tone, he asked, "We're all supposed to be professional aviators, right? So why is it that no other Coveys except Prairie Fire jocks get their planes shot up? What's wrong with you guys? Tom, isn't this the fourth hit you've taken in six months? That must make you either a moron or king of the hotdogs."

My temper instantly flared, and I could feel myself coiling to smash my fist into the arrogant face of my loud-mouthed antagonist. At that moment Evan Quiros grabbed my right arm and s_id calmly, "He's not worth it. And besides, if you hit him you'll tear all the stitches out of your hand. Forget it, he's a jerk."

I walked out into the hallway to cool off, regretting that I had moved into the Muff Divers' Lounge in the first place. The episode only reinforced the fact that the other Coveys didn't understand our mission and never would understand it. Still, it wasn't totally their fault. They flew around at four thousand feet above the ground, and they had no idea that Prairie Fire pilots flew right on top of the trees in some of the most dangerous areas of Vietnam, Laos, and North Vietnam. And with that low altitude came increased exposure to ground fire. Nevertheless, being called a "hotdog," with all its negative implications, was as hurtful as it was insulting.

Sitting around still stewing the next day, I was absolutely obsessed about getting airborne again. I assumed that my injury, although it wasn't at all serious, would keep me off the flying schedule for a while. But we were short-handed since Bob Meadows and Gary Pavlu had just finished their tours, and my hanging around the barracks wasn't helping the cause. Then I remembered a loophole that might offer a way out. The medical grounding of a pilot required that he sign a document called *Air Force Form 1042*; I had signed nothing. Using that rather flimsy technicality, I went to Covey Ops and nonchalantly added my name to the flying schedule for the following afternoon.

Due to mechanical problems, I was late taking off from Da Nang for Quang Tri. Once airborne, though, my right hand felt fine and presented no problems flying the aircraft, other than the fact that the bandages made it difficult to wear a glove. En route I checked in with the MLT to discover that my package had already launched and was heading for Khe Sanh. This mission was an ultrasecret one that we had been standing by to execute for several days. Normally, we had very few operational dealings with the CIA, but on this occasion we were going to extract one of their teams that had run into trouble. Referred to as "CAS" teams (short for Controlled American Source), their activities were shrouded in more secrecy than our own SOG missions. We had no idea what this team was up to, and we weren't even sure how many members were on the team.

Since I was running late, I made a fateful decision to head straight for Khe Sanh rather than stop to pick up a Covey rider. Cruising at four thousand feet, I led the package to a prearranged rendezvous along Route 9 where we set up an orbit as we waited for the CAS team to establish radio contact. On about the second lap of our imaginary racetrack pattern, someone in the package keyed his microphone and shouted, "Jesus, we're in big trouble!" Looking across at my Hueys, I could see about ten black flak bursts coming from several 37mm positions somewhere down along the Trail. Most of the 101st helicopter pilots had never seen the "big stuff" before and were a little unnerved, so to settle them down I announced, "Okay, everybody relax. Let's move about five klicks to the east and we'll avoid the whole issue."

As my package sprinted to the east, I was just banking into a right turn to follow them when several huge explosions threw me back against my ejection seat, then forward into the instrument panel. Almost immediately the aircraft yawed hard to the right. Fighting the yaw with corrective stick and left rudder, I looked to my right and saw the problem. Through the badly pitted canopy I could see that the right engine was hanging down almost vertically in its mount with small fingers of flame shooting out in four or five different places. Then, out of the corner of my eye, I saw several 37mm rounds explode just to my left. Turning to look in that direction, the sight was unnerving: the left engine was engulfed in a sheet of fire that plumed back over the top of the wing. As much as I dreaded the thought, it was clearly time to get out of my burning Bronco.

In all the panic and confusion, I did remember to tighten my shoulder harness straps and to get a radio call off to the package. "Mayday, Mayday, Mayday. This is Covey 221. I'm hit and bailing out just southeast of Tchepone. Slick Lead, I hope you're there to pick me up when my feet touch the ground!" Then, reaching down between my legs, I pulled the ejection D-ring as hard as I could.

In the several seconds that followed, the nightmare worsened. In the OV-10 ejection sequence, the rear seat fires first, followed 0.4 seconds later by the front seat. As the rear seat crashed up through the top of the canopy, evidently the vacuum created sucked the blazing engine fire into the front cockpit, instantly surrounding me in a huge fireball. As my seat ignited and began to rocket me out of the aircraft, I could see the bare skin on both my forearms burning furiously.

Before I could even react, my parachute opened automatically and jerked me up short, literally pulling me out of one of my boots. As I looked down, all I could see was the white sock on my left foot and the boot falling rapidly toward the ground thirty-five hundred feet below. The good news was that the wind blast had blown out the flames on my arms—but the bad news kept on coming.

As I began floating down, a noise from above and behind startled me. Looking back, I spotted my OV-10 in a lazy right-hand spiral—heading straight for me. Helpless to do anything about it, I held my breath as the aircraft passed within one hundred feet of me and continued on its erratic flight path to the south. I never did see it crash. Then several new sounds grabbed my attention. It didn't register at first, but the most prominent noise turned out to be intermittent bursts of small arms fire. Somebody down there was doing a lot of shooting, and I could only assume that it was aimed at me. Then, in between bursts, I thought I heard dogs barking. In my agitated state of mind, I just knew the bad guys had bloodhounds ready to track me down the minute I landed.

Descending under my twenty-eight-foot canopy at a rate of about fifteen feet per second, I was in the air roughly four minutes, which gave me plenty of time to panic and worry. And the biggest worry was that I was coming down very near one of the most heavily defended sections of the Ho Chi Minh Trail. It had to be swarming with bad guys intent on killing me; they didn't take prisoners in Laos. That was a frightening thought even sitting around in the relative safety of the Muff Divers' Lounge, but to be facing the real thing was generating the kind of paralyzing fear that I wasn't sure I could handle.

As I drifted lower, the firing and barking seemed to stop, giving me a chance to regain a little composure and to begin preparing for the landing. One of the first items of business was to figure out what to do with the fiberglass seat pack still strapped to my rear end. Normally, the pilot pulled a quick-release handle that opened the seat pack and deployed a life raft and survival gear on a twenty-five-foot lanyard. For landing in trees, however, we had been advised to retain the seat pack for protection against injury or even impalement. And since there were so many trees below me, I kept the heavy seat pack attached and began thinking about possible problems associated with being hung up in the top of the jungle canopy. In case I made it all the way to the ground, I also gave a little thought to the techniques for a parachute landing fall, or PLF. The theory was to absorb the landing impact by rolling into the ground along the side of the body.

In the last ten seconds, I cringed on realizing that I was about to drift over the trees and land in a good-sized clearing; there was no time to release the survival kit. Then I hit the ground like a ton of bricks and performed the world's worst PLF: feet, knees, and a pitch-over onto my face. Besides knocking the wind out of me, the seat pack gouged two large cuts into the back of my calves. As I struggled back to my knees and began to remove the survival kit, I spotted the bloodstains beginning to soak through on the back of my flight suit and thought to myself, "You idiot. You're really gonna make it easy for the bloodhounds." On that somewhat irrational and negative thought, I scooped up the 'chute and seat pack and hobbled fifty yards to the nearest tree line.

Crawling into the thickest foliage in the vicinity, I lay perfectly still listening for sounds of the enemy soldiers I knew must be searching for me. Ironically, the only sound was my own heavy breathing. Just to have something to occupy my mind while waiting, I inexplicably began loading and unloading my .38 revolver with tracer ammunition. Then, after resting a few more minutes, I stashed the survival kit and parachute and began moving carefully south away from Route 9. At some point I became terribly thirsty and slightly nauseated by a very dry, metallic taste in my mouth. When I reached into my lower flight suit pocket for my baby bottle full of water, it was gone. It must have popped out during the ejection. Angry with myself for losing the water, I continued working my way through the dense brush near the south end of the clearing, all the while swatting at huge swarms of gnats that seemed to be following me. Finally, climbing a small mound to get my bearings, I heard the unmistakable "whopping" of helicopter blades.

With equal portions of excitement and fear, I took out my UHF survival radio, set it to channel "D," then transmitted my first distress call since hitting the ground. "Slick Lead, Slick Lead, this is Covey 221 on Prairie Fire common. How copy, over?"

The reply was about the sweetest sound I had ever heard. "Read you five by, 221. Glad you're okay. Talk us into your position." No longer feeling alone, my spirits soared. Then I began the process of vectoring the UH-1 Huey to me strictly by the sound of his engines. It reminded me of playing the children's game of "hot or cold." After I finally got a visual on Slick Lead and his escorting Cobra, they were able to identify the right clearing and my rough position. All that was left was to go for a pickup.

On the first attempt, as the very slow and vulnerable helicopter crossed the tree line forming the eastern edge of the clearing, heavy machine gun and AK-47 fire erupted from an area some distance north of the field I had landed in. Slick Lead broke off his approach and headed south, but as the firing continued, I could see some muzzle flashes and smoke, so I got on the radio to the Cobras. "Cobra Lead, the fire is coming from a .51-cal position on that first little ridge about three hundred meters north of the clearing. He's in the center of the ridge just below the crest. Put a couple of HEs in there and I'll adjust your fire." After several passes, the Cobra seemed to be right on the money. At that point the Huey tried a second approach and touched down in the clearing about fifty meters in front of me. I bolted from the trees and ran as fast as my one boot and one socked foot would carry me. As I made a dive for the open troop door, the door gunner grabbed me by the collar and roughly pulled me aboard just as the chopper lifted off.

As we climbed away at full power, the door gunner, in a very tender motion, took my face between his two hands and shouted, "Are you okay? Are you okay?" At first I thought he was going to kiss me; at that point I probably would have let him. After I drained his canteen, he grinned and shouted in my ear, "We really like working with you on these missions. You always find new ways to keep things interesting."

Slick Lead bypassed the MLT and flew me straight to the MASH at Quang Tri where the docs and nurses cleaned up my cuts and treated the burns on my arms and on the back of my neck, then left me sitting there for two hours. During the lull, I couldn't stop thinking about the Huey pilots and door gunners who had rescued me. What kind of men were these who would risk everything to go in harm's way to pluck me off the Ho Chi Minh Trail right under the noses of the enemy? The more I thought about them, the more my eyes kept welling up with tears.

After the umteenth time of having my blood pressure and pulse taken, one of the doctors finally walked back into the treatment room. When I complained about the long wait, he laughed right out loud and said, "They told me you were on the ground about thirty-five minutes before the rescue. Now you've been here almost two hours and your pulse is still around 140. When you come down off that adrenaline high, I'll let you go."

Late that night a chopper gave me a ride back to Da Nang, and the real ordeal began. The Covey boss, Ed Cullivan, was absolutely furious with me. As he chewed me out, he used every profanity he could think of, including a threat to "Have your ass medically grounded until hell freezes over." Then the good colonel's mood mellowed slightly, and with a sad, haunted look on his face, he told me, "Dammit, Tom, I can't stand the thought of losing another one of you guys. Promise me you won't do this again." Before I could answer, his temper flared a second time. "Do you realize that every big shot at MACV and Seventh Air Force has called me tonight on secure voice? There's a complete clampdown and blackout on your mission—no inquiries, no investigation boards, and no questions of any kind. What have you gotten yourself mixed up in?" Ironically, I wasn't even sure.

When I finally got back to the Muff Divers' Lounge, there was one more indignity to suffer. As I climbed into my bunk, there was a brown paper bag on my pillow. Opening it, I frowned, then had to laugh. Inside was a whole package of hotdogs.

This time, there was no escaping the flight surgeon or Air Force Form 1042. Much to my displeasure, the net result was a medical grounding called "DNIF": duty not involving flying. Although I couldn't prove it, I felt certain that Ed Cullivan conspired with the flight surgeon to keep me off the schedule much longer than necessary, supposedly for my own good. On the first day, I was probably still on an adrenaline rush, so sitting around didn't bother me. I wrote a bunch of letters, listened to music on a Teac 4010S reel-to-reel tape deck, and consumed several "medicinal" glasses of scotch. Even the second day wasn't too bad, but by the third day, I started climbing the walls. Just sitting around in the Muff Divers' Lounge grew old quickly, and with my two new roommates out flying all day long, there wasn't anyone to talk to. And because of the night schedule, the Covey O-2 pilots and navigators slept all day, so I ended up trapped with my own thoughts. As I sat there sipping scotch and contemplating my circumstances, several long-held but still half-baked notions began to crystallize.

I realized that I had changed radically in my six months of flying combat missions. The mechanics of being a FAC, so complex and mystifying to me in the beginning, had become second nature. My old instructors, John Tait, Don Jensen, and Norm Edgar, all long since returned to the States, would have been pleased with my progress. The things they harped on, such as developing a knack for listening to all five radios at once, no longer bothered me. In fact, I couldn't even remember why it had seemed so difficult. And the maps: When I got another new set built, I knew I would be able to reach into the bag and automatically grab the right one without missing a beat. As for controlling fighters, the Spads and the Cobras, I found myself able to do it with a certain rhythm and a kind of natural flow that seemed to relax the pilots and hopefully inspire a little confidence. Most of all, in a really hot situation, my combat reflexes had developed to the point where they could instinctively handle the present while my mind's eye projected ahead, anticipating. Coupled with a confidence in the Bronco and in my own ability to fly her out of the worst of scrapes, I saw myself for the first time as being truly combat ready.

During my recuperation in the Muff Divers' Lounge, one other notion began creeping into my conscious thoughts for the first time. In view of my tendency to attract enemy flak, accentuated by the ejection episode, I began to consider my own mortality. Until then it had always been a totally abstract idea, one that surfaced only when some other Prairie Fire participant had been unlucky enough to catch the golden BB. Yet the undeniable truth was that I had come very close on several occasions. Did that mean there was an inevitability to the spiral of violence I found myself caught up in? As I pondered the question, no immediate answer came to mind. Like the other Prairie Fire pilots, I approached any thoughts about my own death with mixed feelings. On the one hand, none of us could wait to get up in the morning and go perform this best of all possible FAC jobs. On the other hand, we all felt a certain fatalism about a mission that was brutal, harsh, and forced us on a daily basis to confront a stunning overload of sensation and crushing reality. Looking deep inside ourselves in search of that reality, each of us knew we would rather die than let that team down.

Armed with a clearer picture of my own capabilities and limitations as a FAC, I was genuinely looking forward to strapping into my OV-10 after the long layoff. On the twenty-third I finally got airborne again, but not quite in the way I had expected. Looking down at the Ho Chi Minh Trail from the right seat of an O-2 didn't thrill me, especially since I was only a passenger being hauled from Da Nang to Nakhon Phanom Air Base in Thailand. In what I perceived to be another one of those unexplainable bits of military logic, the head Covey decided I needed yet more rest from the war and that a three-day pass in Bangkok was just the ticket. Evidently my ten days of sitting around didn't count. I pleaded my case carefully, since I wasn't at liberty to talk about the pending SOG missions, not even to Colonel Cullivan. But when the boss finally stated that in his view I needed a change of scenery, there was no way out.

The flight to NKP would allow me to hitch a ride the following day on one of the many transport aircraft flying to Don Muang Airport in Bangkok. The layover also gave me a chance to talk to one of the C-123 crews at NKP. Their mission was anything but a typical airlift job. These guys were pilots on C-123s known as "Candle Stick" birds, and as unlikely as it seemed, they performed a modified FAC mission. The crazy fools would fly around over the Trail at night searching for trucks. When they found something, the Candle would call in the night fighters, drop flares and ground marks, then direct the air strike. The cargo-plane-turned-FAC could carry huge loads of flares and could loiter over the Trail for hours. From all indications, the Candle Stick crews were responsible for busting large numbers of enemy trucks. The old workhorse C-123 Provider finally had itself a glamorous mission.

The following day I linked up with Captain Stu Stewart, a Covey navigator who evidently also needed a rest. A native Californian, Stu Stewart looked the part: tall, blond, a quick smile, and a willingness to party. We hopped a C-130 to Bangkok and ended up at the infamous Florida Hotel, right across the street from the Chao Phya, the U.S. military hotel and officers' club in Bangkok. Using the two hotels as a combined base of operations, we proceeded to attack the city with a vengeance, just like every other tourist GI faced with the dilemma of a huge city and only limited time to take it all in.

There is nothing subtle about Bangkok. It invades your senses with exotic sights, sounds, and smells. Stu Stewart and I immersed ourselves completely. We took in the Grand Palace and the Emerald Buddha. We toured Wat Po to see the famous Reclining Buddha. We sampled spicy-hot Thai food from noodle carts along the street. We went on the Floating Market tour through Bangkok's famous canals. Sandwiched among all the sightseeing, we spent lots of time and cash in the countless jewelry stores on every cor-

ner. Then at night, we hit all the bars, always ending up
back on the top floor of the Florida Hotel at a steamy place
called the Bora Bora Room. During the forty-eight-hour
blitz, I don't think we ever slept.

Early on the morning of the twenty-sixth, we hired a
Thai taxi to drive us fifty miles south to U Tapao Air Base,
home of the large KC-135 tanker and B-52 bomber force
supporting the war effort in Southeast Asia. From there we
would hop a military flight back to Da Nang. On the drive
south, we hoped to catch a few winks, but our driver turned
out to be a frustrated kamikaze pilot. In spite of the steady
stream of oncoming traffic, he couldn't resist pulling out
into the other lane to pass some slowpoke. With horns wailing, brakes screeching, and our hearts pounding in our ears,
our daredevil driver somehow managed to duck back into
his lane at the last possible moment. When we finally made
it to U Tapao's front gate, both Stu and I were on the verge
of hyperventilating. That unforgettable ride may have been
the closest either of us came to being killed in the war.
After three or four hours at Base Ops, we boarded a C-123
headed for Da Nang. Late that afternoon, we collapsed in
our rooms back at the Covey barracks, frightened, exhausted, and much worse for the wear than when we'd left
four days earlier. I wasn't sure about Stu, but I couldn't
take another "rest" like the one that had just ended. Flying
combat missions would be a lot less tiring and probably
not as dangerous.

But the Bangkok blitz had served its purpose. During
most of the time, I had pushed the Prairie Fire mission to
the back of my mind. Yet once we were back home, I
couldn't wait to get back in the saddle.

November

Even in a combat zone, a certain amount of quality control was to be expected. Since most Covey pilots flew missions over the Trail every day, their opportunities to practice simulated airborne emergencies were limited. To make sure all of us remained current and capable of handling those emergencies, we were required to fly a midtour check ride with one of the 20th TASS instructor pilots. The drill normally occurred six months after a pilot became combat ready, and the process included a one-hundred-question open-book exam on aircraft systems, operating procedures, and limitations. There was also a short test on emergency procedures. Most of us considered the check ride a waste of time and an insult to our prowess as pilots, but there was a good reason for our suffering the indignation. Our leaders saw what we couldn't. For six months the individual FAC had been a free spirit, answering to nobody and generally accustomed to having his own way. At that point we thought we knew it all, that we could handle anything. Our bosses knew better. They had gone through the same euphoric stage years earlier and knew that young pilots were most prone to get in trouble early in the combat tour when they were green or at the six-month point when they were cocky. The midtour check was a scathingly brilliant way of pulling in the reins.

My chance to excel came on the fifth of November. These check rides were similar to any other graded test, and a certain amount of anxiety was involved. Fortunately, my old friend Carl D'Benedetto would be my flight examiner. After taking the written tests, I preflighted our OV-10 and got us airborne. Looking in the mirror, I could see Carl sitting in the back seat, cool as always, debonair and dashing with his bushy black mustache. Carl had me demonstrate a traffic pattern stall series and some slow flight, then we flew to Phu Bai for some landings. We started off with a simulated single engine. Carl was aware that I had handled the real thing a month earlier under tougher circumstances, but we pressed on anyway. I entered high key directly over the field at twenty-five hundred feet, then executed a shallow-bank descending turn to downwind at fifteen hundred feet. From there we turned final, threw the gear down, and landed.

Staying in the closed pattern, I set us up for a normal landing when Carl came up on intercom. "A beer says I can do a better spot landing than you. The one who touches main gear closest to the top of the runway numbers wins. You first."

"You gotta bet," I responded.

By all rights I should have won easily. From the front seat, I had great visibility. From the back Carl would have to peek around my ejection seat and my helmet even to glimpse the target. Thinking about how easy it should be, I set up a steady glide angle and held one hundred knots as we crabbed down final toward the concrete runway. Just before touchdown I lowered the right wing into the wind and eased in left rudder to align the fuselage axis with the runway. We touched down on the right main tire, maybe a foot or two short of the target.

On takeoff leg Carl took the controls. His pattern was much like mine except his final was a bit steeper, and he kicked the crab out before we crossed the overrun. Tracking wing low, only a few feet above the surface, Carl had dead aim on the runway numbers. Slightly past the point where I thought we would touch, Carl rapidly retarded the throttles, settling us in exactly on the target—not an inch off either way. It had been a remarkable piece of flying.

From Phu Bai we flew north to my old stomping ground

at Quang Tri. After a no-flap touch-and-go, I dialed in the MLT-2 administrative frequency to say hello. Top answered right away and asked for some help. He had no idea I was unarmed and on a check ride.

"Listen, that team you put in the DMZ a couple of days ago has a problem. How 'bout swinging over their position and find out what's going on."

"We're on the way, Top. I'll get back to you in a few minutes." Then I said to Carl, "Babe, the check ride has to wait. You ever been in the DMZ before?" I knew he hadn't.

With no maps, no guns, and no rockets, I felt naked. There was no telling what kind of trouble the team had stumbled across, and I wasn't sure what help we could be. Still, we couldn't just desert them, so it was worth a try. From Cam Lo I pointed the Bronco northwest on track across two prominent terrain features, the Rock Pile and the Razor Back. We flew into the DMZ and crossed the Song Ben Hai River into the north. On a finger-shaped ridge near Dong Cam, I set up an orbit over the last known position of our team. After I gunned the engines a few times to get their attention, the One-Zero came up on Prairie Fire Common Fox Mike radio frequency.

In a muffled but clear voice, he asked, "Covey circling my pos, how do you read, over."

"Covey 221 at your service. What's your situation?"

"We've got a lot of movement about four hundred meters to our west. If you can distract them, I want to move to a new position one hill to the east. Can you cover us?"

The problem was I didn't know exactly where they were. With no maps the only choice was to have the team mark their location, a risky proposition under the best of circumstances. Once I talked the One-Zero into flashing a signal mirror for me, it became easy. With Carl sitting silently in the back seat, I made four or five low passes on suspected bad guy positions, hoping the simulated machine-gun runs would do the trick. While we buzzed the bomb-cratered hills, the team moved swiftly and silently to a more secure position. Thirty minutes later, the One-Zero came back up on frequency. In a whisper he said simply, "Team okay. Thanks for the help." Carl's only comment was, "Do you guys always fly that low?" When we finally landed at Da Nang, the one-hour check ride had stretched to two hours. With a smile and a shake of the head, Carl passed me with flying colors.

Following the check ride, I spent the next several weeks handling my duties as Prairie Fire training officer. I really enjoyed working with the new recruits, teaching them, worrying about them, and generally carrying on like a mother hen. There was, however, one disadvantage. On early training sorties, I sometimes had to ride shotgun in the right seat of the O-2. While most of the O-2 jocks thought fondly of their war bird, I had a real problem getting used to it. To me, flying the Oscar Deuce in combat seemed to be more of an exercise in energy management. When my eager young trainee would dive on a target to fire a willie pete, things really got interesting. On the pull-up, we didn't go anywhere. The heavy, underpowered Cessna just couldn't zoom back to altitude as my Bronco could. On each pass we'd end up lower and lower, out of ideas, airspeed, and altitude. In spite of what I saw as a definite disadvantage in equipment, our O-2 jocks took it all in stride and ended up running some of the most hairy Prairie Fire missions of the war.

In conversations with the Covey riders, I learned that they generally liked flying in the Oscar Deuce. While the Bronco offered better overall performance and firepower, Satan and Blister found a real advantage in sitting side by side with the pilot as opposed to the tandem arrangement in the OV-10. In the O-2 the Covey rider could react to hand signals and could interpret body language and the facial expressions of his pilot. The two could share maps, cigarettes, and companionship. In general, the more personal communication made for better teamwork. To emphasize his point, Satan took delight in reminding me how close he had come to ejecting when a month earlier our canopy had been shot away and we couldn't communicate.

One other attribute made the Oscar Deuce a favorite among Covey riders: In the event the pilot became incapacitated, there was at least the chance the SOG troop could land the aircraft from the right seat. Most had practiced a few landings under the watchful eyes of their pilot. But in the OV-10, landings were very difficult from the back seat, even for experienced pilots.

There was one other intriguing aspect about flying in the right seat of the Oscar Deuce. On one of my first training rides with a new Prairie Fire candidate, the student had me open the right window, a novel experience for me since I was used to being totally closed in by the canopy in the OV-10. Then he handed me his M16 and told me to fire a few clips through the open window. Obligingly, I set the weapon to full automatic, referred to by the grunts as "rock and roll," and blasted away. I concluded it would take a lot of practice to actually hit anything, but evidently the Covey riders were pretty good at it. Although it was never publicized, they had been known to lend their own form of strafe to a team in trouble by hosing nearby enemy positions with M16 fire. I had also heard that they occasionally employed an M79 grenade launcher from the right seat. And although no one would ever confirm it, there were even rumors that the Covey riders would take a live hand grenade, pull the pin, then place the armed weapon in a glass jar. When tossed out the open window of the O-2, the glass broke on impact with the ground and set off the grenade. Of course any hope of accuracy required the pilot to fly right down in the weeds, but that was something our Prairie Fire O-2 jocks did on a routine basis—and they were good at it.

In between training missions and normal OV-10 sorties, we occasionally got mixed up in off-the-wall episodes. The last half of November turned out to be nonstandard on all counts.

By the eighteenth one of our teams had been sitting around for a week waiting to be inserted. One delay after another had forced a postponement. Not only was the team getting antsy, the indig members were tired of eating GI food. They began complaining and asking for food more to their liking. Since things were slow, we mounted an airborne hunting safari to keep peace in the family. With Satan in my back seat, we drafted one Huey Slick and one Cobra gunship to go with us, our objective being a marshy area at the base of Tiger Tooth Mountain, near Khe Sanh and the Laotian border. En route our Cobra had the first success when he spotted several wild boar ambling along a trail. With ruthless efficiency the Cobra crew nailed the tail-end Charlie. The Huey swooped in, hovered, and retrieved the small pig.

Several miles east of the marsh, we put our choppers in a holding pattern, while Marty and I pressed on, climbing to three thousand feet. As we flew over the rain-soaked ground, we could see hundreds of ducks floating quietly on the seasonal ponds below us. "Marty," I asked, "have you ever strafed ducks?" He replied, "Never have. Does Sir have a hunting license?" Arming up all four machine guns, I ignored Marty's question, eased out to our west, and descended to treetop altitude. As we pressed in on the deck, surprisingly few of the ducks seemed upset by our approach. At point-blank range I squeezed the trigger, spraying hundreds of 7.62mm bullets across the surface of the pond. As the huge flock struggled into the air, we banked hard to our left to avoid the wall of ducks directly in front of us. Between the terrified birds and my machine-gun fire, the placid pond had become a churning sea of water.

For the next twenty minutes, we circled the scene while the door gunner aboard the Slick employed a long stick resembling a shepherd's crook to retrieve the dead ducks scattered about the pond. For all of the rounds I fired, we only managed to bag about fifteen birds. Still, our indig enjoyed a hearty feast of pork and fowl over the next several days.

On a different type of hunting trip late that same afternoon, I teamed up with an ARVN ranger, *Daiwe* Zinh, to pick out an LZ for an all-indig mission. Originally from Haiphong, he and his family had fled the communist regime when the country became divided in 1954. It was apparent to all of us that Zinh had a very personal stake in the war.

We concentrated on the line of hills north of Route 9, just to the east of Tchepone, scene of my recent run-in with the 37mm guns that had turned me into a pedestrian. As we circled one potential LZ, I noticed several flak bursts well to our north. There was nobody else in the area, so I couldn't imagine at whom the gunner might be firing. As we approached, the gunner kept up the tempo, firing clip after clip straight up into the air. He obligingly kept on firing while I plotted his position.

My ARVN back-seater and I weren't looking for trouble, but I couldn't resist asking Hillsboro for some air. To my way of thinking, the 23mm gun crew had gone off the deep end and deserved to be put out of their misery—before they killed someone. Evidently the controller aboard the big EC-130 felt the same way. Within minutes, Dudley Flight, a four-ship of F-4s, checked in with us. I gave the circling Phantoms a quick brief, then rolled in from the south right on the deck. With five degrees of dive angle at a slant range of two thousand feet, I popped off two willie petes as my pipper superimposed on the gun pit. Then I racked it hard to the west for a climb into the late afternoon sun.

Out the top of the canopy, we could see the marks were right on. I advised my fighters, "Okay, gents, hit my smoke. Whoever's in position is cleared in hot. I'll be holding low, just south of the target."

The gunfire had stopped. The ranger and I watched as Dudley Lead rolled into a steep dive from the east. At about five thousand feet, Lead pickled off several canisters of CBU-24. Roughly halfway to the target, the bombs split in two, releasing hundreds of spin-armed bomblets. On impact, each bomblet exploded, propelling tiny steel balls in all directions. The overall explosion pattern as seen from above resembled a giant doughnut, complete with a hollow center. In succession, we cleared Two, Three, and Four in to give the gun more of the same. After the smoke cleared, we watched as ten to fifteen rounds of exploding 23mm ammo cooked off inside what had been the gun pit. With the F-4s covering me, we made one low pass over the position. In the dark shadows, the gun sat upright with its barrel drooping, pointing into the ground. There was no trace of the crew.

In the last rays of light, we headed back to Quang Tri. In spite of the darkness, we could see several rain showers in the vicinity of the runway. Coming in from the west, I entered downwind and turned a left base. On very short final, maybe fifty feet in the air, we crossed the perimeter road and ran smack into a solid wall of black rain. My forward visibility was instantly reduced to zero. For a split second, I thought to myself, "Just hold this attitude and we should touch down right on centerline. You've done it a thousand times." Instead, I cobbed the power and pulled the nose up in a desperate attempt to put altitude between the runway and me. When I had positive climb indications on the altimeter and vertical velocity indicator, I sucked up the gear and put us in a gentle bank to the west. Within seconds we were out of the rain, into the clear night sky. Climbing back to pattern altitude, I could see that the south end of Quang Tri's runway had disappeared in the squall. On the other end the dim white runway lights outlined a clear slab of concrete. This time I turned a right base for the opposite runway and landed uneventfully. On the landing roll-out, we coasted back into the driving rain at the other end of the field. Slowly I taxied us clear of the active and toward Barky Operations, without even waiting for the de-arming crew. When we climbed out, my passenger smiled from ear to ear. I couldn't even force a grin. For the first time in the war, I looked down to see both my hands shaking. It was terrifying to think about what a stupid thing I had almost let myself do.

Following the strange episodes involving ducks, 23mm guns, and rain squalls, an old-fashioned Prairie Fire mission would have been a welcome change. It wasn't in the cards. Several days later Blister, the Covey rider with the gaudy gold chain, jumped in the back seat of my OV-10 for what we thought would be a routine baby-sitting mission. A few minutes past noon, we headed into Laos, with Blister cheerfully munching away on his favorite sandwich, raw hamburger meat on French bread. Neither of us anticipated much action. Unlike the normal five- to seven-man team, the group we were going to support was large enough to take care of itself. Early the same morning, a twenty-four-man SOG team stumbled out of an armada of Huey Slicks, and sprinted off an LZ located in the middle of an area known as the Laotian salient. On our maps, the salient resembled the business end of a hatchet, with its blade roughly five miles wide and its body jutting about eight miles due north into Vietnam.

When we arrived overhead, the One-Zero of the reconnaissance-in-force team complained about sporadic sniper fire from several sides. As I worked a couple of Cobra gunships around the flanks, I heard Blister's voice become deadly serious as he talked to the team leader.

"I don't like this. You're letting these snipers herd you south. There's lots of cover and well-used trails that way. You've got the muscle, so keep moving east."

Several exchanges later, I heard Blister say, "It's a setup. I'm advising you to move any direction but south."

For whatever reason, the team leader continued the sweep due south for another hour. Shortly after the One-Zero reported the sniper fire had ceased, a new voice began screaming at us: "Prairie Fire! Prairie Fire! We're in contact. The One-Zero's down. Get us out!"

In the confusion I had no idea where the enemy fire was coming from. Blister, in his inimitable gruff but calming voice, fired off a few questions and gave me all the data we needed to get started. Using directions from the assistant team leader, I turned the Cobras loose on the pocket of small-arms and automatic-weapons fire. From the radio chatter, I gathered the team had begun an organized withdrawal to the north. We pounded the area around the team for twenty minutes, hoping to break the contact and give

them a chance to move to a more defensible position, pref-
erably close to a usable LZ. Hillsboro responded to my
emergency call for help by diverting six flights of fighters.
Using the flights with soft ordnance first, I put a wall of
snake and nape in close around the friendlies. Then I ex-
pended the flights with slick bombs around the periphery,
hoping to disrupt any enemy reinforcements trying to move
against our team.

While Blister called back to the launch site for some
Hueys, I asked the team, "How's the One-Zero?"

The One-One answered, "The *bac si* is working on him
now. It's a flesh wound in the groin. Doesn't look too bad."

Thirty minutes later, we put five Hueys into a nearby
LZ for an unopposed extraction while I simultaneously directed a flight of Navy A-4s into the area just south of the
LZ. As my package lifted off and headed back toward
Quang Tri, Slick Lead relayed the disturbing news. The
One-Zero had gone into massive shock and was in critical
condition. After we landed Blister and I talked to the *bac
si*. The young medic stood there, rocking back and forth,
looking old and drawn, concerned that the One-Zero's condition was somehow his fault. When we asked him what
had happened, he stopped rocking for a few seconds, then
said hoarsely, "We did everything we could. He's not hurt
that bad. I think he just gave up. He quit fighting. I've never
seen anything like it."

Several days later I found myself involved in one of the
more exotic interludes of my tour at Rocket City, an episode proving that even military guys took to heart the message of "Make love, not war." Here was the recipe: Take
a bunch of young Air Force pilots, put them in a war, then
impose almost total celibacy on them, and you've got yourself a hormonal Richter Scale reading that was off the
charts. The dangerous levels of adrenaline and testosterone
tended to generate a lot of "tension" as well as some funny
but strange stories. For example, after I had been at Da
Nang for a while, one of my friends from Hurlburt Field
joined the Coveys. After about three months, Dan and a

cute little Air Force nurse named Cindy fell madly in love.
I can only guess that the excitement of snuggling during
rocket attacks lost its appeal, so one night after we'd put a
big dent in a bottle of scotch, Dan and Cindy came to me
with a strange request. They knew I often flew with lots of
weird characters from the Special Forces and that I had a
reputation for pushing the envelope where flying rules and
regulations were concerned.

Dan and Cindy had a scathingly perverted idea. Suspended behind the cockpit and between the twin tail booms
of the Bronco was a small cargo bay capable of holding
three or four paratroopers. We never used it to haul people,
but they wanted me to fly them in my OV-10 so they could
join the "mile high club." Always willing to do a favor for
a fellow pilot, I foolishly agreed. Several days later we
arranged for a predawn takeoff, and the two lovers showed
up on the flight line—with a sleeping bag. Cindy sported
a raincoat to conceal the fact that otherwise she was wearing nothing, and she took offense when I made both of
them wear a parachute harness; she said it destroyed the
mood, but I had to tie them in some way. After helping
them climb into the 3' × 4' × 8' bay, and with considerable
apprehension, I closed the clamshell door on their little love
nest. We finally got airborne, and to make sure it would be
"official," I leveled off at 7,500 feet and cruised up and
down the coast of Vietnam for about an hour, listening to
the BBC on the HF radio and trying not to think about
what was going on ten feet behind me. When we landed
and I let them out of the cargo bay, both were smiling, so
I assumed it was a successful mission. The next day when
I showed up to fly, Dan had one of the crew chiefs paint a
new name on the nose of my airplane: "Love Machine."

November's strange turns of events kept right on coming. On the morning of the twenty-third, as I cruised around
the north end of the A Shau, a mayday call from a battle-
damaged F-105 drew everyone's attention. The distressed
aircraft, Dallas 01, relayed his position to the search-and-
rescue HC-130, King, and I knew we were in the same

neighborhood. Several minutes later, five miles away and well above me, I saw the burning Thud. Within a matter of seconds, the F-105 veered sharply to its left, and a parachute appeared. The whole sequence happened so fast I never actually saw the ejection.

Evidently I wasn't the only FAC in the vicinity. One of the O-2 FACs supporting the 101st, call sign "Bilk," notified King that he had a tally on the 'chute and was assuming the job as on-scene commander for the rescue. Since we were in his assigned sector, I had no problem with Bilk's initiative, but instinctively, I felt better qualified to run a SAR. It was right up my alley, precisely what I'd been doing for the past five months. Somewhat grudgingly, I kept my mouth shut until Bilk elected to do things the hard way, calling for a scramble of Air Force Jolly Green helicopters from Da Nang. Those aircrews included some of the bravest, most dedicated aviators in the world. To emphasize the point, the only Jolly Green pilot to receive the Medal of Honor, Captain Gerald Young, had earned his medal during a nighttime rescue attempt of a SOG team deep in Laos. But in this case, time—not the Jollies—was the problem, since it would take the H-53s forty-five minutes to arrive. From experience, I knew I could have an Army chopper on the scene in five minutes.

One quick call to my helicopter buddies in the 101st produced all the help we needed. An OH-6 Loach contacted me for the downed pilot's position, then headed straight for our boy. Somewhat guiltily, I thought about the ramifications of upstaging the other FAC. It wasn't his fault he'd never run a SAR before; he was simply doing it by the book. Reluctantly, I had the Loach contact Bilk.

In the radio exchange that followed, the Bilk FAC seemed pleased to have the help. In a very professional manner, he talked the Loach into Dallas 01, who appeared to be stuck up to his armpits in mud on the bank of a small stream. With no hesitation and no cover, the Loach landed near the pilot, discharged a copilot, and continued to sit there brazenly while the spare crewmember tried to pull the pilot free. When the copilot ran back to his helicopter, I could tell there was trouble. While the Loach pilot and the FAC discussed options for freeing the stuck Thud pilot, I got on the horn and asked the 101st to divert a medical evacuation helicopter, known throughout Vietnam as "Dust-Off." Within minutes the Dust-Off contacted the orbiting O-2, and that's when the turf battle got out of control.

Up to that point, King, the orbiting HC-130 SAR coordinator, had been fairly quiet, asking a few questions and passing along the progress of the Jolly Green. But when the Dust-Off showed up, King became very vocal. With a definite edge in his voice, the controller aboard King interrupted. "Dust-Off, this is King 24. Request you remain clear of the area. We have a Jolly Green inbound at this time. He's equipped with a hoist and medical help for this rescue."

The Dust-Off shot back, "We're hoist equipped and have a medic on board also. I've got your pilot in sight at this time."

In an even more agitated voice, King countered, "I say again. Remain clear of the area. The Jolly is ten minutes out and will make the pickup. This is an Air Force rescue. Acknowledge."

Nobody said a word for about fifteen seconds. During the silence, the tension was thick enough to cut with a knife. Then, without identifying himself, a voice said disgustedly, "King 24, you're an ass." That comment voiced the sentiments of all of us watching the fiasco. With that, the Dust-Off executed a 180-degree turn and headed back to Phu Bai. Twenty minutes later, the Jolly Green pulled the downed pilot aboard and retraced its flight path back to Da Nang. In spite of everything, the rescue had turned out okay, but it wasn't exactly a red letter day in the annals of interservice cooperation.

Fortunately, the rift wasn't permanent. The day before Thanksgiving, the news in the *Stars and Stripes* captured everyone's attention. In bold one-inch letters, the headlines declared: "RAID ON POW CAMP." Colonel Arthur "Bull" Simons, a legend in Special Forces circles and former commander of MACSOG, had led a fifty-six-man team in a daring rescue raid on the Son Tay Prison, twenty miles west of Hanoi. Supported by Air Force H-53 Jolly Green helicopters and A-1 Skyraiders, the SF volunteers stormed the prison in a perfectly executed plan—only to find all Americans had been moved. It was a bitter disappointment. Still, the audacity of pulling off a mission right under Uncle Ho's spiritual nose electrified the SOG community and shocked the North Vietnamese.

Immediately after the Son Tay raid, CCN executed another spectacular first, this time via parachute. In an effort to insert teams at night when no NVA LZ watchers operated, SOG decided to attempt the first combat HALO (high altitude, low opening) parachute drop in history. The concept resembled sport parachuting free-fall jumps, including a steerable parachute, but unlike the sport, in HALO the free-fall was only a means to a very dangerous end. Dipping into its pool of talented, dedicated warriors, CCN recruited three of the best to form RT Florida. The One-Zero on the mission was none other than Staff Sergeant Cliff Newman, one of the most experienced recon leaders in the business. His One-One was Sergeant First Class Sammy Hernandez, a veteran of seventy-five HALO training jumps. The final member of the trio was Sergeant First Class Melvin Hill, a former HALO instructor at Fort Bragg. Rounding out the team were an ARVN officer and two Montagnards. RT Florida's mission involved a wiretap on a main NVA telephone line along the Ho Chi Minh Trail.

At 2 A.M. the team jumped into heavy weather from a specially outfitted MC-130 aircraft known as a "Blackbird." Exiting the aircraft at 18,000 feet, each team member began a long free fall, finally opening their parachutes at 1,500 feet. Because of the darkness, rain, and cloud cover, the team lost visual contact and ended up scattered over a wide area on the ground; fortunately, none was injured during the landing.

As the first Covey FAC to arrive on station at daylight,

Evan Quiros determined that the team had inadvertently become three separate two-man units. He also found that they had been dropped miles from the intended drop zone, a situation complicated by the fact that the new area was completely off the team's maps. Nevertheless, RT Florida had landed undetected, and the three elements pushed on with individual reconnaissance missions deep in enemy territory.

By the fifth morning SOG decided to pull the entire team. For Evan Quiros, that meant three individual extracts, each with all the attendant difficulties of a search-and-rescue operation. Instead of using UH-1 Hueys from the 101st, Evan called on the services of Air Force long-range H-53 helicopters from Thailand. Operating from SOG's "Heavy Hook" detachment at NKP, the helicopters, call sign "Knife," swooped in and plucked each element from the menacing jungle. Evan covered the complicated extraction by blanketing the surrounding area with ordnance from F-4 Phantoms and A-1 Skyraiders. As with all SOG operations, there was absolutely no public disclosure about the world's first combat HALO mission.

On the twenty-seventh I spent the night at MLT-2. As we sat around the newly constructed dayroom/kitchen/party hooch sipping beer, unaware that the HALO mission was underway, the Son Tay raid dominated conversation. Speculation became the order of the evening. The Green Berets sprawled around the smoke-filled little room took turns guessing which of their SF buddies had been on the raid. Someone would offer, "I'll bet old so-and-so was on it. He always was in the right place at the right time." From across the room, a slurred voice countered, "Nah, he's a jerk and a lousy shot. Bull would never pick him." This type of banter continued well into the wee hours. Through it all, the sense of pride came through loud and clear. Every man in the room would have given up practically anything to have been part of the Son Tay raid.

In my five months as a Prairie Fire pilot, that night was the first time I had a chance to see and hear the personal side of the men with whom I'd been working. Sitting there on their home turf, their inhibitions melted away by too many beers, I listened to them ramble on about friends, ex-wives, gripes, retirement plans. In their maudlin moods, much to my embarrassment, they couldn't say enough nice things about the Air Force FACs who supported them. The bond was genuine and the sentiment sincere. I was deeply touched by their words, but for whatever reasons, I was too hung up to show it. Instead of accepting their compliments graciously, I retreated behind a façade of jokes and laughing denials.

My SF friends had their hang-ups, too. As we continued to drink and talk, each story became part of a composite forming in my mind. A definite pattern emerged. Every Green Beret in the room was serving on at least his second tour in Vietnam. Most were on a third or even fourth tour. Most had already suffered through at least one bad marriage, aggravated by long separations. All of these men had an abiding love for Special Forces and the values the Green Berets represented. Yet they seemed to be trapped in a push-pull situation. On the one hand, they were drawn by the freewheeling adventure and unconventional war of Southeast Asia. On the other hand, they seemed repelled by the Regular Army with its spit and polish, garrison duty, and stateside rules. To a man they bemoaned the fate of any of their number who rotated home only to become part of the bureaucracy at Fort Bragg charged with training sullen antiwar draftees. Rather than face that prospect, most of the MLT-2 troops chose to extend their tour in Vietnam indefinitely, until the war ended—or it killed them.

Shortly after midnight a change in mood rippled through the hooch. A mischievous feeling replaced the melancholy. Before I could figure out what was happening, my hosts swept me out the door into a jeep. In addition to the five of us crammed into the M-151, another half-dozen limber bodies piled into a three-quarter-ton truck. With beers in each hand and shouts of encouragement all around, we set off down the bumpy road toward Quang Tri Army Base.

Nearing the center of the sleeping base, our drivers turned off their headlights, and everyone in the convoy became deadly quiet. At a snail's pace, we motored silently down several side streets and through a back alley or two. My companions in the jeep became tense and alert, displaying just the sort of composure I imagined they'd have on a Prairie Fire mission. After a few more turns, we stopped behind a nondescript one-story building. A porch light at the far end of the long building seemed to be the only light around. Amid groans and giggles, the men in the back seat with me climbed out and sprinted to the lighted end of the structure. Quickly and silently, they blended into the night shadows. Simultaneously, the crew in the truck moved swiftly to the back door of the building and disappeared inside.

Finally I whispered to the driver, "Will somebody tell me what the hell's going on?"

He whispered back, "Be quiet. Here, have another beer."

Obediently I accepted the can. For the next ten minutes, the two of us sat there, the only sounds coming when we slapped a mosquito or gulped down a big swallow of beer. I couldn't imagine what my SF friends were doing inside that building, but instinctively I sensed they were up to no good. Helped by the alcohol, my mind reeled. Panty raid? Nurse napping? God help us, bank robbery?

A dark figure whistled softly, then the truck started up and backed up to the rear door. Straining, I thought I saw several men load a large rectangular shape into the truck. Seconds later one troop climbed back in our jeep. Again with headlights out, we fell in behind the truck, retracing our route out of Quang Tri Army Base. When I asked about the missing men from our jeep, the driver simply jerked a thumb to the rear. Looking back, I saw another jeep, lights out, in trail behind us.

Once we reentered the MLT-2 perimeter, my jeep mates began hooting and laughing between chants of "popcorn, popcorn." I still didn't have a clue. The pieces fell into place when I saw a shouting, groaning team of men unload a full-sized popcorn machine, just like the ones in movie theaters back in the States. To the cheers of onlookers, the crew carefully carried it inside, placed it in an empty corner, then plugged it in. From the looks of anticipation on their faces, the assembled Green Berets could already taste the fresh, hot popcorn. But, just as quickly, the smiles turned to frowns. Members of the road crew began a frantic search for something, dashing to the truck, then back to the hooch. After inspecting every door and every corner of the popcorn machine, the men slumped dejectedly into chairs. In the darkness and confusion, they had forgotten to "borrow" the bags of unpopped kernels and the oil. The popcorn party would have to wait.

When I finally crawled out of bed the next morning, the MLT-2 troops were already hard at work. The focus of most of the activity appeared to be a strange jeep bearing the markings of the 18th MASH, the hospital on Quang Tri Army Base. Several indig were busy painting the vehicle black. I decided to ask no questions. I couldn't swear it was the jeep from last night's adventure, and I really didn't want to know for sure.

Late that afternoon as I was preparing for the flight back to Da Nang, several SOG troops jokingly presented me with a hastily framed sheet of paper. Reading it, I found the part about stealing jeeps struck particularly close to home. The framed document read:

THE FAC

As seen by Seventh Air Force: A drunken, brawling, jeep-stealing, woman-corrupting liar with a star sapphire ring, Seiko watch, and a pearl-handled .38.

As seen by himself: A tall, handsome, highly trained professional killer, gentleman idol of women, with a star sapphire ring, wearing a pearl-handled .38, who is always on time due to the reliability of his Seiko watch.

As seen by his wife: A stinking member of the family who staggers into town about every year or so with a B-4 bag full of dirty underwear and fornication on his mind.

As seen by his commander: A fine specimen of a drunken, brawling, jeep-stealing, woman-corrupting liar with a star sapphire ring, Seiko watch, and a pearl-handled .38.

As seen by the Department of the Air Force: An overpaid, over-ranked tax burden who is indispensable because he has volunteered to go anywhere and do anything as long as he can booze it up, brawl, steal jeeps, corrupt women, lie, wear a star sapphire ring, a Seiko watch, and carry a pearl-handled .38.

December

THE COVEY BOMB DUMP

As the war eased into the final month of 1970, I found myself on more than one occasion remembering my pilot training days at Laughlin AFB. The month of December had been a particularly trying time for our instructors. To a man they hated the thought of Christmas break. The IPs complained bitterly that their boneheaded students spent more time daydreaming about the upcoming holidays than learning to fly. The preoccupation with family, girlfriends, and Christmas manifested itself in several disturbing statistics. Whether by design or coincidence, December always spawned a rash of automobile accidents and airplane crashes among student pilots. It was the best of times and the worst of times.

On December 4, 1970, I came within a cat's whisker of becoming one of those dreaded statistics and of succumbing to the lack of concentration I supposedly outgrew three years earlier at Laughlin. Instead of channeling my energies into tackling the horrible weather around Quang Tri, I let my mind race toward the end of the month when I would be meeting my wife in Hawaii. We hadn't seen each other in nine long months. On top of that, Jane didn't have a clue about what I was doing in the Prairie Fire mission, and since I wasn't allowed to tell her about it, I gave a lot of thought to how I'd dodge the subject. An assistant professor at Louisiana Tech University, the lady was no dummy. Furthermore, as an Air Force brat, Jane knew a lot about the flying game. I wasn't at all certain about how I'd handle the situation.

In Quang Tri Province, gloomy gray clouds socked in the entire area. A low, ragged ceiling held steady at about two to three hundred feet. After landing special VFR, I got word through Barky Ops radio that one of our teams was in trouble. Without waiting for a Covey rider to arrive, I launched into the scud. Imitating Army chopper pilots, I elected to remain below the deck as I hedgehopped toward Laos. For ease of navigation I pointed the Bronco northwest toward Dong Ha. From there I turned west to Cam Lo, then picked up Route 9 as it wound through the hills toward Khe Sanh. As I approached the abandoned airstrip from the east, the cloud deck dropped even lower. Several miles away, the terrain and sky blended together into a solid, dark gray curtain. In an all-out effort to get to the team, but with thoughts of R and R buzzing in my brain, I piloted my craft into the Rao Quan River gorge.

The Bronco seemed alive as we glided through the narrow gorge, just below the rim of the jagged cliffs on either side. Maneuvering space in the gorge was minimal, but visibility proved to be excellent. With only a few clicks of the trim button, I could will the aircraft into gentle climbs or banks. The control stick responded to the slightest pressure from my hand. In addition to the sheer thrill of flying, I took a few moments to enjoy the scenery. In contrast to the swirling gray mist only a few feet above, the gorge was alive with green tropical vegetation, boulders with seal-slick texture, and whitewater cascading along the bottom, swollen by the monsoon rains. The Bronco and I faithfully followed each S-turn of the river, completely absorbed by the primordial scene.

Two minutes after entering the gorge, I rolled into ninety degrees of left bank to negotiate a particularly tight hairpin turn in the river. As I centered the stick, the sight in front of me made me gasp out loud. Approximately one-half mile ahead of me, a solid wall of rain obliterated the gorge. With less than fifty feet separating each of my wing tips from the rocky sides, a retreat was impossible. I knew that flying into the rain squall would result in a fiery crash against

an unseen wall of the gorge. My only chance was lady luck
and the climbing power of the OV-10.

Pulse pounding in my temples, I shoved the throttles
forward to full military power, then set a twenty-degree
nose-high climb on the attitude indicator. Seconds later we
slipped into the dark clouds. As the Bronco struggled to
gain altitude, I fully expected to slam into one of the many
three-thousand-foot mountains on either side of the Rao
Quan River. Flying on instruments, I could only guess at
my position relative to the mountains. Since the river generally ran to the northwest, I held that heading and watched
as the altimeter slowly wound up—one thousand, fifteen
hundred, two thousand. I began talking to my mechanical
partner. "Come on, baby. Climb. Climb. Get us out of this.
A little more back pressure and trim to keep this angle of
climb. Twenty-five hundred feet. We've almost got it
whipped. Keep climbing. Don't stall on me."

Passing three thousand on the altimeter, I let out a war
whoop. The threat had to be to my right, so I eased in a
little left aileron and rudder to give us more room. At thirty-
five hundred feet, we broke out of the soup between layers
of stratus clouds. Nothing had ever looked so beautiful.
Roughly one mile off the right wing tip, the barren, bald
top of Hill 1015 jutted into the gray drizzle, an ugly reminder of how close I had come to being the worst kind
of statistic.

Fortified with a renewed sense of respect for the anonymous sage who coined the adage about keeping your mind
on your work, I mentally got myself back in the war. Several days after the close call in the Rao Quan River gorge,
I stumbled headlong into a different type of distraction. The
day started innocently enough. The head Covey, Lieutenant
Colonel Ed Cullivan, hopped in my back seat for a lift north
to Quang Tri. When we landed, Ed remained on the airfield
to conduct some negotiations with Barky Operations while
I pressed on with my secret Prairie Fire mission. I think the
situation made us both a little uneasy. Even in his position
as Covey commander, Colonel Cullivan didn't have oper-

ational control over the six Prairie Fire pilots. We operated a completely independent schedule and mission from the Trail Coveys. He didn't even possess the necessary SOG security clearances to enter our top secret Prairie Fire briefing room at Da Nang. He had a vague idea of what we did, but his knowledge stopped there. Our tactics and standard operating procedures remained off-limits. I knew for a fact the convoluted situation troubled him. Since the only Covey combat losses during Ed's command involved Prairie Fire pilots, he felt a genuine sadness and sense of helplessness over the turn of events. On more than one occasion, Colonel Cullivan would shake his head and mutter, "What a way to run a railroad."

By midafternoon the head Covey met me planeside for the flight back to Da Nang. Out of habit I left all our radios tuned to operational frequencies. Just as we became airborne, a distress call blasted through our earphones. Unaware that Colonel Cullivan was listening, the O-2 jock filled me in over a secure voice encryption gadget known as the KY-28. In between squelch breaks and beeps, Ed heard the pilot announce, "Tom, I've got a TAC E going and no close air support. I'd like to expend your ordnance before I commit the Hueys. How copy, over?"

My passenger and I heard it loud and clear. My mind raced as I formulated an answer. The situation sounded hot, and my guns and rockets might make a big difference. On the flip side, playing fighter with the uncleared commander in my back seat presented a different kind of risk, not to mention an unwelcome distraction. With mixed emotions and no real conviction in my voice, I finally replied, "Covey 221 inbound to you with a flight of one. I've got fourteen each willie petes and HEs, and two thousand rounds of pop gun."

As we slipped across the fence, the boss didn't have much to say, and I made no effort to steel him for what lay ahead. Thankfully, we each had the good sense to leave the other alone. Still, I couldn't help thanking the weather gods for a high broken cloud ceiling and plenty of sunshine.

The very thought of hugging the top of the triple-canopy jungle made me feel squeamish. Even at fifteen hundred feet, I could have sworn I felt Ed's dark eyes burning disapproving holes into the back of my head.

The target loomed straight in front of us, a large emerald green field surrounded by scrub brush and scrawny trees. Several low hills immediately to the northwest, casting afternoon shadows across the landscape, created the illusion of an overgrown crater or a shallow soup bowl. The SOG team had managed to get itself into a firefight at the geographic center of the field, one of those rare occasions when the good guys and bad guys chose to fight right out in the open. As luck would have it, my passenger was going to get an eyeful.

The Prairie Fire O-2 laid down several well-placed white smokes to mark the target, then cleared us in hot. Out of deference to Colonel Cullivan, I came down the chute a little steeper and higher than normal. With one eye on the smoke and the other on the team seventy-five meters to the south, I lined up the target in my gunsight. Purposely aiming slightly right of the target in the direction of the friendlies, I squeezed off two HE rockets. On the first shot, the One-Zeros preferred that we keep the stuff in close, to drive the enemy away from the explosions and the team rather than forcing them to flee toward the team. At the sight of the dirty little detonations, I completely forgot about my back-seater.

The orbiting FAC, cheered on by enthusiastic corrections from the team, had me dive in for three or four more rocket passes. Then the real excitement started. For good measure we flew multiple machine-gun passes, stitching the green field with long bursts of fire. While I kept the bad guys pinned down, two Hueys swept in for a formation landing. We kept up the figure-eight strafing patterns until the choppers lifted off and climbed to a safe altitude.

As the package took up a heading for Quang Tri and I pointed us south, Slick Lead gave me a call.

"Covey 221, the One-Zero says it's imperative you return to QT. He's got something you've gotta see."

With a shrug of the shoulders, I banked us around to the northeast. To Colonel Cullivan, I explained, "This shouldn't take long." Then somewhat apologetically I added, "They wouldn't call us back unless it was important."

The MLT black jeep was waiting when we landed. Colonel Cullivan strolled back into Barky Ops while I bounced off down the road to the launch site. When we arrived, the driver struck out across the soggy LZ toward a group of figures standing near the choppers. They seemed intent on watching something or someone. As I walked up, the circle of Special Forces troops and helicopter pilots parted, revealing the object of their attention. Squatting flat-footed, balanced perfectly on his haunches in Oriental fashion, a young Vietnamese soldier sat there puffing on a cigarette. He wore a baggy khaki-colored uniform, the shirt conspicuous by the large blood stain on the left side. An army battle dressing was tied around his left bicep.

Sporting a wide grin, one of the troops explained, "We snatched this character during your air strike. We don't know who he is or where he came from, but he was just wandering around out in the middle of the fight like he was lost. The *bac si* says it looks like a couple of pieces of rocket shrapnel creased him. When we told him you did it, he said he'd like to meet you."

Someone said something in Vietnamese, bringing a weak smile to the baby-faced soldier's lips. In between drags on the cigarette, he rattled off a couple of sentences. The translator said that the kid thought I was a good shot. Partly out of curiosity and partly out of meanness, I asked, "What effect did my shooting have on the rest of your buddies?" After hearing the translation, the kid spoke no words, but his defiant glare more than answered my question.

On the flight south to Da Nang, Ed Cullivan chattered away, never once mentioning the curious little battle he had observed out in the middle of Laos. In a breezy, casual manner, he confined most of his comments to the Barky operation, discussing their FAC mission and the problems they faced. As he talked, I only half-paid attention. My mind kept framing pictures of the boyish-looking NVA soldier, his dark eyes with no pupils staring at me. I felt a certain twinge of remorse at being responsible for his wounds, yet that same little guy, armed with an AK-47, had probably been a dangerous adversary only minutes before. Still, I derived no sense of pleasure in shooting him. In fact, the down side to meeting him face-to-face outweighed the novelty of meeting him at all. In a passing thought, I worried that on my next mission, taking aim through the gunsight, I might see his smooth, expressionless face instead of a fleeting target. Hashing the episode around one last time before we landed, I arrived at only one clear conclusion. Temperamentally, I was much better suited to the impersonal air war than to the close-up, blood-and-guts side of the fighting.

As if in a self-fulfilling prophecy, for the next few days I had trouble shaking the vision of the baby-faced soldier at Quang Tri. The episode never seemed to bother me during the workday, but at night, during lulls inside the Muff Divers' Lounge, I could visualize the blood-soaked shirt in vivid detail. The preoccupation finally took care of itself as I became absorbed in setting up and trying out my newly arrived stereo gear: Teac tape deck and Pioneer tuner and speakers. That simple diversion did the trick for me. Other Coveys handled the tension in other ways.

To take their minds off the fighting, the troops in Vietnam devised some inspired ways to let off steam. A few of the less rowdy troops tried losing themselves in hobbies or in reading. Others opted for marathon card games. The more active ones participated in roughhouse games of volleyball, playing by "jungle rules"—anything goes. The whole idea was to find a distraction to occupy the time between combat missions. This safety valve came naturally to most, as if bred into the soldiers, sailors, and airmen by design. But a few always hung back, almost brooding, the stress eating away at them. Such men tended to lose themselves in a fog of whiskey or depression. One of our own Prairie Fire pilots resigned from the program, claiming too much was expected from him. Unable to cope with the stress, the man became physically ill.

Sometimes a little artificial help was needed to lower the stress level. On December 11 the Coveys instinctively knew the time had come for a rip-roaring bash. From all over the main compound, a crush of bodies packed the Muff Divers' Lounge. Coveys, Spads, Jolly Greens, nurses, intel, maintenance—everybody crowded in. As nominal hosts, Sonny, Larry, and I picked the theme. We decided on a "Yucca Flats" party. Into a large steel kettle, we poured gallons of vodka and grain alcohol. To mask the awful taste, we stirred in sliced oranges, jars of maraschino cherries, and a little sugar. The potent concoction easily lived up to its namesake in the Nevada desert. One sip would start a chain reaction that could blow the top of your head off.

A simple dip of a cup into the vat would have been the obvious, conventional way of serving our thirsty guests. But in honor of our unconventional war, our Yucca Flats punch needed a unique touch, a bit of flair, and a dose of the dramatic equal to the high spirits of the evening. The solution was simple. One of the nurses donated a pair of black silk panties. Someone else chipped in with an old tennis shoe. The Big Bippy did the honors by stirring both deep into the vat. Then we announced the rules of engagement. Anyone wanting a drink had to wring the soaked panties into his cup until it was half full. The tennis shoe became a ladle to fill the cup to the brim. Amid yowls of laughter, everyone followed the rules to the letter.

One of the more bizarre incidents of the party occurred when Lieutenant Arch Batista, who had just landed after a mission over the Trail, came strolling into the Muff Divers' Lounge looking for a cup of punch. Much to the distress of most of us, one of the Coveys had been scaring everyone with an incredibly realistic looking rubber snake. As Arch bent over the vat, the Covey tossed the snake at him. In what must have been reflex, Arch caught the snake and in the next instant bit its head off. One of the nurses broke the silence by saying to me, "No way he knew that was a fake snake. It had to be pure adrenaline. Remind me never to get you guys mad at me right after you come back from a mission."

Later in the party, armed with a full cup of punch guaranteed to cure shyness, I struck up a conversation with two other Air Force nurses. Lieutenant Pat Orowski, a pretty, blonde Yankee, had the most intriguing Maine accent I'd ever heard. Her sidekick, Lieutenant Sherdeane Kinney, was a slender, good-looking auburn-haired Southern belle from Mobile, Alabama, by way of Woodstock, New York. At first I asked a lot of dumb questions just to hear the two contrasting accents. Then as Pat and Sherdeane began talking about their jobs at the Air Force hospital, I found myself listening for content. Their professional lives revolved around an endless stream of badly wounded GIs, most waiting for medical evacuation back to the States. On each shift the nurses dealt with sucking chest wounds, shattered limbs, and mutilated bodies. Along with the gory dressing and bandaging of wounds, the nurses were drafted by their patients into the emotional roles of friend, confidante, pseudo-mother, sister, or even girlfriend. I listened as the two ladies described laughing and teasing with a young man with both legs blown off. Then, with knots in their stomachs, they walked out of the ward and into the corridor to cry. And the same scene repeated itself, day after day. If anyone ever deserved a chance to unwind, these very professional Air Force nurses did.

Eventually the conversation lightened up. As we talked, Pat and Sherdeane brought up the possibility of visiting a few nurse buddies at Quang Tri. Rumor had it I flew up there every day, and they wondered if I would give one of them a ride in my OV-10. At first I dismissed the notion as party chatter, but in her deep Southern drawl, Sherdeane persisted, demanding a definite yes or no. As she tried to convince me, it occurred to me whom she reminded me of.

THE COVEY BOMB DUMP 233

She could have been the personification of Holly Golightly, the free spirit of *Breakfast at Tiffany's*. And the similarity went deeper than looks. Like the character Holly, Sherdeane struck me as being capable of operating comfortably in the conventional world, then easing right into the flower child scene. She was a hawk on the war, but her heart was in Haight Ashbury—she was a hippy in uniform! Finally, at two in the morning, with some strong-arm help from her buddy Sonny Haynes, I agreed to fly Sherdeane to Quang Tri.

The Yucca Flats party generated two casualties. The first was my old friend Norm Komich from pilot training days. On the day of the party, Norm decided to move out of his Jolly Green quarters and into the Muff Divers' Lounge. We knew he wouldn't last. Norm's clean living and Spartan habits doomed the experiment to failure. The drinking, the loud music, and the round-the-clock tempo were too much. The next morning, Norm apologetically moved back in with the other helicopter pilots. In his heavy Boston accent, he pleaded, "Hey, it's not you guys. Honest. But Tom, Tom, I just couldn't get any Zs. I gotta have my Zs. It was the noise. I really am sorry." All of us fell over laughing. All by itself, Norm's pronunciation of my name, "TOE-UM," cracked us up.

The other casualty was our maid, Mamma San. When she walked in and saw the mess, she almost cried. Bottles, cups, and potato chips lay strewn about the room. The floor was gummy from spilled punch, and soot from several large candles had blackened the white tile ceiling. Her blood-curdling scream echoed through the place as she dug through the remnants of the Yucca Flats vat. She was calm as she fished out the panties and the tennis shoe. She maintained her composure as she gingerly scooped out someone's partial denture plate. But when Mamma San reached in and pulled out the life-size realistic-looking rubber snake, she ran screaming from the Muff Divers' Lounge. It took two days of bribing with food and presents to coax her into returning.

In the late morning sunshine on the day after the party, I walked nervously across the ramp to my airplane, with my back-seater matching me stride for stride. Suffering from a mild case of paranoia, I searched the faces of the staring crew chiefs, wondering which of them would be the first to recognize Lieutenant Kinney, even with her long red hair cleverly hidden under the helmet she wore. Their expressions revealed nothing. The troops were conditioned to seeing me show up with an oddball assortment of Green Berets or indig, so I hoped they'd pay no attention to my latest passenger. Unfortunately, the young airmen spotted Sherdeane's shape in spite of the baggy fatigues she wore. By the time we reached the plane, half a dozen grinning crew chiefs greeted us, each gushing for a chance to help the Air Force nurse climb into the waiting airplane.

I growled at them, "Knock it off, gents." Then to the only one of them wearing a shirt, I snapped, "You, help the lieutenant strap in." Without waiting to see the reaction, I climbed into the front seat and began attaching the survival kit fittings, the lap belt, and the shoulder harness fittings. Through the mirror I could see the young crew chief, perched on the side of the plane, warming up to his duties. I had to smile when he told Sherdeane, "You sure do smell good, Sir."

Once airborne, my initial uneasiness disappeared until Lieutenant Kinney asked, "Tom, what happens if we have to bail out?"

"You just pull the ejection D-ring like I showed you." Then I added sarcastically, "Once you're clear, then I'll fly into the nearest mountain peak, because if anything happened to you, the brass would kill me anyway."

On the flight north, I let my passenger fly the aircraft while I gently guarded the controls. I even talked her through a pretty decent aileron roll. She handled it so well that I decided to give her the acid test.

In an open area a few miles south of Khe Sanh on the Laotian border, a deserted thatch hooch stood innocently, the victim of monsoon weather and hundreds of practice rocket attacks by passing FACs and gunship pilots. Over the months I had fired at that blasted hooch dozens of times and never hit it once. As we flew over it, I set the hook.

"Hey, Sher, I just saw some bad guys run into that hooch. Hold on while I blast 'em."

With a flip of the wrist, I put the Bronco on her back, all the while feeding in the back pressure to pull the nose down to the target four thousand feet below. When the hooch disappeared underneath us, I rudder-rolled back to wings-level and popped off one willie pete as we stabilized in a forty-five-degree dive. Out of consideration to my back-seater, I executed a weak pull-off of three Gs. When I looked back at the target, white smoke came belching out a hole in the roof and through the door. The temptation was too much. In mock horror I yelled, "Damn! Did you see that? Did you see those two bad guys run outside? Their clothes were on fire from the burning phosphorous!"

Not knowing how far to carry the hoax, I shut up to hear what Sherdeane would say. Her answer floored me.

"Go back for another pass and nail their hides!"

I banked around for Quang Tri instead, not willing to press my luck. I could have fired at that hooch all day long and probably never scored another direct hit. Also, I wasn't keen about the game any more. It suddenly felt tacky to tease Sherdeane about something as serious as shooting at people. Still, she had been a real trooper about it. Who would have thought that a sweet little Air Force nurse, an angel of mercy from the Da Nang hospital, could get such a charge out of an ordnance delivery. She was a true warrior.

Several days later I ran into Sherdeane's friend, Pat, and asked if anything had been said about the OV-10 ride. "Not really," Pat answered. "All Sher said was, 'Tom's a good shot.' " I figured that was the end of it until the next day found all of us at Covey Ops for another impromptu cook-out. Evidently word about the unauthorized flight had made the rounds among the Coveys, and Sher and I suddenly found ourselves the object of unwanted attention. At some point in the evening Colonel Cullivan motioned for all of us to fall into some semblance of military formation for the presentation of a medal. I still hadn't caught on until my roomie, Captain Larry Thomas, announced, "Lieutenant Kinney, front and center." When she was in place, Larry read, "Citation to accompany the award of the Special Covey Air Medal to Sherdeane Kinney." At that point I suddenly realized it was going to be a long, embarrassing night. Then Larry read the citation: "Lieutenant Sherdeane Kinney distinguished herself by extraordinary achievement while participating in aerial flight as an airborne Covey nurse on 12 December 1970. On that date Lieutenant Kinney directed the pussy-whipped pilot of her lightly armed OV-10 aircraft in a daring white phosphorous rocket attack against a well-defended military structure located deep within hostile territory. In spite of intense and highly accurate ground fire, Lieutenant Kinney, with complete disregard for her own safety, and with a good deal of contempt for the frayed nerves of her front-seater, was instrumental in destroying the fortified fighting position and its determined defenders. Dismissing the wails, sobs, and pleas of her distraught pilot to leave the hazardous location, Lieutenant Kinney insisted on performing dangerous post strike reconnaissance which revealed that a nearby road was full of ruts, the ruts were full of guts, and there was blood and gore everywhere. The professionalism, aerial skill, and devotion to duty displayed by Lieutenant Kinney reflect great credit upon herself and the United States Air Farce."

In the week following my flying Sherdeane to Quang Tri, I returned to the more familiar turf of Prairie Fire to find myself relegated to the back seat as part of a new Prairie Fire pilot's checkout. Captain Jim Smith was a pleasure to fly with and a quick study. Jim had already served one tour in Vietnam as a Caribou pilot, so he had a lot of air sense. He was picking up on the mission so fast that I had already mentioned to our boss, Bob Denison, that Jim would be a good choice as training officer when I left.

Although my Prairie Fire duties had no tie-in to the normal Covey Trail mission, I managed to hear a few war stories by virtue of my residency in the Muff Divers' Lounge. There was a lot of discussion about the heavy truck traffic moving south through the Covey sector of the Trail, VR-6. A sophisticated network of acoustical sensors, code-named "Igloo White," could actually hear each truck pass a given point along the Trail. Specially equipped orbiting aircraft picked up the signals and relayed them to Task Force Alpha, an enormous concrete building at NKP Air Base, Thailand. There, intelligence analysts studied the raw data and plotted numbers, times, and locations as enemy trucks motored south each night. The wizards at Task Force Alpha could even track individual trucks as they passed consecutive sensors. More important, the analysts could tell when the traffic pulled off the road before reaching the next sensor. The interruption generally meant one thing—a truck park.

On the night of December 18, the Coveys struck the mother lode. At the controls of his Oscar Deuce, Lieutenant John Browning, Covey 281, lifted off Da Nang's Runway 17 Left exactly on time. He began a slow climb to the west and leveled off at eighty-five hundred feet MSL. At the Laotian border, he gave the traditional across-the-fence call to Panama, switched off all outside navigation lights, un-sinked his props, then called "Moon Beam," the nighttime version of Hillsboro. Arriving over the Trail, John took up a heading for a geographic reference point called Delta 43, near the deserted Laotian village of Ban Bak. From sensor movements, the intel types swore there had to be a truck park in the area, and Covey 281 was determined to find it.

In the right seat of the O-2, the forward air navigator, Captain Norm Monnig, broke out his starlight scope and poked it out the open right window to begin the search for any movement on the dark trail thirty-five hundred feet below him. He didn't have long to wait. Shortly after midnight, the nav detected "movers." While Covey 281 radioed Moon Beam for air, Norm picked out a convoy of twelve trucks without lights running south along a relatively clear stretch of road. A convoy of that size was definitely a juicy target, so it was a bitter disappointment when the trucks suddenly turned off the main road and disappeared beneath the jungle canopy.

The two Coveys knew the convoy had to be somewhere down there in the darkness. Rather than go home empty-handed, they decided to probe the area with ordnance from a set of fighters approaching Delta 43. After briefing Iceman flight, Covey 281 dropped a mark that ignited on the ground in the general target area, crossed his fingers, and cleared the fighters in hot. Using the burning log as an aim point, the two F-4s dumped their heavy loads of Mark-82s right on the money. The exploding five-hundred-pounders were always an impressive sight, especially at night, but this time the dark jungle erupted in an old-fashioned fireworks display.

In a matter of minutes, the thick foliage had been ripped and splintered away by twenty-eight secondary explosions. Circling overhead, the Covey FACs also counted seven big fires, including two fiercely burning trucks. Covey 281 thought to himself, "At least part of the convoy will never make it south—chalk up another good mission for the Coveys." As the O-2 crew watched the jungle burn, neither they nor anyone else suspected that the fires and explosions at Ban Bak would continue without letup for another ten days!

At dawn on December 19, the OV-10 Broncos picked up where the Covey night shift had left off. In addition to the daylight, the complexion of the battle also changed. The enemy gunners around Ban Bak reacted fiercely, hosing FACs and fighters with an unusually heavy barrage of 23 and 37mm triple A. Most Coveys were conditioned by regular hampering fire from guns along the Trail, but nobody had ever seen the likes of the flak at Ban Bak. By mid-morning the sector FAC reported, "The stuff's so thick you can get out and walk on it." As an added safety measure, the squadron back at Da Nang launched a second FAC to fly high cover. His job would be to call out the gunfire, allowing the primary FAC to concentrate on directing air strikes.

Flying the second OV-10 mission of the day, my roomie, Captain Larry Thomas, ran through the target briefing with Gunfighter 66 Flight. As he was about to mark the target for the orbiting F-4s, Larry detected a single truck sneaking away from the area through a small streambed. Using a quick movement he had practiced many times, he selected the left outboard rocket pod on his armament panel, flipped on the master arm switch, turned on the gunsight, and dialed in 28 mils. Then he reefed the OV-10 into a near-vertical dive toward the smoke-filled jungle below. When the fleeing truck was lined up perfectly in his sights, Bippy fired two willie petes and then yanked the stick back into an eye-watering five-G climbing right turn. Holding the back pressure, he glanced over his right shoulder just in time to see the white smoke of the first rocket hit short and the second one score a direct hit through the windshield. Jubilant, Larry yelled into the mike, "Hot damn! Scratch one truck and driver!"

Gunfighter Lead began cackling about a lucky shot, but Larry was too busy to trade quips. Three 23mm guns opened up simultaneously, pumping over one hundred rounds at the slow-moving OV-10. No matter how he maneuvered, the guns kept tracking, kept firing, and kept following him with deadly gray and black airbursts. At one point, the high-cover FAC observed the Bippy's aircraft totally bracketed and obscured from view by exploding flak bursts. Miraculously, Larry dished out the bottom of the ugly cloud without a scratch.

After spending three hair-raising hours over Ban Bak, Larry turned control over to our other roommate, Sonny Haynes. Before he had a chance to work a single set of fighters, Sonny watched through his binoculars as fires on the ground from Larry's air strike touched off several more large secondary explosions. It was becoming clear that the Coveys had found something a lot bigger than just a twelve-truck convoy. The target area had assumed the pro-

portions of approximately one kilometer square, with many
fires and detonations visible in all quadrants. The inferno
below him boggled the mind. As Sonny studied the destruction, his UHF radio receiver announced the arrival of another set of fighters. "Covey 262, Black Lion Flight at base
plus 11. We've each got eight Mark-82s, ten minutes of
play time. Gimme a hold down, over."

In his easygoing Texas drawl, Sonny began the briefing
that had become second nature to him. As he talked, a
navigation needle on Black Lion Lead's instrument panel
homed on Sonny's voice, pointing directly at the low-flying
Bronco. Lead banked his flight twenty degrees to the left
and continued homing as the FAC spoke. "Do I have a
good deal for you—trucks and supplies right out in the
open! Target elevation is 2750. High terrain is fifteen miles
east, going up to 4550. Wind is out of the northeast at less
than ten knots. There are at least five 23 and 37mm guns
in the area, all active. If you get in trouble, your best emergency bailout is the high stuff to the east. If you end up on
the ground, stay cool, work with me, and I'll save your butt
for mamma. One last thing. These gunners are really good,
so whatever you do, keep it moving and don't be predictable."

As with all of Covey 262's air strikes, the attack proceeded like a well-choreographed ballet. Black Lion's
bombs touched off thirty secondary explosions. While navigating through the smoke and low clouds trying to determine the nature of those detonations, Sonny ran into an
intense barrage of fire from four 23mm weapons, which
poured out over three hundred rounds in his direction. Several of the airbursts were so close that the concussion jolted
his aircraft. When Sonny Haynes returned to Da Nang and
taxied into the Covey revetments, the ground crew and several other pilots noted that his face was totally covered with
black cordite from the exploding flak.

Over the next three days, the Coveys continued to pound
Ban Bak. Hillsboro cooperated by diverting all available air
to the area, advising the fighters to "Rendezvous with your

FAC over the Covey Bomb Dump." The day-and nightshift Coveys directed thirty-five flights of fighters against the Bomb Dump, setting off thousands of explosions and drawing hundreds of rounds of antiaircraft fire. In one instance the sector FAC observed fuel barrels exploding every few seconds over a period of two-and-one-half hours. During the night of December 22, Covey 276, Lieutenant Gary Beard, and his navigator, Major Hall Elliott, watched in disbelief as the bombs from Wolfpack 72 Flight ignited a spectacular fireball, which reached a height of two thousand feet, turning the black night into day. Detonating tracers from the blast shot up to an altitude of nine thousand feet.

On the twenty-third, weather socked in the Trail, shutting down virtually all bombing missions against Ban Bak. But the sector FACs reported seeing the eerie glow of fires and secondaries reflecting through the layers of clouds shrouding the Bomb Dump. Anyone silly enough to venture under the low ceilings found out that NVA gun crews still seemed well supplied. The rash young pilots always attracted four or five clips of 23 or 37mm fire.

Back in the Muff Divers' Lounge, excitement kept building among the Coveys. The restless pilots stood around talking with their hands and comparing strike results in the best traditions of one-upmanship: "I'll see your two trucks and raise you three more," or "I'll see your five large secondaries and raise you five hundred small ones." There was even a lively debate surrounding reports that NVA gunners were firing red and green tracers, in honor of Christmas. In keeping with the spirit of the season, I had managed to scrounge up one of the tree-shaped acoustical buoys normally dropped along the Ho Chi Minh Trail to monitor trucks. Decorated with tinsel, ornaments, and a star, the pathetic-looking device resembled a surrealistic Christmas tree. It was a perfect addition to the Muff Divers' Lounge, which was doing land-office business, generated partly by sentimental holiday thoughts of family and friends back home and partly by the tension surrounding the life-and-death struggle at the Covey Bomb Dump.

At 6 P.M. on Christmas Eve, a twenty-four-hour ceasefire went into effect. Nobody at Da Nang seemed to notice, especially the Coveys, who continued to fly missions in Laos. Yet the atmosphere around Da Nang was festive and upbeat, due primarily to one enduring tradition: the Bob Hope Christmas show. Over twenty thousand troops packed into the Freedom Hill amphitheater and spilled over onto the neighboring hillside for a glimpse of the renowned comedian. The GIs weren't disappointed. In addition to Bob Hope, the show included the lovely and talented Gloria Loring, six gorgeous singer-dancers called the Gold Diggers, and Johnny Bench, the all-star catcher from the Cincinnati Reds. But everyone's vote for hit of the night went to Lola Falana, a beautiful, sultry actress-dancer who stole the show along with everyone's heart. Just one look at the smiling faces of the wounded soldiers wheeled in by their nurses convinced all of us that the Bob Hope show was better medicine than any hospital could administer.

Christmas Day passed quietly. Most of the Coveys felt an undercurrent of melancholy or even homesickness. There was no denying we missed our families. Yet we were among good friends, thrown together by circumstance and chance. The bonds of friendship and common experience in many cases forged stronger ties than we had back in the world. On reflection, I wanted to be home for Christmas with my wife and family, but selfishly I wanted all my Covey and Prairie Fire buddies there with me. It wouldn't have seemed like Christmas without them.

By late afternoon on December 26, the weather over the Trail broke. The pilots radioed back incredible descriptions. The area around Ban Bak resembled a vast landscape on the surface of the moon. The jungle was gone; bomb craters pitted the black, scorched ground in all directions; and smoldering vehicles were scattered about in twisted, contorted heaps. Through breaks in the clouds, pilots could see the billowing smoke and fires from twenty-five miles away. And the stench. The smell of burning rubber, fuel, and cordite permeated everything—cockpit, flight suit, helmet, eyes, nose, and mouth. It was actually possible to taste the smell. Some of the odors were strange and nauseating. The pilots tried not to think about those smells.

For Lieutenant Rick Ottom, the euphoria of three earlier missions against the Bomb Dump gave way to the grim reality of routine. Tall, slender, introspective, and good at his job, Rick had acquired the embarrassing nickname of "Salvo," referring to the occasion flying with Sonny Haynes when he had inadvertently pickled off all the rocket pods and fuel tank. Although good-natured about the kidding, even Rick began to feel the grind associated with missions over Ban Bak. No matter where he directed the strike aircraft, their bombs always ignited spectacular secondary explosions. And every time Salvo rolled in to mark a specific target, the gunners responded with a vengeance. Rick sincerely believed the missions had become a deadly game, a test of wits and nerve rather than skill. As he pulled off one rocket pass, a pair of 23mm guns opened up with seventy rounds in a classic tail shoot. This time, the play backfired. Tide 71 Flight, holding over the target, spotted the gun, and after receiving clearance from Rick, blew the position away with well-placed canisters of CBU-24. In addition to taking out the gun, the exploding bomblets set off hundreds of small secondary explosions and seven sustained fires.

The incredible destruction continued through the night, but by the morning of the twenty-seventh, a perceptible decrease in secondaries was evident. During the remainder of the day, the Coveys used thirteen sets of fighters to destroy seven trucks and seventy-five stacks of camouflaged supplies.

The Bomb Dump finally played out on the twenty-eighth. During ten incredible days, Coveys logged more than two hundred hours over one of the most heavily defended targets in Southeast Asia. Flying low and slow, the Coveys jinked and maneuvered through thousands of rounds of antiaircraft fire without a single loss. By contrast, the enemy on the ground suffered horribly in lives and treasure. FAC-directed fighters destroyed forty-six trucks, ten thousand rounds of ammunition, countless drums of fuel, and over one thousand tons of supplies. During the bombardment, aircrews counted over 6,500 secondary explosions and 225 sustained fires. By any standard, the Covey Bomb Dump was one of the largest and most successful interdiction efforts waged against the Ho Chi Minh Trail. In a letter of appreciation, General Lucius D. Clay Jr., the Seventh Air Force commander, relayed the following message from the Chairman of the Joint Chiefs of Staff, General William C. Westmoreland:

> The effectiveness of U.S. air operations in Steel Tiger was most clearly demonstrated by the outstanding success achieved by the TACAIR sorties directed against the truck park and storage complex in the vicinity of Ban Bak. We may never know precisely the degree to which the destruction of this storage complex affected the enemy's logistic capability, however, I am convinced that his capability to support combat operations has been seriously degraded and the damage to the enemy represents one of the most outstanding achievements by TACAIR in Commando Hunt operations. The success of this strike effort is due in large measure to the courage and determination of the Covey FACs in their surveillance of the suspected area. The Joint Chiefs of Staff congratulate all officers and men involved in this most productive strike effort.

As the last strikes were going in against the Bomb Dump, my thoughts couldn't have been more noncombative. With my B-4 bag draped across the bunk bed, I happily packed clothes for the R and R flight to Hawaii the next morning. The war was on hold for me. I was putting the finishing touches to the folding and stuffing when a voice yelled to me from the hall door, "Hey, Tom, telephone." Shuffling down the hallway, I wondered who could be calling me. In my nine months at Da Nang, I could count on one hand the number of phone calls I'd received.

When I picked up the receiver, the duty officer began talking in a low, apologetic tone of voice. "The Ops officer told me to call you. Evan Quiros just radioed us that Jim Smith is overdue by a couple of hours. Evan thinks he must be down. You want us to get you a plane ready?"

I looked at my watch—3 P.M. Not much time to launch, find Jim, and mount a SAR before dark. "Yeah," I answered. "Get somebody to preflight it for me. I'll be there in fifteen minutes."

On the short jeep ride to Covey Ops, I tried to force myself to stop thinking about R and R. Think about the mission; think about Jim. In my mind it had to be a mistake. Jim was too good to be cannon fodder for the bad guys. Even though he had only been combat-ready in Prairie Fire for two weeks, he was a natural. He must have landed at Phu Bai without telling MLT-2. The SOG folks must have their wires crossed on this one. I had trained Jim. I had taught him the fine points. Had I glossed over something important? Had I forgotten something in his training?

In spite of the excitement generated by the emergency scramble out of Da Nang, the afternoon sunshine streaming through the canopy made me feel sluggish and listless. More than once on the flight north, I caught myself thinking about the early-morning report time at the MAC passenger terminal. The reverie didn't evaporate until I heard Evan's high-pitched voice on the KY-28. Evan explained, "There's been no contact with Jim since noon. He can't still be airborne. He had dry tanks two hours ago. Let's spread out and start looking. Any place in particular you want to search?"

I didn't have a clue. For lack of a better plan, Evan concentrated on the area around Route 9. I focused on the real estate on the east side of Route 92. We crisscrossed the terrain time after time for two hours. As the sun got lower, our sense of urgency got higher. A few minutes before sunset, Larry Thomas diverted into the area to help. We couldn't find a trace of a crash, a parachute, a signal mirror, or a flare. The three of us searched until dark with no luck.

Frustrated and tired, we were about to call off the effort when the obvious hit me between the eyes. Jim and his Covey rider, Roger Teeter, code-named "Buffalo," must have been in contact at some point with our only team on the ground. Disgusted with myself for not having thought of it sooner, I attempted to hide the anger in my voice as I asked Evan to get the team up to find out what they might know. Fifteen minutes later, I braced myself as Evan relayed his conversation with the One-Zero. The team reported radio contact with Jim overhead at 12:40. Because of a low cloud deck, there was no visual contact. Several minutes later, they heard several long bursts from what sounded like a 14.5mm ZSU heavy machine. They heard the distinctive turboprop engines increase to full power, then there was a loud explosion. The One-Zero estimated the map coordinates, based strictly on sound, to be about a thousand meters from his position. According to the plot, the impact point was near a steep cliff socked in by mist and low clouds.

Cruising south to Da Nang, I set the Bronco's air vents to scoop up the maximum flow of cool night air. With the refreshing stream blowing in my face, I tried to sort out my feelings. I didn't want to believe Jim and Buffalo had crashed. But nothing else made any sense, and no other scenario matched the few facts we had. Reluctantly I concluded our troops really were down. At best they might have ejected and be evading through the jungle. But if that were the case, we would have heard the emergency beepers from their survival radios. Deep inside, I knew they were dead. Emotionally, I felt like a traitor for giving up on them.

The next morning, as I stepped on the R and R bird for Hawaii, guilt riddled me from the top of my head to the soles of my feet. The other Prairie Fire Coveys had already launched to resume the search. They were flying combat missions while I sat in seat 15A of a comfortable Boeing

707 bound for paradise. My stomach churned as I rationalized. My fellow Prairie Fire pilots didn't need my help to pull off the grim task they faced. I wanted to be with them, but after six months of SOG flying, I desperately needed to get away from it for a few days. I couldn't wait any longer to see my wife. Somehow, I hoped, Jim Smith and Buffalo would understand.

January

The Army personnel at the Fort DeRussy R and R Center in Honolulu ran an amazing operation, around the clock, 365 days a year. At least several times daily, a Boeing 707 or Convair 880 cleared Honolulu International Airport's main runway and taxied to the terminal. Between 165 and 200 tired but anxious GIs filed stiffly out of each bird and onto waiting Army buses for the short ride to DeRussy, located on Waikiki Beach, right next door to the Hilton Hawaiian Village. At each of the daily reenactments, the buses pulled up to a one-story, nondescript-looking welcoming center. Inside, the Army had cleverly stashed the dozens of waiting wives or girlfriends; unleashing them at the airport would have caused total pandemonium.

As we piled off the buses and walked inside, none of us was ready for the sight that greeted us. Standing expectantly two rows deep along each side of the long corridor painted latrine green, excited ladies hopped, waved, whistled, and called out first names or pet names to their loved ones: "Bill, over here!" or "Honey, sweetie, here I am!" A dozen confused GIs pivoted first in one direction, then another as they searched the crowd, trying desperately to match the shouts with that one all-important face. As each match occurred, the result was a predictable squeal of delight from both parties, followed by a flurry of tears, hugs, and kisses.

As I inched my way between the rows, two outrageous thoughts filled my mind. First, the scene somehow reminded me of an experience years earlier as a Boy Scout, when for punishment or amusement we ran a gauntlet known as the belt line. The object was to run as fast as possible through two rows of belt-wielding Scouts, each one intent on landing a solid blow across the victim's backside. Now, as I looked around the R and R center, the parallel was unmistakable. My other thought was much more worrisome. I hadn't seen Jane in nine months. What if in the commotion I inadvertently walked right by her? Worse still, what if I didn't recognize her? My anxiety intensified as I approached the end of the gauntlet.

That first glimpse of my wife is one of those memories etched permanently on my brain. I spotted her standing quietly toward the end of the right-hand row—small, shy, and beautiful, with long blond hair and a short miniskirt, looking like a composite of Catherine Deneuve and Grace Kelly. As we embraced, the smell of her hair and the softness of her cheek against mine were overpowering. For a brief second the tears welled up in my eyes. Deftly, I wiped them away in Jane's hair. She might have been embarrassed to see her combat-pilot husband cry in public.

For six glorious days we indulged in a whirlwind of sightseeing, restaurants, and tourist traps. In addition to the obligatory time on the sands of Waikiki, we took in Pearl Harbor, Diamond Head, the Dole pineapple fields, the International Market, and a dinner show performed by the well-known Hawaiian singer Don Ho.

During our time together, Jane and I only occasionally talked about the war and my specific job. I fended off most of her questions by maneuvering the conversation toward the lighthearted and insignificant events that were part of our existence at Da Nang. I told her about the rowdy hail-and-farewell parties, the cookouts, the funny incidents. Part of my ploy was to protect the secret nature of SOG's mission. The other was to spare her the details, some gory, of what I actually did. In a nutshell, I didn't want her to worry about me. I desperately wanted to tell her about Jim Smith, about Prairie Fire, about the secret war we were fighting in Laos, but I couldn't—and I didn't. Every time the subject of flying came up, I would look into Jane's beautiful blue eyes and see genuine sadness, a forlorn reflection telling me that she knew I was either lying or purposely evading. She instinctively knew something was eating away at me, yet she never pressed, and she never tried to confront me with it. With both of us holding back emotionally, the strain that developed was predictable and inevitable.

After six days with Jane at the Ilikai Hotel, I joined the other troops for the return flight to Vietnam. The long ride provided plenty of time to think. It had been a wonderful trip, but the R and R fell short of being the belated dream honeymoon we had both anticipated. No matter how hard I had tried, I could never shake thoughts about the SAR effort for Jim Smith. Jane had picked up on my preoccupation over what was going on back at Da Nang, and although she didn't know exactly what was bothering me, she knew competition when she saw it. Predictably, she felt hurt, and I felt like an insensitive jerk. Worst of all, it would be another four months before I would see her again—and have the chance to make it up to her.

On January 9 I flew to Quang Tri on my first mission since returning from R and R. In the cockpit on the flight north, I smelled a soothing aroma I had truly missed, a strange blend of leather and JP-4. I felt comfortable, back in my element.

The first order of business after landing was resolved as I expected it would be. The Bright Light team had found Jim Smith and his back-seater, Roger Teeter, still strapped in their ejection seats. Their OV-10 had plowed into a box canyon not far from the location guessed at by the reconnaissance team. At the MLT, nobody said much about the crash, a sure sign that the episode was eating away at their insides. A tough situation was made even worse by a small, yellow puppy scampering playfully around the compound. The little mongrel ran from one American to the next, only to be kicked away or ignored. The sight of the corkscrew-tailed little dog was more than the SF troops could bear. During the two weeks prior to the crash, Buffalo and his new puppy had been inseparable.

Late that same afternoon I flew high cover as one of the new O-2 jocks ran a team insert deep in the western DMZ. To me, First Lieutenant Larry Hull seemed an unlikely candidate for the Prairie Fire program. Larry was blond and slender, almost fragile looking. On the surface he flaunted a cocky, devil-may-care attitude, but underneath, a boiling anger or resentment about something made him much more dangerous than his boyish appearance suggested. The SF troops evidently saw something of themselves in Larry because they idolized him, partly as warrior and partly as mascot. For a reason known only to them, the Green Berets decided Larry reminded them of Woodstock, the small yellow bird from the "Peanuts" cartoon strip. They even pasted a Woodstock decal on Larry's helmet.

With all eyes in the package watching, Larry dived his O-2 toward the LZ for the verbal mark. From my vantage point he appeared even lower than normal. When he pulled off without keying his mike, I knew something had gone wrong. "Covey 275, this is 221. What's the problem, over?"

"No big deal," he answered. "I seem to have brushed the tops of the trees. Actually, part of one looks like it's growing out the leading edge of my right wing."

From my height advantage I pulled the Bronco down and to the inside of Larry's turn. With plenty of speed advantage and lots of cutoff, I rejoined on his right wing in a matter of seconds. Sure enough, several small branches and tree limbs lay draped across the midsection of the wing. There was no way to tell whether the wind stream held the branches in place or if they were in fact embedded in the metal skin. As we climbed to an altitude of two thousand feet, Larry performed a controllability check on the battered Oscar Deuce. He claimed handling characteristics were normal, so I sent him home while I continued with the team insert.

By the next morning, Larry's SF buddies at Quang Tri had already written a short poem to commemorate Covey 275's baptism of fire:

The Ballad of Woodstock

I love to fly the Oscar Deuce from channel one-oh-
three.
I fly that dog through rain and fog in the extreme
western DMZ,
And no one knows we're fighting there 'cept Charlie,
you, and me.
So mark my words and heed them well, or you could
end up like me.
I flew down low and got too slow and hit a goddamn
tree!

While Woodstock's brush with the trees made him a
celebrity within Prairie Fire circles, another Prairie Fire
Covey managed to achieve unwanted notoriety on a much
larger scale. January 10 turned out to be Evan Quiros day,
and a memorable one at that. Shortly after noon, the team
Larry and I had inserted the day before ran smack into a
large NVA patrol. The team One-Zero reported his situation
as a "TAC E," or tactical emergency. By using that particular phrase, the One-Zero was letting us know that his situation was tense and fluid. An emergency extraction might
be necessary, but with some close air support, the mission
might be able to continue.

Evan pinpointed the team's position, then began working over the enemy patrol with his M-60s. Like virtually
all our other sorties, this one required placing ordnance well
inside the prescribed safety margins. Since Evan was an
old pro, he didn't even flinch at the prospect. He dived his
OV-10 on multiple strafing passes to within only a few feet
of the friendlies. His deadly aim broke the contact quickly,
allowing the team to move to a safer hiding place. On several of his strafing runs, Evan had been so low that the tips
of his propellers actually touched the tops of the elephant
grass. After things settled down, Evan asked the team if his
machine-gun fire had been close enough for them. In what
was destined to become a legendary SOG war story, the
One-Zero replied, "Let's put it like this. If I'd wanted to

smoke, I could've held a cigarette at arm's length, and your tracers would have lit it for me. Great shooting."

The Prairie Fire pilots always got a tremendous charge out of laying it in really close when one of our teams was in trouble. The invisible bond between that team on the ground and that pilot with his finger on the trigger is beyond explanation. People like Evan Quiros and Larry Hull would break every rule and take any chance to help a reconnaissance team. When the action was super-hot, the One-Zero never gave a second thought to friendly machine-gun fire or rockets kicking dirt up at his feet, as long as it came from one of his Prairie Fire FACs. That mutual respect and commitment formed the lifeblood of our operations so deep in the secret parts of Laos.

On that same afternoon, off the coast of the DMZ, a U.S. Navy destroyer moved in close on a naval gunfire mission. The USS *Lynde McCormick*, DDG-8, had recently arrived in the South China Sea by way of Hong Kong. On her second day in the war zone, the *Lynde McCormick* had already fired one early-morning mission from her five-inch deck guns. As she was about to fire a second mission late that afternoon, Evan Quiros decided to give the crew a thrill.

Evan was still keyed up from his own gun mission in the DMZ. He knew he had made a difference. He felt good about himself. When he spotted that large gray ship off the coast, he saw the perfect opportunity to let off some steam. Without considering the ship's possible mission, Evan dropped to wave-top level and headed for the *Lynde McCormick*. With his Bronco's engines cranked up to full power, he pressed in to a wingspan's separation while flying the length of the ship. Reaching the bow, Evan pulled up and reversed course with the first leaf of a Cuban eight. For the next five minutes, he dazzled the crew of the destroyer with a series of perfectly executed aerobatic maneuvers. Unknown to Evan, the *Lynde McCormick* had been forced to abandon her fire mission because of his air show. That fact finally sank in when the ship broadcast a warning on the emergency radio frequency. Through his helmet earphones Evan heard, "Air Force aircraft operating in the vicinity of the U.S. Navy warship off Ha Loi. You are interfering with a naval gunfire mission. Depart the area immediately!"

I was standing in front of my aircraft, getting ready to fly back to Da Nang, when Evan's OV-10 touched down on the Quang Tri runway. He taxied in, shut down, and walked straight toward me. Something about his gait, something about the way he carried his shoulders and head, signaled that all was not well. Evan poured out the whole story in a briefing-like manner. When he finished, he looked at me with those light blue eyes and asked forlornly, "What do I do now, coach?"

For the next several minutes, we stood there conspiring, trying desperately to invent some plausible explanation for what had happened. We ended up settling on an absolutely absurd rendition of the facts. In our panic to save Evan's rear end, we decided that he was signaling the destroyer to get its attention. He needed its gunfire for a target, and since he didn't know the destroyer's radio frequencies, buzzing the ship at close quarters seemed to be the only choice.

The plan survived about thirty seconds until logic and a twinge of conscience took hold. We knew lying wasn't the answer. We also knew that in the screwed-up world of Vietnam the episode would probably end up buried in the ship's log. We decided to forget about the incident unless the Navy made an issue of it, in which case Evan would confess and take his medicine.

In the remaining twilight, I climbed into my Bronco. Once airborne, I dropped down on the deck and eased out over the sandy beach. The trip was part of our training route for new Prairie Fire pilots. To accustom them to low-level flying, we would use the beach as an altimeter check for absolute sea level. Once the new guy felt comfortable at one hundred feet, we would ease down to fifty feet. When he could handle that reasonably well, we would move inland to mix absolute altitudes with the real world—trees, hooches, hills, power lines. Graduation came with flying nap-of-the-earth over the deadly hills and mountains of Laos.

Flying low-level demanded complete concentration, and I needed that mental stimulus to shake myself loose from Evan's problem. Once over the beach, I dropped to twenty-five feet, then to ten feet, then down to just inches above the mild surf washing up on the sand. Over the past month, I had pushed myself to fly lower and lower, perhaps just to prove that I could hack it. Part of it was an ongoing game with the crew chiefs at Da Nang. When I would land, several would run over. The old head would say to the relatively new crew chief, "See, I told ya." Then to me he'd say, "Captain, I don't know where the hell you fly, but I keep telling these guys every time you come in there's salt-water spray all over your centerline tank."

Larry Hull's close call and Evan's predicament still concerned me, no matter how hard I tried to block them out of my mind. Of all the Prairie Fire pilots, those two were special to me. Like an old mother hen, I hovered around, worried that something bad might happen to my brood of chicks. Still, I had to back off enough to let them do their jobs—and I had my own to do. Through it all, the missions kept coming and the sorties continued to mount for all of us. The deadly grind, however, was not without some lighter moments.

On my next flight to Quang Tri, Kim Budrow, instead of using my regular Covey call sign, kept referring to me over the radio as "Snow Leopard." Since I had no clue as to the meaning of the strange phrase, I asked him about it later that afternoon. He burst out laughing, pointing to an unsightly series of white spots on both my forearms, souvenirs from my walk through Laos in October. The burns I had received on ejection had healed with virtually no scar tissue, but a curious phenomenon had occurred. For some reason the fire had burned most of the pigment from my skin, resulting in a number of white spots, each about the size of a dime. The Special Forces troops thought the effect was hilarious, hence the new nickname. From that time on they delighted in poking fun my way by calling me "Snow Leopard."

Armed with my new nickname, on the fourteenth I logged a healthy 9.2 hours in the OV-10, with a routine insert along Route 9, then an emergency extraction. All the missions seemed to be running together in my mind. The normal tour for a Prairie Fire pilot was about six months. So far, half our pilots never lived that long—and here I was, into my seventh month in Prairie Fire, with two more months to go. The nonstop pace began to take its toll in subtle ways.

At 1400 a new Covey rider jumped in my back seat for my fourth sortie of the day. I felt dog-tired, and the low scud and rain moving in made the flight even trickier. Our mission was to find one of our teams in the DMZ, and unlike most teams, this one had been on the ground for a complete term of seven days. By now they were probably out of food and exhausted.

As we leapfrogged across the rain-soaked ground at tree-top level, I somehow missed the Song Ben Hai River, where I needed to hang a left to navigate to the team. My back-seater noticed but said nothing, figuring I knew what I was doing. As we pressed farther north, the scenery didn't look right. At first subtly, then more rapidly, the terrain changed from moonscape bomb craters to cultivated green fields. I realized with a shock where we were when I saw two hooches just in front of us and saw figures running toward three 57mm gun positions. We were well into North Vietnam.

I jammed the stick to the left, racking us into ninety degrees of left bank. Then I fed in the Gs to keep the turn as tight as possible. As the OV-10 shuddered through the near-stall-producing 180-degree turn, I kept my eyes riveted on the soggy terrain only a few feet below us. I could just make out the four red spoiler plates on top of the left wing, each sticking out in the wind stream to kill lift on the low wing, enabling me to keep the roll and high-G turn going.

Once we returned to a southerly heading, I rolled us out abruptly, then added several spirited jinks to throw off the aiming solution of any would-be gunners. As I rolled back to wings-level, the view through my gunsight sent my pulse into overdrive. A quarter of a mile in front of us, a long column of North Vietnamese troops marched south along a muddy road, strung out along the trail in three long files. I estimated at least three hundred troops were down there. From our height of fifty feet, and with a fast closure rate at full power, there wasn't even time to charge my machine guns. This was the best target I had ever seen, and I wasn't even in position to strafe them out of existence.

The sound of the Garrett AiResearch turboprop engines running at full military power finally reached the rear of the enemy column. The figures looked like falling dominoes as the sound traveled the length of the procession. From rear to front, row after row of troops tumbled or dived to the ground as the roar of our OV-10 registered in their brains. As we streaked overhead, tracers came at us from all directions. Unlike some of the other times I had been hosed and hit, this time I heard the impact. A series of sharp thumps registered somewhere in the nose section. Through the rudder pedals, the bottom of my feet felt the vibrations as the bullets found their mark.

As fast as it started, it was over. Within seconds the firing troops were behind us, masked from view by veils of drizzle and low clouds. My back-seater was philosophical about the ordeal. As we retreated back to Quang Tri, he mused, "Hey, Snow Leopard. Wish we could have iced those bastards." Then as an afterthought he added, "Even a camera would have been okay. I'd love to have just one eight-by-ten glossy to toss on the table the next time some antiwar creep shouts all that dribble about how the North isn't the aggressor or doesn't infiltrate troops south." He received no argument from me.

After we landed the Barky crew chiefs needed only about an hour to work their magic. From somewhere they scrounged a spare nose-gear door to replace the ragged one unceremoniously dumped on them. Three well-placed AK-47 rounds had done a number on the original. Miraculously, there was no other damage. For the third time in the war, a crew chief, noting the battle damage to my airplane, told me how lucky I was.

That evening at Da Nang, I dropped into the Covey intel shop to talk with our intel officer, Captain Duane Andrews. Normally Prairie Fire pilots handled their own debriefings via a top secret events log maintained in their special room. Since my mission contained a few peculiar twists not having much to do with Prairie Fire, I decided to share them with the Covey intel officer. I gave Duane my best guess on coordinates for the three gun positions. Then I told him about the troop column moving south. After copying the information, he looked up with a smile and said, "Actually, unless you were on a mission number fragging you into the North, you really shouldn't have been up there. Your report might generate a few questions along those lines. Just out of curiosity, what were you doing up there?"

Smiling back, I told the intel officer, "If anybody asks, just tell them the weather was bad and that I got lost."

Shaking his head from side to side, Duane responded, "They'll never buy that one."

"It's the truth," I said, shrugging my shoulders. Then I turned around and walked out the door. We never heard another word about that mission.

A week later Evan and I got mixed up in another strange episode, this time involving the cargo-carrying capacity of our OV-10s. We had several teams on the ground along Route 9, one of the primary east–west infiltration routes into Quang Tri Province. The team working the south side of the road encountered no problems. They did, however, find an odd assortment of NVA supply items, including several tins of processed meat from Czechoslovakia. In an even more bizarre discovery, they stumbled across a bootleg cache of empty Coca-Cola cans and a worn pair of Keds tennis shoes. Ironically, the Communist meat tins had been discarded unopened.

The team on the north side of Route 9 ran into a buzz saw. In the heavy fighting, they suffered two indig killed in action, or KIA. Through the team's heroics and the bravery of the chopper pilots and the A-1 jocks, we managed to extract the team, including their KIAs.

Back at Quang Tri, the MLT-2 troops placed the body bags in a secured building near the runway. Dedicated SOG airlift from Nha Trang would pick up the remains and return them to the grieving families. Unfortunately, four days passed with no airlift in sight. With the delay, the families at Da Nang were beginning to raise a stink equal to the one emanating from the makeshift morgue. In a fit of desperation, somebody remembered the cargo bay in the OV-10.

When North American Rockwell designed the OV-10, they included a small cargo bay as part of the fuselage behind the cockpit section. Covered by a tapered, side-hinged clamshell door, the cargo bay measured roughly three-by-four-by-eight feet, for a total of about seventy cubic feet of space. The ingenious Special Forces troops quickly calculated that the cargo bay was the perfect size for a coffin.

Evan agreed to give it a shot. Even though this particular situation wasn't covered in the FAC mission description, he genuinely wanted to help out. And how much could the dead solder weigh—maybe 120 pounds? Evan knew he was in trouble when a truck backed up to his bird and a small army of SF types began straining to lift a wooden box into the cargo bay. As they slid the coffin inside, the Bronco's main landing gear struts compressed noticeably from the heavy weight. For a guess, the SOG troops estimated the coffin tipped in at five hundred pounds. To cover the overpowering stench, they had doused the body in formaldehyde, then filled the coffin with heavy stones and sand.

On his takeoff roll, Evan used every inch of Quang Tri's runway. As the last few feet of concrete disappeared under the aircraft nose, Evan pulled the protesting bird into the air. With the Bronco staggering forward at just ten feet off the ground, Evan carefully milked the flaps up in increments. A full mile off the end of the runway, he finally gained enough flying speed to begin a slow climbing turn to the south.

The next day, I had my chance. Learning from Evan's experience, I carried empty rocket pods and only enough gas to get us to Da Nang. As the troops loaded the heavy coffin, we all knew the extra day had been a mistake. Even with the light breeze blowing off the ocean, most of the loading crew became nauseated in a matter of seconds. My only hope was that the ram air effect during the flight would keep the stench behind me.

I got airborne without incident. Cruising southeast along the coast, I soon realized the ventilation system wasn't going to work. For some reason, that sickening sweet formaldehyde aroma circulated through the cockpit. During the remaining twenty minutes of flight, it took all my concentration to keep from gagging and retching.

After landing, with absolutely no reverence or ceremony due a fallen warrior, I turned the remains over to the waiting CCN delegation, then made a beeline for the Covey barracks. It took three long showers before I felt relatively free of the death smell. Repeated washings of my flight suit never did rid it of the smell. I finally gave up and threw it away.

Because of the constant pressures from daily combat missions, all of us looked for ways to decompress, and one of the best releases was available right in the Muff Divers' Lounge. Every night a group of us gathered to watch and listen to an extraordinarily talented singer and musician, Lieutenant Ollie "Skip" Franklin. An O-2 Covey, Skip kept us entertained and amused with his almost limitless supply of songs. Before joining the Air Force, Skip had been a professional musician, playing and singing backup for several big stars, including the "Killer" himself, Jerry Lee Lewis. When Skip wasn't out flying, he could usually be found in the Muff Divers' Lounge leading us in a singalong or recording his own dual-track renditions of various pop songs or country and western favorites. At the end of one of those recording sessions, Skip was rewinding the finished tape when my Teac tape deck "ate" the last half of his program. Frustrated and angry, Skip slammed his right fist into the door. Two hours later, he walked back in escorted by our favorite nurse, Sherdeane Kinney. Somewhat sheepishly, Skip held up his right hand, gleaming white in its new cast. There would clearly be no more guitar playing for weeks. Several bottles of scotch later, someone remembered that my tape deck had been the culprit, and it was unanimously decided that an execution was in order. With great ceremony, we hauled the tape deck outdoors and handed the M16 to Skip, who put it on full rock and roll, emptying an entire clip into the offending machine. We doubled over with laughter as pieces flew in all directions. The party broke up abruptly when the Air Police arrived, questioning the wisdom and sanity of a bunch of slightly intoxicated pilots firing weapons inside the main compound. The next morning, surveying the results of our firing squad, I had to agree with the Air Police; in the light of day, none of it seemed very funny, especially since I was out four hundred dollars!

By the end of the month, we were well into the training program for Jim Smith's replacement, First Lieutenant Henry Yeackle III. A baby-faced cherub, Henry's good nature and even-keeled outlook masked his aggressive, tenacious approach to flying as a Covey FAC. Because of his appearance, the Coveys had already christened our pilot with one of those inexplicable nicknames destined to stick with him for life. For some reason, Henry reminded us of a cartoon character from one of the Saturday morning cereal commercials. Everybody in the squadron simply referred to him as "Sugar Bear."

Early on the morning of the twenty-eighth, Henry and I got airborne and took a detour into the normal Covey AO to look at a large enemy truck convoy trapped in the open during the preceding night. The sector FAC had wisely directed his fighters against the lead truck and at the tail-end

charlie. Stranded on the face of a cliff with no way to move
around the burning roadblocks at either end of the procession, the helpless enemy trucks sat awaiting their fate.

Since the Trail Coveys rarely flew low and almost never
used their machine guns, I decided the convoy would be
good practice for Henry. With a little coaching from me,
Henry dropped down to an altitude level with the road cut
into the ridge. Only a few days earlier, my front-seater had
been a Trail Covey, cruising over this same sector at three
to four thousand feet.

As we pressed in perpendicular to the line of trucks and
at precisely their level, Henry armed up all four guns. While
he chose an individual target, I reminded him, "Sugar Bear,
to compensate for our forward momentum, keep your tracers impacting on the bottom of the truck. The other four
ball rounds will be hitting a little higher, probably right on
the money. You'll actually be bunting forward with the
stick to keep that sight picture."

Our M-60 machine guns weren't known for their hitting
power and, as Henry opened fire, I wasn't sure what effect
our pop guns would have against a heavy truck. We got
the answer fast. To my surprise, the truck vibrated and
bounced up and down in a pronounced fashion as Sugar
Bear poured long bursts into it. It was clear our 7.62mm
bullets were beating the hell out of that truck. Our target
never did explode à la World War II gun camera films, but
the truck would never run again. Rather than press our luck,
we scooted out of the area with a newfound respect for the
firepower of our OV-10.

That afternoon at Quang Tri, I came to a decision about
something that had been kicking around in my mind for a
couple of weeks. Buffalo's golden puppy had grown pretty
large. He was a good-looking animal as Vietnamese dogs
went, but he still got a cold shoulder from everyone at the
MLT. Now, instead of romping around the compound looking for friends, the little dog would lay off to the side,
chops resting on crossed front paws, watching each pas-
serby with his sad brown eyes. I was convinced the SF

troops didn't realize how they were reacting to a situation that wasn't the puppy's fault. I also knew the treatment was breaking my heart.

Without revealing my motives, I casually asked if they would mind if I took charge of the puppy. I laid it on a little thick, explaining that I wanted to take the dog to Da Nang to be the Covey mascot. They thought it was a great idea.

The next problem was getting our new mascot to Da Nang. I wanted to take him with me in the OV-10, but that squirming bundle of fur inside the cockpit would be more than three handfuls. The SF medic came up with what seemed like a workable solution. While Henry and I held the puppy, the *bac si* grabbed a handful of skin on the back of the dog's neck and injected him with some sort of knockout drug. Within a few minutes, the pup was sound asleep. Next we took gauze and tied the dog's front legs together, then the rear legs together. As a final precaution, we wrapped several layers of gauze around the animal's eyes to form a blindfold. With no small amount of trepidation, we climbed in a jeep and headed for the airfield.

After I strapped in the back seat, Henry and a crew chief lifted the sleeping puppy up and laid him across my lap. As we taxied out, I said to Henry, "Keep it smooth, and no emergencies. In case he starts wiggling around, I'm gonna have to leave the pin in my ejection seat."

Halfway to Da Nang the little beast started coming to. For several moments he became violent as he tried desperately to use his front paws to swipe at the blindfold. All of the movement and banging into the control stick made it tough for Sugar Bear to keep us in level flight. In a last-ditch effort to regain control, I reached out and pulled the blindfold away from the puppy's eyes. As another precaution, I slid it down and tightened the gauze around his mouth in a makeshift muzzle. Right away he settled down, looking around the cockpit curiously. He even stood up in my lap and looked outside. With his legs still tied, he wobbled and lurched badly but would have no part of my attempts to make him lie down. When he started gasping and whimpering, I became concerned he couldn't breathe. Cautiously, I removed the muzzle. Again he settled down, but first rewarded me with a series of wet licks across my face.

Once he could pant and look around, our furry passenger took to flying like a natural. The only other tense moment came when I looked up to see him happily chewing away on one of the fire T-handles. Pulling one of those would have shut the engine down instantly.

Following Henry's smooth landing, we taxied into the de-arming area. Before the crews would go under the aircraft to install safety pins in the guns and rockets, they insisted that pilots hold up both hands to show that nobody was moving switches around on the armament panel, a drill designed for the ground crew's protection. Trying to control the dog's movements, I wasn't able to put my hands up, prompting several angry signals from the de-arming team leader. It was a Mexican standoff, and tempers were getting short. Finally, I lifted the dog above the canopy rails so everyone could see the problem. The crusty old crew chief shook his head in disgust, then waved his troops under the aircraft.

When we had shut down in the revetments, Henry and I began tossing helmets and map bags to the waiting crew chief just like after any other mission. As the young troop walked away with our gear, I yelled to him, "Wait a minute. I got something else." When I handed the wide-awake puppy over the side, the crew chief's eyes bugged right out of his head. From the corner of my eye I saw the line chief get out of his jeep and trot over for a firsthand look at the strange scene. While I climbed down out of the back seat, the line chief stared at me for a few moments, then he announced, "If that dog crapped in that airplane, you're gonna clean it up yourself. And, Sir, I just gotta tell you this. You pilots might be college graduates, but you don't have a lick of common sense." Sugar Bear and I just smiled as we loaded our dog into the jeep for the short ride to Ops.

The puppy took to the Muff Divers' Lounge as if it had

always been his home. There was no end of Coveys to spoil him, and the little rascal seemed deliriously happy, running from one outstretched hand to another. By acclamation we decided to name him Muff. Only a few people ever knew the sad story of Muff's original owner at Quang Tri or how the Covey mascot made the trip to Da Nang. But I felt certain about one thing: Roger "Buffalo" Teeter would have been pleased with the puppy's new home.

The next morning, at 0400 hours on January 29, units of the U.S. Army's First Brigade, Fifth Mechanized Infantry Division pushed out of Dong Ha along Route 9 westward toward Khe Sanh and the Laotian border. They constituted the lead elements of Operation Dewey Canyon II, the last major American combat operation of the war. The objective of the long column of M-48 tanks, M-551 armored reconnaissance assault vehicles, and M-113 armored personnel carriers was to secure Khe Sanh, Lang Vei, and all the real estate up to the Laotian border. Once under U.S. control, the border area around Khe Sanh would become the jumping-off point for a massive, though temporary, ARVN invasion of Laos, code-named Lam Son 719. The ARVN force hoped to push out along Route 9 to Tchepone, with the stated objective of disrupting the whole NVA logistics network flowing down the Ho Chi Minh Trail.

When we heard about the plan, all of the SOG troops and most of the Prairie Fire pilots smiled nervously and began fidgeting. The consensus of opinion was that the ARVN troops were in for a rough time. The SOG teams were the only ones who had any firsthand knowledge about Laos. From personal experience, they suspected the ARVN force was about to walk into a buzz saw.

We figured a sense of humor would help. Since Laos was our stomping ground, we decided to make the Fifth Mech troops feel welcome when they reached Khe Sanh. With two Cobras and my OV-10 providing the cover, we escorted a UH-1 directly to the deserted Khe Sanh airstrip. Under our watchful eyes, the Slick landed in the middle of the old runway. Several figures darted from the chopper to the edge of the strip. Carefully, the two Green Berets planted a large sign in the red dirt. Then they hustled back aboard their chopper for the ride back to MLT-2. For grins, I made a low-level pass the length of the east–west runway, just to savor the effect of the sign. In big letters it said:

WELCOME TO CCN COUNTRY

February

VALLEY OF THE SHADOW OF DEATH

February 1 literally came in with a bang. Around Da Nang things had been relatively quiet, due in all probability to the Tet ceasefire from January 24 through 26. Then, at midnight on the first and again at 2 A.M., the VC lobbed several rockets in, probably to let us know they were still around. They saved the best for last. At 0405, eight deadly 122mm rockets crashed into Da Nang Air Base, lighting up the perimeter like day. We were helpless against the barrage, so to shake off the tension, somebody in the Muff Divers' Lounge passed out the shot glasses, poured the scotch, and offered a toast to combat pay. We sat there quietly, sipping and looking at each other, wondering how bad things would get. Everybody had expected the action to pick up with the onset of the dry season. Maybe the increasingly frequent rocket attacks were telling us something.

Approximately an hour before sunrise on February 8, I took off into the darkness and began a gentle turn to the northwest. The day was destined to be a special one. The night before, CCN had briefed us that the eighth was D-day. A large force of ARVN infantry and armor was scheduled to move out on Operation Lam Son 719, the invasion of Laos. Although MACSOG had no role in the actual assault, their recon teams had performed all preinvasion intel along Route 9. Now I would have the chance to carry the SOG banner, figuratively, on the initial thrust across the border. Somebody must have figured that it might be handy to have a Prairie Fire FAC on the scene.

Lam Son 719 kicked off on schedule at 0700 hours. As

the lead elements prepared to cross into Laos, my Covey rider and I circled over Co Roc, waiting for the Huey Slicks carrying the pathfinder troops of the ARVN First Infantry Division. Our job was to mark the LZs verbally for our helicopter buddies from the 101st Airborne. Since Co Roc was the prominent terrain feature south of Route 9, it made sense to secure the ridge with its commanding view before the armored units pushed west. There were plenty of old heads around who remembered the murderous enemy artillery fire three years earlier when NVA gunners, shooting from the top of Co Roc's steep cliffs, zeroed in on the U.S. Marines at Khe Sanh. A repeat performance against ARVN tank columns in the open would have finished Lam Son 719 before it started.

The first batch of six Hueys checked in with us right on time. As the serpentine procession flew over Co Roc east to west, I dived in from the opposite direction so they could see us as we overflew their LZ. There was no ground fire as we trolled along at treetop height, but there was an anxious moment pulling off the LZ. It took some fast stick-and-rudder work to avoid colliding with several command and control Hueys darting around the area. They seemed to be everywhere.

When Slick Lead confirmed he had a tally on the LZ, I climbed above the traffic to watch the drama unfold. While we circled, chopper after chopper touched down uneventfully, off-loaded its troops, and then flew back for another load. The shuttle continued throughout the morning, lifting ARVN troops to a number of LZs on either side of Route 9. By the end of the day, helicopters from the 101st had carried over six thousand troops into Laos. By contrast, my single mission in support of Lam Son 719 had been tame and insignificant. Still, there was an indescribable sense of satisfaction and pride in being even a small part of a history-making event.

While the ARVN forces fought their way west along Route 9, we inserted several reconnaissance teams roughly twenty klicks to the north to get a feel for how fast the

NVA might try to reinforce the area. We got our answer on February 12. When the ARVN columns closed in on the intersection of routes 9 and 92, they ran into the first sustained heavy fighting of the invasion. Everyone except the SOG teams seemed surprised by how quickly the enemy was able to move in reinforcements. They were also shocked by the toughness of the NVA soldiers and their willingness to stand and fight.

We got our first chance to see big enemy troop concentrations on Valentine's Day. At 1300 I got airborne from Quang Tri for the return trip to Da Nang. Rather than go home by way of the beach as usual, I decided to swing out over the triborder area. As soon as I crossed into Laos, one of our indig teams began yelling for help. Four days earlier, I had inserted the eight-man team on a karst ridge overlooking Route 92 near the North Vietnamese border. On our maps the place was named Ban Chay. I recognized the One-Zero's voice and headed straight to him.

When I arrived overhead, the team leader explained, "They've got us pinned down with mortar and .51-cal fire. There's a company-size force climbing up a draw three hundred meters northwest of us. It should be very prominent from the air. We need some stuff all along that gully."

I had no trouble spotting the little wash he described. But from my altitude of three thousand feet, I couldn't see any movement, only the scrub brush and trees growing along either side. To do the job right, I needed a set of fighters with lots of soft ordnance. When I relayed my request to Hillsboro, the controller had absolutely nothing available. He offered to scramble a flight from one of the Thailand bases, but it would be at least thirty minutes before the cavalry would arrive. Judging from the high pitch in the One-Zero's voice, we didn't have that kind of time.

Arming up the high-explosive rocket pods, I began a fast spiral down to working altitude. From the insert I recalled that the run-in was going to be a little tricky. Another karst ridge just to the north of our team severely limited our maneuvering space. The only low-altitude approach was through the valley between the two ridges. To keep from firing in the team's direction, it was necessary to make each pass from east to west. Directly abeam the team, I would bank sharply left into the karst, pickle off a rocket into the gully, then execute a hard rolling turn back to the west.

After the first few identical passes, the bad guys caught on to the plan. From then on, they threw up everything except the kitchen sink. A pair of 12.7mm machine guns was pouring out the lead. The situation got even hotter when a 37mm gun joined in the fight and began firing flat-trajectory shots at me. The exploding flak bursts at eye level sent the One-Zero into convulsions. He'd never seen anything like that before. He pleaded with me over the radio to "be careful of the big stuff," but I was much more concerned by the machine-gun fire. To counter the 37mm, I dropped to the bottom of the valley floor, doubting that he could shoot down on me. And rather than pull up after each pass, I merely set up a low-level race track by flying one valley farther to the north. Now, on the eastbound leg of each circuit, the intervening ridge protected me from the ground fire.

In between passes, I asked the launch site to send a package for an emergency extraction. With the help of the HE rockets, the team's situation seemed to be improving. They were no longer in contact, and the attacking force was moving back down the gully. We needed to pull our troops while there was a break in the action.

The lull only lasted a few minutes. Pulling off the final rocket pass, I spotted an unnerving sight. On the valley floor, a group of about one hundred enemy troops had fanned out for a dash across the open area between the karst ridges. Our team was obviously their objective. No longer constrained by restrictive run-in headings, I armed up all four M-60s and rolled in west to east. Using a ten-degree dive angle, I fired burst after long burst into the advancing troops. In all, I made four strafing runs before the survivors melted into the vegetation at the base of the karst. As I lined up the target in my gunsight, the view made me think of Pickett's charge across the open ground at Gettysburg.

By the time Larry Hull arrived with the package, I was "Winchester," or out of ammo. On the valley floor, we counted twenty bodies scattered about. Larry called to me, "Hey, 221, you're a real killer. You bagged the limit today!"

Before he could say anything more, I snapped, "Shut up, Larry. Let's worry about getting the team out."

I wasn't actually mad at Larry Hull. Looking down at the scene below, I suddenly felt tired, emotionally drained, and irritable. He clearly didn't mean anything by his comment. It was me. In ten months of combat flying, I had fired a lot of rockets and bullets at the bad guys, but this was my first time to actually see dead bodies as a direct consequence of my actions. The sight of those lifeless forms left me with an unsettling panicky feeling. The mood passed after only a few minutes, but the vivid picture of two of the enemy soldiers sprawled on top of each other lasted for days.

While Larry worked over the area with the set of F-4s I had ordered, I ducked into Quang Tri for a quick rearming. When I returned, any doubts about having the stomach for the job evaporated instantly. Shortly after the fighters left, the enemy launched another charge across the valley. With Larry running the extraction, I concentrated on the new threat. I lost count of the number of strafing passes and only stopped when I ran out of bullets. Between the F-4s, the Cobras, and my OV-10, the team confirmed an additional forty enemy troops KBA—killed by air. One of the SOG team members with a flair for the dramatic dubbed the action "The Saint Valentine's Day Massacre—Laos Chapter."

Two days later, we ran an instant replay on the same ridge. This time, the team was again all indig, and the weather was terrible.

I had the early-morning go to Quang Tri. For some unexplainable reason, I flew straight to the AO instead of swinging by to pick up a Covey rider. Lately, I felt much

more comfortable flying alone than with the new crop of
SF back-seaters. It was nothing personal—they were great
guys—but they weren't Blister or Satan, and the bond just
wasn't there. My thinking on the matter had really become
twisted: I was the old head; nobody had ever done this as
long as I had; the new troops slowed me down; I could
handle the hot situations better and faster alone.

When the One-Zero came up on Fox Mike in his broken
English, I wasn't at all surprised. In fact, I had suspected
the night before that the team would be in trouble by morning. Smiling at his choice of words, I listened to the ARVN
team leader's whining voice: "Cubby, Cubby. This is Papa
Delta. Have very bad situation. Many VC. You bring big
bomb right now."

As a general rule, our ARVN teams had a knack for
overstating the threat. This time, however, I believed him.
Papa Delta was working on top of the same karst ridge from
the action two days before. Because of the invasion, the
place had to be crawling with bad guys.

When I arrived overhead, there was nothing visible below except a solid stratus deck of dingy gray clouds. To
help, I would need to fly below the stuff. Luckily I had
calculated an accurate bearing and distance from Quang
Tri's TACAN during the earlier action, so I had a good
instrument fix on a relatively large valley slightly northwest
of my team. My problem was the three-thousand-foot peaks
jutting up around the valley. If my altitude calculations
were off or if the TACAN signal developed a false lock-
on, I could end up splattering myself and aircraft 831
against jagged limestone karst—the irresistible force meeting the immovable object.

On entering the cloud deck, the cockpit became very
dark. I strained to see the instruments before me while simultaneously peering out the front windscreen for a
glimpse of ground I knew was getting close. The pitot
boom mounted on the Bronco's nose represented the limit
of my forward visibility. Back inside, I fought to hold a
picture on the attitude indicator that would give me a very

shallow rate of descent, between two hundred and three hundred feet per minute on the vertical velocity indicator.

Easing below three thousand feet indicated altitude, I was committed. From here on, I needed luck and patience. Descending the next thousand feet seemed to take forever; losing the final eight hundred feet took an eternity. With sweat dripping into my eyes, it took a moment before the visual cues registered when I finally broke out of the clouds.

The scene in front of me was devoid of color. The valley stretched out slightly to my north, draped in dark shadows, like in a black-and-white film. Two hundred feet directly below me, patches of fog clung to the karst and trees. I made a mental note to add another two miles to my TACAN DME reading.

After a quick swig of water, I pointed the Bronco eastward down the familiar little valley. As I approached the team's position on the east end of the ridge, the One-Zero kept moaning, "Cubby, bring big bomb right now."

Contemptuously, I thought to myself: What a doofus. He must realize fighters can't work below all this crud. Then, as if he were reading my mind, the indig team leader played me like a Stradivarius. He cooed, "Cubbies always help us. We need big bomb—now!"

The karst ridge sloped gradually up from west to east, reaching a height of about eighteen hundred feet on my altimeter. On the north face, the steep cliffs gave way to a flat valley four hundred feet below. The Saint Valentine's Day Massacre had occurred on the center section of the ridge, directly opposite another karst, but this team would be easier to support. The northern ridge abruptly ended a mile to the west, leaving me a clean run-in to the target.

After the team marked their position with an orange panel, I went to work. The One-Zero reported a company of NVA regulars moving against him in a pincer movement. While one group climbed the karst directly below him, the other one was angling in from the west. Since the climbers were closest, I went after them first.

Flying due south at three hundred feet, I zeroed in on the ridge directly in front of me. At approximately fifteen-hundred-feet slant range, I put the pipper on some heavy brush one hundred feet below my team and opened up with all four machine guns. I held the trigger down until the last possible second, then jinked up and over the ridge. For several seconds I inadvertently slipped into the base of the clouds hanging only a few hundred feet above the crest. I had to maneuver for several minutes to get back in position for another strafing run.

After my third or fourth pass, the bad guys began returning fire with a vengeance. Small-arms fire chattered away from the western attack force. With each jink up to miss the ridge looming in front of me, a trio of 12.7mm machine guns located south of the team got in on the act, spraying tracers and smoke all over the dark morning sky. The One-Zero, in a genuine show of concern, dropped his monotonous chant about big bombs and replaced it with a warning. On each pass he'd yell, "Cubby, you be careful. Many VC shoot at you. Please be careful."

In an effort to extract more precise information, I responded, "Papa Delta, tell me exactly where the fire is coming from."

Without missing a beat, the voice replied, "Everywhere! Everywhere!"

Several minutes later, I had fired off all two thousand rounds of 7.62. I quickly adjusted the mil setting on my gunsight and switched over to rockets, a move that proved to be a costly mistake. Taking aim on a pocket of troops one hundred meters west and just below the team, I fired a pair of marking rockets into the side of the karst. When I completed the 360-degree circuit for a second pass, I was horrified to see the brush on top of the ridge burning fiercely, apparently ignited by my rockets. Even more disturbing, the light westerly wind pushed the flames toward the team. As the fire grew, I couldn't believe the mess I had created. The team had no choice but to start moving to the east. Once they reached the end of the karst, only five hundred meters away, there was no place to go but straight down.

First in pairs, then singly, I fired all my remaining HE and willie pete rockets into the bad guys to the west, hoping to slow if not disrupt their movement. When I was Winchester, I threw in a couple of dry runs to keep everyone's head down—and as a necessary penance for my own stupidity. Then, trying to sound as confident as possible, I told the team the fire would keep the NVA away long enough for me to rearm and return with the rescue helicopters. The One-Zero acknowledged calmly and asked me to hurry. Climbing back through the clouds, I felt sick about leaving the team in such a jam. Cobbing the power, I coaxed the Bronco back to Quang Tri as fast as she would fly.

The Barky crew chiefs refueled and rearmed my OV-10 in a blur of churning legs, bending arms, and sweaty bodies. In record time Sergeant First Class Jim Parry and I were back in the air and across the fence. It was a relief to have a partner. Although Parry was new to the business, he possessed the natural instincts of the best, Marty Martin. Jim had a more rugged-looking face and a quieter demeanor than Satan, but he was hard-core Green Beret and a welcome addition to the depleted Covey rider ranks.

En route to the battle, two Cobras and three Slicks joined us. As we flew over the solid cloud deck below, I was really scared wondering about the team's situation. I hoped we could get to them before the fire or the bad guys did.

At the adjusted TACAN let-down point, I turned my navigation lights on full bright. Leaving the Slicks in the holding pattern, I had the Cobras tuck in as close to my wing tips as possible. Since they weren't trained instrument pilots, my OV-10 was about to become their total frame of reference. Slowly at first, with careful, deliberate stick movements, I eased the strange formation into the weather. Through the colorless mist I could just make out the two helicopters with their pilots watching me intently, mirroring every move of the Bronco. By the end of the first racetrack pattern, the bouncing had stopped and everyone settled down into a smooth, functioning unit.

Three thousand feet and five minutes later, we coasted out of the dreary soup and into the clear. This time we ended up on the north side of the valley. Once everyone had his bearings, I poured on the coals and told the Cobras to follow me.

As we approached the target area, Jim Parry began calling the team on Fox Mike while I searched for the fire. For the life of me, I couldn't see anything burning. For one brief, heart-stopping second, I thought I was lost. Then a heavily accented voice brought a big smile to my face. In broken English, the One-Zero picked up where he had left off. It was a relief to hear his familiar refrain, "Cubby, Cubby. Very bad situation. You bring big bomb right now."

Miraculously the fire had apparently burned itself out in the wet brush, with only a 150-meter stretch of scorched ground to mark its passing. Taking advantage of the burned-off area, the cagey One-Zero dug his team in with weapons pointed in that direction, ready to cut down any fool who might try to cross the open ground.

While we circled, my back-seater digested the tactical situation as explained by Papa Delta. From what Jim could piece together, the determined enemy troops were below the crest, working their way east along the steep sides of the karst. The closest bunch was on a ledge only thirty-five meters from the team. The bad guys were in no position to fire, but they kept climbing.

The first order of business was to mark some targets and put the Cobras to work. Not wanting to take a chance on starting another fire with the willie petes, I shot several HE rockets into the ledge. It felt like old home week as we jinked up and over the ridge, greeted by familiar volleys of fire from the 12.7mm positions. As I banked us hard to the left, Jim Parry spotted one of the machine-gun pits. He didn't exactly suggest we go after it, but we both knew that gun would cut our Hueys to pieces as they hovered to pick up the team. With Jim directing, I snapped us into a turn back to the right. In what amounted to a sneak attack, we maneuvered well to the south before heading north toward the gun. I positioned us right at the base of the clouds, two hundred feet above the terrain. As a diversion, Cobra Lead began the attack on the ledge.

We were on top of the gun so fast that it surprised me. There was almost no time to aim and fire. I pressed the red pickle button on the control stick twice, sending two high-explosive rockets with ten-pound warheads streaking toward the pit. The startled three-man crew had just begun swinging their weapon in our direction when they disappeared in an explosion of gray smoke and flying brown dirt.

While the Cobras worked over the karst, I pointed the Bronco's nose up for the three-thousand-foot climb through the weather to our orbiting Slicks. Breaking out into the blue sky and bright sunshine, we spotted the Hueys several miles farther east. As I flew toward them, the warm sun streaming into the cockpit seemed to sap the strength right out of me. I dreaded going back down into that repulsive weather, so cleverly hiding the mountain peaks, karst rock formations, and enemy fire. Inexplicably, I thought about the Prairie Fire business cards most of us carried. The front of each card included the particular pilot's name, rank, call sign, and a series of gag boasts: casual war hero, world traveler, philanthropist, hero of the oppressed. On the back of my cards, there was a short spoof of the Twenty-third Psalm:

> *Yea, though I fly through the valley of the shadow of*
> *death,*
> *I shall fear no evil,*
> *For I am the meanest son of a bitch in the valley*

It had been my choice to make that bit of biblical verse part of my Prairie Fire image. Now it was time to live up to the boastful arrogance. For the third time in four hours, I throttled back for the let-down. With the third Slick remaining on top in reserve and the other two invisibly linked

278 DA NANG DIARY

to my aircraft, we slid into the waiting cloud deck. Throughout the descent I kept wondering if fate had or- dained the fight in the valley below to fulfill the prophecy on the back of my cards.

The Slick pilots hung in there beautifully. With my land- ing gear and flaps down, our speeds matched perfectly. We were in passable fingertip formation when we finally glided out of the clouds and into the valley of the shadow of death.

In our absence the Cobras had done a great job of beat- ing up the area. Following a brief conversation with the team and the Cobras, we knew it was time to go for the extraction. Our problem would be lack of air space for ma- neuvering. During most extractions we had the luxury of operating in all three dimensions. On this one the low cloud ceilings compressed us into two dimensions, with virtually no use of the vertical. Studying the situation, I could see there wasn't going to be room in the small valley for two Cobras, two Hueys, and one OV-10, all maneuvering to- ward the same spot on top of the karst ridge.

With a certain amount of guilt, I sent the package in for the pickup while Jim and I moved roughly one klick to the north to watch. I should have never given the decision a second thought. As the Slicks started their runs to the make- shift LZ with the Cobras providing covering fire, Jim and I got caught up in our own private little war. From one of the mountains immediately to our west, a pair of 23mm guns opened up on us. Although their fire was flat trajectory at maximum range, the exploding flak appeared more frightening than normal. With the surrounding ridges and the ragged ceiling of clouds only a few hundred feet above us, I felt trapped, hemmed in. No matter which way we jinked, the nasty little white airbursts followed us. In a fit of desperation, I yelled to Jim, "How 'bout singing a verse of 'The Ballad of the Green Beret.' "

Probably thinking I had lost my mind, Jim shouted back, "What on earth are you talking about?" A new Covey rider, he evidently didn't know the story of Satan's famous ren- ditions of the song.

Humming the melody softly to myself, I racked us into a vision-tunneling high-G diving turn to the west. As we scooted down the valley away from our team, all I could think about was getting the northern karst between us and the guns. For the first time in what seemed like an eternity, I heard the radio chatter between the team and the choppers. Slick Lead was in a hover about to pull half the eight-man team. Several anxious moments followed before he called, "Lead's off and heading north to your position, Covey."

The thought of the two 23mm guns blasting the unsuspecting choppers sent shivers down my spine. As I screamed a terrified "NO!" into my boom mike, a 37mm drew a bead on us and hosed away, probably the same rascal who had tried it two days earlier. Jim held his breath as I executed a chandelle up into the clouds, the only way I could see to get us going the other way in a hurry. At the top I kicked in some bottom rudder, crossed my fingers, then zoomed back down on a reciprocal heading. If we hit one of the karsts in a steep dive, I reasoned, we would never feel a thing.

In a stroke of luck, we came out of the clouds at about the same place we entered. Seconds after we reappeared, the gray airbursts strung out behind us. For the first time I found the voice to talk to the Slicks. Moving at full speed due east down the floor of the valley, I advised the Hueys, "Whatever you do, don't move to the north. A couple of 23s sitting up there will have your lunch. Set up a tight orbit where I dropped you off, and keep it very low."

Pulling off the LZ with the rest of the team, Slick Two picked up a few B-40 grenade fragments and some AK-47 rounds in the belly, but nobody was hurt and the bird was flyable. Jim and I dived in behind them, firing an entire pod of HE rockets into enemy positions on the karst.

With the big guns to our north and fire still coming our way from the ridge, there was no time or room to form the package up for an instrument climb back through the weather. Instead, I gave the Cobras a heading to climb on while I safed up my switches and joined up with the damaged Slicks. Once again with gear and flaps hanging, I led the Hueys into the soup and to the salvation waiting for us on top. When we broke into the clear at five thousand feet, the sun directly overhead had never looked so good.

I never did find the Cobras, who apparently had rendezvoused with the spare Slick and were well on the way back to Quang Tri. We could hear them talking, though. I had to smile when the Slick asked, "How was it down there?"

One of the Cobras answered, "No sweat. This was an easy one."

The following day, the Prairie Fire action shifted south from the valley of the shadow of death to a new and equally deadly location, the A Shau Valley. Launching out of MLT-1 at Phu Bai, we inserted two teams, one on each wall of the A Shau. Each RT had an identical mission. The small teams had the impossible task of setting up surveillance and roadblocks against NVA units attempting to move north against Lam Son 719.

The first real trouble began late on the afternoon of February 18. The area was infested with the usual LZ watchers and tracker teams, but the NVA had also moved at least ten counterrecon companies into the area, a fair indication of the importance the North Vietnamese placed on trying stop SOG teams. Unfortunately, RT Intruder on the west wall made contact with part of that large enemy force. Faced with insurmountable odds, surrounded and unable to move through the dense jungle underbrush growing on the steep slope of the ridge, the One-Zero, Captain Ronald "Doc" Watson, had no choice but to call for an extraction. With a Ph.D. in history from the University of California at Berkeley, Doc Watson was checking out as a One-Zero in order to get a feel for SOG missions so he could write a book on the subject. His One-One was Sergeant Allen "Little Jesus" Lloyd, and the evaluator on the mission was Sammy Hernandez, fresh off his HALO mission. When the package arrived on the scene, it was clear to everyone that the team could never make it to the nearest LZ. The decision was made to pull the indig team members out on strings. A second UH-1 arrived with a ladder to extract the three Americans. With Larry Hull running the extract, I arrived on station to provide extra firepower. While the Slick moved into position to pick up the remaining SF troops, Larry asked me to beat up the high ground to the west with HE rockets. In a truly remarkable display of bravery, the Huey went into a stationary hover while the team scurried to climb up the flimsy ladder dangling just a few feet from the ground. The intense ground fire coming from all directions proved to be more than even the agile Cobras could handle. Riddled with bullets, the hovering Huey lurched forward in a drunken fashion, inadvertently snagging the ladder, along with the three clinging team members, in the tops of the trees. Acting like an unbreakable leash on a straining dog, the tangled ladder jerked the chopper up short, sending it plunging nose first into the dense jungle. At first contact, the rotor blades sprayed branches and wood chips in all directions. Then the UH-1 evaporated in a huge orange fireball right on the Laotian–Vietnamese border.

At that point Larry sent the rest of the package back to Phu Bai due to low fuel, while we trolled the treetops searching for survivors. Tired and disgusted after taking five AK rounds somewhere in the bottom of my aircraft, I finally went home when the cockpit floor began filling up with hydraulic fluid and smoke. Larry Hull remained on station until dark, shooting off all his remaining willie petes and HE rockets at the sporadic ground fire still coming from the ridge. For all his trouble, he caught a few AK-47 rounds in the passenger door. It was a miracle that his Covey rider in the right seat, Sergeant First Class Bill Fernandez, wasn't even scratched.

That night in the Muff Divers' Lounge sleep was hard to come by. My mind reeled from the day's events. There had been more U.S. troops killed on this one mission than on any other one we had ever run. From the team we had lost Doc Watson, Little Jesus, and Sammy Hernandez. George Berg, Gerry Woods, Gary Johnson, and Walt Dem-

sey were missing on the downed Huey. Stretched out on
my bunk in the dark, I felt like I was about to come out of
my skin; the guilt and grief were overpowering. I kept
thinking to myself, "If I got those fine men killed, then I
deserve to burn in hell for all eternity."

At dawn the next morning I landed at Phu Bai to pick
up one of the new Covey riders. We headed directly to the
crash site and began a slow low-altitude search on the outside chance one of our troops might still be alive. As the
sun rose above the hills on the east wall of the A Shau, I
picked up what looked like a mirror flash a hundred meters
down the slope from the crash. On our second pass at treetop height, a lone figure stepped out of the shadows and
waved to us. I rocked the wings to let him know we had a
tally on him, then we got on the horn to put the wheels of
the rescue in motion.

An hour later a helicopter package rendezvoused with
us in the middle of the A Shau. Since I couldn't be sure
there weren't other survivors wandering around the area, I
gave strict orders to the Cobras and the Slick door gunners.
The only permissible use of guns was to return fire for fire.
There would be no LZ prepping and no suppressing fire.

Under the circumstances all of us were extremely nervous as Slick Lead inched over the spot I had verbally
marked, then dropped his ladder. Fighting the heavy rotor
wash, our survivor limped out of his hiding place and
climbed onto the swaying contraption. Working his cyclic
to perfection, the Huey pilot carefully lifted his precious
cargo up and clear of the trees before transitioning into
forward flight. We flew alongside the incredibly lucky
Sammy Hernandez all the way back to Phu Bai.

At midmorning I launched on my third sortie of the day,
this time escorting RT Habu, a Bright Light team whose
mission was to recover the bodies of our comrades. Commanded by the incomparable Cliff Newman, and assisted
by a true SOG legend, Sergeant Major Billy Waugh, RT
Habu was inserted several klicks away from the crashed
Huey, but it was the best we could do. We managed to get

the Bright Light team in without a hitch, although a heavy machine-gun position did take a few pot shots at us.

At noon Larry Hull relieved me. As I headed in to land at Phu Bai, I cautioned him, "Larry, the Bright Light has a hell of a long way to go. My guess is they'll need lots of air support as they move. Be on the lookout for a 14.5mm gun somewhere on the ridge just above the team. He could give your choppers problems."

I was refueled and halfway to Da Nang when the call came in from the MLT. The Bright Light team relayed that Woodstock's O-2 had been blasted by the 14.5mm and had spun in several miles northwest of them. At the moment there were no emergency radio beepers to indicate survivors.

The crash site sat on top of the west rim of the A Shau, just inside Laos. The Bright Light team had been correct. From the air the plane appeared to be still intact, so it must have come down in some kind of crash landing. As I circled over the small meadow with its grisly new centerpiece, I felt dazed and, for the first time, demoralized. I simply wanted to fly back to Da Nang, crawl into my bunk, and sleep out the remainder of my tour. I had finally had enough.

Reluctantly, I stood by while the MLT put together a second Bright Light team. When the choppers finally arrived late that afternoon, I led them to the scene and covered them while they inserted the team next to the O-2. On the ground the twelve-man team found the damage to be much more extensive than we could see from above. With a great deal of difficulty, they managed to remove and recover Bill Fernandez's body. But no matter how hard they tried, they couldn't get Larry's body out of the twisted wreckage. As it began to get dark, we called off the effort and headed home, leaving Woodstock still sitting at the controls of his Oscar Deuce.

At first light on the twentieth, I banked my OV-10 out of the Da Nang traffic pattern. Following the beach north, I spotted a large school of sharks gliding effortlessly through the clear, blue water just off the cost of Monkey Mountain, an eighteen-hundred-foot peak covered with sophisticated radar antennas. In an uncharacteristic move I couldn't even explain to myself, I charged up the M-60s and attacked the unoffending creatures for no other reason than blood lust. As the hail of bullets churned the water's surface, the sharks darted off in all directions, apparently frightened but unharmed by the fusillade. For a few terrible seconds, I trembled in wild rage, infuriated that I had missed, that the sharks had escaped. I slammed the stick first right, then left, trying to line up one of the despicable monsters in my gunsight. Overcome with frustration, I finally gave up. As fast as it had possessed me, the fight drained out of me. I slumped back in the seat, gasping for breath.

Perhaps out of intuition or perhaps out of embarrassment, I realized I was in no mood to deal with a Covey rider. Disregarding a recent promise I had made to myself—never to fly without an SF alter ego in the back seat—I pressed into the A Shau Valley solo.

As I flew overhead, all was relatively quiet for the team on the east wall. On the west wall, it was a different story. RT Habu was still bogged down in the heavy brush just short of the helicopter crash site. Cliff Newman asked for an air strike against a concentration of enemy troops to his southwest. For the past two hours, his team had been taking a beating from an 82mm mortar. The tube represented more of a nuisance than a threat, but the One-Zero's voice sounded like I felt. He wanted to get even. After plotting out the coordinates, I gave a halfhearted call to Hillsboro, figuring all tactical air would be tied up supporting the ARVN troops fighting for their lives along Highway 9. Much to my surprise, Hillsboro sent a flight of F-4s directly to my location. My spirits picked up considerably.

The sight of the first string of Mark-82s exploding against the west wall had a cathartic effect on me. The jumpiness, the anger seemed to melt. My perspective balanced out when the bad guys fired a few feeble tracers at the fighters. In response, the Phantoms kept pressing in, dropping their loads wherever I directed. The blast patterns looked great, probably because each bomb sported a Daisy Cutter, a three- to four-foot-long fuse extender protruding from the nose. Instead of burrowing into the dirt, the five-hundred-pounders detonated when the Daisy Cutter contacted the ground, lethally blasting the surrounding jungle. With each explosion I could hear the Bright Light team cheering us on over the radio.

Shortly after the air strike, my attention shifted to inside the cockpit. The fuel quantity indicator registered a little low, considering I had the external transfer switch turned on. If working properly, the transfer pump in the external fuel transfer line should have been pumping 845 pounds of JP-4 per hour from the 230-gallon centerline tank into my main wing tanks. I cycled the switch on and off several times, then watched the gauge for any sign of filling. Nothing. As a last resort, I pumped the stick forward and aft rapidly in order to porpoise the aircraft, hoping the sloshing fuel would begin feeding. That didn't work either. I decided to give it a rest for a few minutes, hoping the half-full centerline tank would fix itself.

Before I had time to troubleshoot the problem any further, a scream over the radio made the hair on the back of my neck stand straight up. At full volume the voice screeched, "Prairie Fire! Prairie Fire! We're in heavy contact. We need an emergency extract right now!"

I recognized the voice as that of Captain Jim Butler, the One-Zero of RT Python. Jim was highly experienced and one of the best team leaders around. We had worked together before on several hot ones, and I knew that if Butler was that agitated, his situation must really be bad. I rolled into a steep bank and struck out across the A Shau Valley for the east wall. Until that moment all my attention had been focused on the other side of the valley.

The fourteen-man team was located on top of a bald, dusty hill once known as Fire Base Thor. A few of the old sandbag walls were still visible around the summit. Over the past three days, Jim and his crew of two Green Berets and eleven indig had been fighting a running battle against determined NVA probes aimed at the tiny fortress. So far, RT Python had been holding its own. As a sign of their defiance, the team had run an American flag up a long pole for the whole world to see—and the bad guys to aim at. While fending off the round-the-clock attacks, several of the team had been wounded. Jim probably should have called for extraction earlier, but he knew we had our hands full across the valley. Like the pro he was, he gutted it out.

Once I reached his position, Jim broadsided me with a torrent of excited, jumbled words. I couldn't make any sense of them and the pitch of his voice actually scared me. Meaning no disrespect to a soldier I deeply admired, I shouted back at him, "Dammit, Jim, get hold of yourself. Stop feeding me this stream of consciousness crap. I can't help you unless you settle down and tell me slowly and clearly exactly what the problem is."

After a few deep breaths, the feisty team leader regained his cool. In measured tones he explained that his team was up against a massive attack in force. The lead enemy elements were already on the northwest perimeter, about to spill over the top. He said prophetically, "We can't hold 'em much longer. Get us out of here."

Arming up the HE rocket pods, I spiraled down to the base of the hill. Sure enough, a pocket of enemy troops sat huddled against the outside sandbag fortification. Every few seconds, several more raced out of the brush at the base of the hill and scampered twenty or thirty yards up the slope to join their buddies.

I yelled to the One-Zero, "Get your heads down. I'm gonna put it in close along the western perimeter." Diving in from the north at a shallow angle, I let the pipper drift up to the crouching figures before I squeezed off a pair of rockets. Pulling up in a hard rolling turn to the west, I couldn't see the impact. I asked Jim, "How was that?"

Laughing, he shouted, "You're blowing dirt and rocks all over us. It's great. Keep it coming."

I made one more pass before backing off. The enemy troops were climbing the hill faster than the team or my rockets could mow them down. What we needed was some big-time help. Switching to emergency transmit, I bypassed Hillsboro with a call to anyone listening: "This is Covey 221, transmitting in the blind on Guard. I've got troops in contact in the A Shau. Any fighter aircraft with soft ordnance, give me a call."

As if in answer to a prayer, a two-ship of A-1s en route from NKP to Da Nang came to the rescue. Within ten minutes I had the Spads dropping napalm canisters on the hiding troops at the base of the hill. Then we worked over the slopes with CBU-25 and strafe. I marveled at how accurately the big prop-driven machines could lay down the ordnance. When we got back to Da Nang, I planned to buy the two Spad pilots all the beer they could drink. Just as the A-1s departed, however, I found myself on the receiving end of the NVA's retaliation.

I was just pulling out of a low-level strafing pass when an RPG-2 slammed into the bottom of my aircraft, the projectile piercing the fuselage and exploding directly under the front cockpit with a tremendous wallop. Some of the shrapnel penetrated my ejection seat and survival kit, embedding itself in my buttocks and the back of my thighs. Although the circumstances were completely different, this was the second time the ejection seat had saved my life.

Once I determined that the aircraft was still flyable and that I could still function, I called MLT-1 to get a package moving in our direction. The young MLT commander, Captain Robert Leong, had been monitoring my conversations with RT Python, so he knew they were in a world of hurt. Unfortunately, Bob relayed that all the 101st helicopters were committed to one of the big Lam Son battles. Cobra support was out of the question; however, he had managed to scrounge up two Slicks, if I wanted to take a chance on committing them with no covering fire. As I saw it, we had no choice. I told him to launch the fleet.

As the One-Zero's shouts alerted me to another pending

disaster, I couldn't help thinking about the old cliché: When
it rains, it pours. Butler was beside himself. The bad guys
were attacking the opposite end of the fort with infantry
and a barrage of B-40 rockets. One of the explosions had
blown an indig down the slope of the hill into the advancing
troops. The One-One, Staff Sergeant Leslie Chapman,
climbed over the barricade and ran down the hill to retrieve
his unconscious comrade. Before I could get in position to
help, Chapman had killed four NVA soldiers at point-blank
range. Then he threw the injured trooper on his back and
started up the steep slope.

I reefed the Bronco around for a west to east run-in. At
one hundred yards, I aimed at Chapman's heels and pulled
the trigger. The left-hand sponson belched out a twin stream
of tracers into the bare ground slightly behind the struggling
American. As the red dust and smoke swirled around, I let
the bullets walk into a row of bushes. Several figures
pitched over into contorted heaps. Zooming straight up to
stay in tight, I sucked in my breath when several grenade
blasts knocked Sergeant Chapman to the ground. By the
time I had fired a second long burst, he was on his feet and
climbing. At the top of the hill, RT Python blasted the
hillside with deadly covering fire. I broke off the run when
the dust became so bad that I could no longer see anything.
Butler had to tell me when Chapman finally staggered back
into the RT's small defensive perimeter.

I had aged at least ten years by the time the two Hueys
checked in on my frequency. In addition to the battle raging
below, a serious problem in the cockpit had me worried.
The fuel-low caution light had been glowing a bright yellow for some time, indicating something less than 220
pounds of gas remaining. With all the low-altitude rocket
and strafing passes, I was burning up the juice at a wicked
rate. I cursed the centerline tank for picking such a critical
time to act up. Fortunately, the runway at Phu Bai was only
thirty miles away.

Quickly briefing the orbiting Slicks, I tried to give them
an accurate picture of what they were up against. Dug in

around the old firebase, an estimated 350 enemy troops would be aiming their weapons at the helicopters. Except for the door gunners, my Bronco was the only other covering fire available. To complicate things even more, each Slick would have to lift out seven team members, a heavy load under ideal conditions. When I finished talking, the Huey pilots didn't show the slightest signs of apprehension or hesitation. Using my own trademark phrase, Slick Lead said simply, "Let's do it."

We decided to make the run from the southwest, the corridor where I had taken the lightest ground fire. With the team laying down their maximum rate of fire, we started down the chute. I concentrated my smoke rockets in the southern quadrant while the door gunner fired his M-60 along the steep slope. Crossing the hilltop perimeter, the Huey shook violently from the blasts of several RPG explosions, but the pilot held on and touched down in a blinding cloud of red dust. After an agonizingly long wait, Lead lifted off. To cover his escape, I laid down a wall of strafe from one end of the eastern slope to the other, then racked my bird into a high-G climbing turn to the west to link up with Slick Two.

In formation, we ran a carbon copy of the original effort. I fired off all my remaining rockets and added a few bursts from the guns as Two slid into the LZ. When he finally lifted off, I roared in from the south, finger on the trigger. A second later the M-60s went dead. My effort as a fighter pilot was over. The helicopter, unfortunately, paid the price. Unopposed, the bad guys riddled Slick Two from stem to stern. Somehow, the courageous crew kept their chopper flying.

Heading eastbound with my little flock, I was ecstatic. We had done it. I wasn't sure how, but we had pulled it off. Out of habit, I asked each Slick to confirm a head count on the team. Slick Lead reported seven aboard. I literally felt faint when Two reported six. A recount turned up the same numbers. We were missing a man.

Although Slick Two had the short load, the battered UH-

1 was in no condition to make a second run into the LZ. Without being asked, Slick Lead executed a 180-degree turn and followed me back to the A Shau.

The pucker factor forced a lump in my throat. The needle on my fuel gauge bounced around the bottom gradation, the one-hundred-pound mark. Frightened and exhausted, I started to turn around and make a run for Phu Bai with what little fuel I had left. Then I looked down at the LZ and saw a solitary figure stand up, pop a quick hand salute, and dive back into a foxhole. Our boy was down there alone, still fighting. He deserved something better than a cowardly FAC leaving him to his fate.

As Slick Lead set up for his approach, I dived in on a simulated strafing pass, hoping the ploy would make a few of the bad guys duck. When Lead was ready, I rolled in to support him, only this time I had a surprise for the waiting enemy troops. Taking aim at a couple of machine gun positions near the base of the hill, I placed the rocket pod toggle switches on the armament panel to the drop position. At fifty feet, just like in the low-angle event on the scorable range at Hurlburt, I hit the pickle button, sending the four LAU-59 pods tumbling end over end into the red dirt. The odds were against my hitting anything, but the feeble effort made me feel like I was contributing.

While Slick Lead hovered a few inches off the ground, our boy dived in the left troop door. As the Huey struggled into the air, I came in on the deck from the south, saving the best for last. Moving the number three station toggle switch to drop, I ducked under the Huey and pickled off the half-full centerline tank. It had come in handy after all.

We climbed away from the bald hilltop and the A Shau on a straight line for Phu Bai. Although shot full of holes, both Slicks reported they could make it home. Lead did pass along the sad news that the indig soldier rescued by Sergeant Chapman had died.

I had the runway in sight and three thousand feet of altitude before the red fuel feed warning light blinked on, indicating roughly fifty pounds of fuel left to make a safe landing. There was no time to set up for a flame-out pattern, so I entered on a high base leg, slipped off the excess altitude in a steep final turn, threw the gear down, and pranged the Bronco onto the concrete—with a huge sigh of relief. Once clear of the runway, I watched in a drunken stupor as a jeep pulled up with the de-arming crew. Before they could crawl out, both engines flamed out. Looking at the damage to my aircraft, one of the crew chiefs kept muttering, "Jesus, Jesus." When he helped me out of the cockpit and saw all the blood, he moaned, "Triple Jesus. I think I'm gonna puke!"

Face down on an examination table inside the MASH, I lay stark naked except for a green sheet draped across my buttocks. A young Army captain nurse who reminded me of the singer Connie Francis was evidently assigned to take care of me. The disconcerting part was that every few minutes she appeared with another female nurse, and much to my embarrassment, Nurse Connie would lift my sheet and proceed to give the new visitor a medical tour of my backside. Evidently the concern wasn't about the shards of metal and fiberglass that had already been removed from my buttocks and thighs. Instead, each nurse seemed to take great delight in probing around with tweezers and a magnifying glass, searching for cloth threads from my shredded underwear or flight suit that might cause infection in the series of small cuts.

When Nurse Connie showed up with yet another buddy, I finally said somewhat irritably, "Why don't you go round up the whole shift, bring them in all at once, and let's get this over with."

Connie's sidekick, a beautiful, willowy, blonde first lieutenant, snapped back, "Oh shut up and stop complaining. You pilots are such babies."

Before I could respond, Connie started in on me. "You know," she said, while still working me over with the tweezers, "you're sort of a celebrity around here. You're the first Air Force pilot we've ever treated." Then, out of what I regarded as pure meanness, she added, "Did you know you came within about an inch of being a soprano?"

Then Lieutenant Blondie chimed in. "Yeah, it's also the

first time we've seen a hotshot flyboy with his ass shot off.
You're lucky we're not charging admission." With that sarcastic observation, she began to wash me down with some
kind of diabolic solution that stung so bad it made me see
stars; it hurt a lot worse than the original wounds. Finally
she tossed me a pair of pajamas and said, "Okay, flyboy.
Put these on, then I'll walk you down to the ward."

The next day Nurse Connie gave me a very painful tet-
anus shot, an Army flight suit, and a rubber inflatable
doughnut to sit on. When I asked one of the doctors about
flying, he just shrugged and said, "That's up to you. If
you're not too tender, have at it." With that they sent me
out the door and back to work. Instinctively, I knew the
Air Force flight surgeons would ground me, but for the
moment, the Army doctors had indirectly blessed my plan
to continue flying.

During my short stay as a guest at the Phu Bai hospital,
several of the Coveys managed to pull RT Habu out of the
A Shau. Cliff Newman and his team actually located the
bodies of Doc Watson and Allen Lloyd, but when a reinforced NVA company attacked, they were forced to leave
the bodies and jump off a cliff to escape. In the daring
firefight, half the team was wounded. The heartbreaking
part of the story was that for months the enemy left Watson's and Lloyd's body bags in a clearing, hoping SOG
would take the bait and try to retrieve their friends. The
bodies were never recovered.*

Since my squadron was unaware that I had been injured,
they obligingly had two Coveys ferry a spare OV-10 to Phu
Bai. On the morning of February 23, I gingerly positioned
myself on the rubber doughnut and blasted off for the return
flight to Da Nang, but instead of heading straight home, I
broke my promise again by flying solo into the A Shau
Valley. In the early morning light, forward visibility was

---

*Although teams from Joint Task Force Full Accounting have
searched the area extensively, the UH-1 wreckage containing the bodies of George Berg, Gerry Woods, Gary Johnson, and Walt Demsey
has never been located.

extremely limited because of smoke and haze. In an age-old practice, the local farmers were busy burning off their rice fields and reclaiming the intruding jungle by use of the torch. In the still air, the gray smoke hung in thick layers, easily matching the worst smoggy day in the Los Angeles basin.

I was inexorably drawn to the little meadow on the west wall of the valley. Sitting there peacefully, Larry's O-2 was just visible through the veil of haze. Dropping down lower for one last look, I froze on the control stick when four or five shapes ran out from under the left wing. As I circled a few feet above their heads, the green clad soldiers disappeared into the tall elephant grass. Outraged at the thought of what the enemy soldiers might be up to, I fired a couple of HE rockets into the tall grass with no apparent effect. I had never felt so angry and out of control in my life. My hands shook, just as in the shark attack episode a few days earlier. It seemed like years ago.

When I asked for air from Hillsboro, the controller hedged on me, obviously lukewarm about the idea of diverting badly needed fighters to such a strange mission. When he wouldn't commit, I signed off with a rude "Screw you bastards."

The MLT at Phu Bai was more accommodating. The SOG troops still had a special feeling for Woodstock, so without demanding any explanation, Bob Leong sent me two Cobras. In the thick haze, the rendezvous was tough; it took us twenty minutes to find each other. Once we joined up, I led the gunships to the meadow.

Buzzing over the crash, I was horrified to see that NVA troops were once again milling around the O-2. At the top of my voice, I screamed into the radio, "Those sadistic little bastards are back!"

When I attempted to give the Cobras a verbal mark, they lost sight of me in the haze. We tried it twice more, with the same result. In frustration I armed up the willie petes and rolled in. My intention was to put a smoke down near the O-2. When the bad guys ran, I would direct the Cobras using the white smoke for reference.

Either my shot was lousy or my subconscious took over. The willie pete roared out of the tube and streaked down

to the target, impacting in the center of the right wing on
the Oscar Deuce. In a matter of seconds the fuel blew up,
engulfing the airplane in a ball of orange flame. As the
plane burned, black smoke swirled straight up, mixing with
the already dirty air.

Nobody said a word as we watched the strange funeral
pyre below. After five minutes of circling, one of the Cobras broke the strained silence. "We're gonna head on
home, Covey." Then in a hushed tone he added, "Sorry
about your friend, but it's better this way. Shake it off and
come on back with us." I couldn't trust myself to talk.
Clicking the mike button twice, I moved the control stick
mechanically through an aileron roll over Woodstock's final resting place, then pointed the Bronco toward Da Nang.

On short final to Runway 17 Left, I had trouble seeing
the approach end numbers. Automatically I rubbed at my
eyes with the back of my left hand. My glove came away
wet. When I reached up again, I felt a stream of tears rolling
down both cheeks, a stream I couldn't control and couldn't
stop. A sickening feeling swept over me. The thought of
what I had done to Larry Hull crushed me with guilt at
least as consequential as original sin.

After landing, I skipped the customary stops at the personal equipment and the intel shops. Instead, I stole the first
jeep I found and drove straight to the Covey barracks. Still
wearing my survival vest and parachute harness, I bolted
past several wide-eyed Coveys and into the first latrine stall
in the long row outside the community shower. I threw up
for thirty minutes, until there was nothing left inside me.*

---

*In 1997 a joint U.S./Lao team located a crash site believed to be that
of Larry Hull. Various pieces of aircraft wreckage and life support
equipment found definitely correlate this site to Larry's O-2 aircraft.
Unfortunately, the team was unable to recover any remains. The site
has been recommended for full excavation, but because of protocols
and scheduling restrictions, it may be several more years before the
excavation can begin.

March

For all practical purposes, the Prairie Fire mission died on the west wall of the A Shau Valley, along with Larry Hull. During the month of March, we couldn't have mounted a team insert if we had wanted to. The teams were ready; the FACs were ready; the Covey riders were ready. The missing vital element proved to be helicopters.

Like a giant sponge, Lam Son 719 continued to soak up men and equipment. During the first week of March, the ARVN had first call on all 101st helicopters for the final big push toward Tchepone. When they finally achieved the objective at the bombed-out crossroads, the ARVN disengaged and started the deadly return to the border, again via helicopter. Overloaded UH-1 Hueys and CH-47 Chinooks shuttled back and forth to hellholes named LZ Lolo, Liz, and Sophia Two. The valiant chopper crews kept at it until they dropped from exhaustion or from enemy ground fire.

By March 24 the last ARVN troops had been lifted out of Laos, and all that remained was the withdrawal from the border back to Dong Ha and Quang Tri. With the main part of the battle over, SOG was anxious to saddle up and put its own teams across the fence. It wasn't in the cards. The lack of helicopters was still the limiting factor. During the forty-five days of Lam Son 719, enemy gunners shot down over one hundred U.S. helicopters and damaged another six hundred. As those of us who had been flying there on a steady basis knew, the arena on the ground and in the air over the Ho Chi Minh Trail was one of the most desolate and deadly of the entire war.

Throughout the intense fighting during the first two weeks of March, I never even got airborne. With no helicopters, we had no job. Consequently, the Prairie Fire pilots sat idle. The inactivity became a tough pill to swallow, especially since two weeks earlier we had been logging seven to nine hours of combat time each day.

To keep me gainfully employed, and to give my wounds more healing time, the head Covey asked me to write a detailed narrative on the Covey Bomb Dump. For almost two weeks I sat in the intel shop poring over records, after-action reports, and debriefs relating to the missions flown around Ban Bak. I also interviewed all the Covey pilots and navigators who flew those missions. Their firsthand accounts of the sights, smells, and sounds of an aerial battle were captivating. The events they described to me were far more fascinating and entertaining than any article in an adventure magazine.

My writing efforts also kept my mind off the moral and ethical questions that had been eating away at me ever since the burning of Larry Hull's airplane. The sick feeling was never far away, but the Bomb Dump project helped me cope. Turning out fifty pages of text, I was immersed in the effort when an offhand comment jolted me into wanting to fly more missions.

Late one night in the Muff Divers' Lounge, I tried to doze off while an animated bull session raged on in the party half of the lounge. Evidently the participants assumed I was asleep, because the conversation became hushed as they began discussing me. One of the Coveys remarked, "Nah, don't sweat getting grounded. That stuff about two hits and they ground you is a bunch of bull. Hell, Tom's been hit at least ten times that I know of and had his plane shot out from under him on another occasion. Nobody grounded him."

Somebody else offered the rebuttal: "Well, he's not officially grounded, but why do you think they've got him doing that busywork over at intel? I heard the bosses want to wean him from flying combat for the next month. Otherwise, they think he'll go out and get himself killed."

Not surprisingly, I never went to sleep that night. An odd mixture of gratitude and anger buzzed through my mind. On the one hand, I marveled at the totally plausible logic my commanders had used on me, assuming they were trying to wean me off the flying schedule. Their concern flattered me. On the other hand, the implication that I had some kind of death wish really rankled me. Because of the nature of the job, the Prairie Fire pilots necessarily saw a lot of action and took some chances. But they were usually calculated risks, intended to save a team or one of our chopper crews. On any number of occasions my judgment could be called into question, but I sincerely believed any shortcomings were positively motivated, no matter how flawed my logic might have been. As for all the ground-fire hits I had taken, they were proportionally about the same as the other Prairie Fire pilots had chalked up; I had more simply because I'd been doing it much longer than they had. Perhaps increased exposure was the culprit. The eight combat losses in Covey aircraft during the past ten months had all been in Prairie Fire; maybe it was logical to assume the next one would be too. Still, I didn't believe any of the arguments and speculation supported anything as ridiculous as an operative death wish.

The following day I put the finishing touches on my writing project and turned it over to the 20th TASS historian. Then, leaning back in my chair, I began rehearsing the speech I planned to deliver to the Covey commander. My concentration came apart when someone told me the news about Evan Quiros.

Some sneaky devil aboard the USS *Lynde McCormick* had filmed Evan's famous air show. To make matters worse, they sent the film through the chain of command. Eventually, somebody in Saigon saw the flick and decided to make an example of one Captain Quiros. Evan was grounded in disgrace for the remainder of his tour and ordered to Saigon to confess his sins before an assembled group of new pilots.

That did it. One grounded Prairie Fire pilot was enough. When I stomped into the commander's tiny office, the words of my carefully planned speech had evaporated into alphabet heaven but, instead, I stammered and stuttered, demanding to be put back on the flying schedule as a regular Trail Covey. The new Covey boss, a lieutenant colonel with a kindly face and short, graying hair, stared at me for a few agonizingly long moments before nodding his head. Ken Summers said quietly, "Okay, you got it. Just remember, you've got less than a month to go on your tour. You've seen more action than any other pilot in this squadron, and you've got nothing to prove to anybody, so take it easy out there."

I couldn't believe it. I'd walked in the door ready to do battle to get my way. Instead, the boss had not only said yes, he had done it with poise, consideration, and caring. He could have ripped me a new one for being so impertinent. I came away from the encounter thinking how lucky the Coveys were to have had such high-caliber leaders in command; men like Ken Summers, Bob Denison and Ed Cullivan; men who genuinely cared about the feelings, the motivations, the natural exuberance of a bunch of young combat pilots and navigators.

Along with the new leadership within the organization came a different kind of sad but predictable changing of the guard. Shortly after my conversation with Colonel Summers, I found myself at the Da Nang terminal saying goodbye to old friends. We'd been through a lot together, in many cases we'd grown up together, and we'd shared experiences that would bond us for life. It was tough to see Evan Quiros, Sonny Haynes, and Carl D'Benedetto get on the Freedom Bird and fly out of my life. They'd been not only friends but also the support network that kept me going. Their departure left a void, which I chose not to fill with new friends. It wouldn't have been the same. Instead, I made up my mind to make the remaining time go quickly by flying as many combat missions as possible.

Before saddling up again, an opportunity presented itself for me to visit Vietnam's most famous city, Saigon. Because of the temporary stand-down at CCN, SOG extended to several Prairie Fire FACs an invitation to tour MACSOG headquarters. We made the trip south aboard an Air Force MC-130 "Blackbird," one of the supersecret aircraft serving in SOG's flight detachment at Nha Trang Air Base. Equipped with advanced avionics, special electronic countermeasures equipment, Doppler radar, and the highly classified forward-looking infrared night vision system, the Blackbirds routinely flew extremely dangerous night resupply and deception parachute drops over North Vietnam. The aircrews for these "spy" missions came from the 90th Special Operations Squadron.

During our orientation at SOG headquarters, it was an honor to meet the dedicated staff members who planned so many of the missions we had flown. Additionally, there was something comforting about putting a face with a name; the MACSOG folks expressed the same sentiment on meeting us. One of the executive officers put it best. "I see your FAC call sign in all the reports, and I've always wondered what a crazy bastard looked like. Now I know!"

One of the most interesting sections we visited was OP 75, the operational air arm within SOG that handled all the tactical airlift, Blackbirds, helicopters, and FACs supporting the mission. Our briefer was particularly keen about the Air Force helicopters involved with SOG. The most famous was the 20th Special Operations Squadron "Green Hornets," operating N model UH-1 Hueys. Flying for CCS teams ranging into Cambodia, the Green Hornets were idolized by their SOG teams for their courage and audacity. Part of that well deserved reputation came from the 20th SOS's only Medal of Honor recipient, Lieutenant Jim

Fleming, who executed an incredible feat of bravery and flying by piloting his shot-up Huey into a totally exposed riverbank and then snatching a trapped SOG team from certain death.

Next we proceeded to "House Ten," a SOG-operated safe house in Saigon where team members could grab a hot shower, a clean bed, and cheap drinks in the bar. Using House Ten as our base of operations, several Green Berets took us on a wild night tour of Saigon's more sordid locations, including most of the bars on the infamous Tu Do Street and to a Special Forces favorite known as the "Artistic Hand Massage Parlor." The following morning, much worse for wear and tear, we hitched a ride back to Da Nang on another Blackbird.

True to his word, Colonel Summers got me back on the schedule. By March 15 I was cruising up and down the Ho Chi Minh Trail looking for trucks. After the camaraderie and intensity of Prairie Fire, the solo missions over the maze of dirt roads seemed long and lonely, but one thing hadn't changed. The gunners along the Trail still had plenty of ammo.

On my first venture out, I worked a flight of Navy A-6 Intruders against two river fords near an area known as Delta 87. The A-6s carried an unusual seeding ordnance with delayed fusing. In theory, the bomblets spread out over the area and lay dormant until any metal object approached. Small antennas on the bomblet sensed the metal, then detonated the explosive, hopefully catching a juicy truck loaded with supplies. Because of the risk, the trucks were forced to avoid the bombed area and to delay their journeys by as much as thirty-six hours. On this occasion we had a hard time getting the ordnance on the target.

After marking the fords, I cleared the lead A-6 in hot. As soon as he rolled in, a trio of 37mm guns opened up, spewing flak all around the diving jet. The gunners tracked him all the way down the chute, through the pull-off, and through most of the climb away from the target. Then the gunners gave the wingman the same treatment. They pumped clip after clip into the hazy morning sky, with no indication of a desire to conserve ammo. In my eleven months of flying combat, I had never seen so many 37mm shells fired in such a short interval.

As I began flying my final combat missions, the never-ending stream of new pilots continued to flow into the unit, each eager to become combat ready. According to my roomie, Larry "Big Bippy" Thomas, one of the best prospects was a young lieutenant named Jack Butcher, Covey 231. The Big Bippy claimed Jack, with his short-clipped dark hair and even darker smoldering eyes, was the fastest study among the new group. Just before going on two weeks of leave, Larry sang the praises of his student and asked me to keep an eye on Lieutenant Jack Butcher. The opportunity presented itself on March 24.

We took off in formation at first light, Butcher tucked in close on my right wing. As part of his training, Jack had to fly some solo observer missions over the Trail, where he practiced his visual reconnaissance techniques or observed experienced Coveys direct air strikes. The specific training for the day involved Jack's watching me run an Igloo White sensor mission. Once across the fence, we headed for Delta 43, a ninety-degree bend in the Xe Kong River near the now infamous village of Ban Bak.

Our target was a small segment of Route 92 running between two high ridges. From the air the steep tree-covered slopes resembled a dark green shag carpet. The red dirt of Route 92 was clearly visible, accentuated by scores of bomb craters along either side of the road scratched out along the narrow valley floor. Somewhere in the green shag, we knew several NVA triple-A positions sat waiting and watching.

The two-ship of F-4 Phantoms checked in with me on schedule. My job was to mark a precise stretch of road approximately three hundred meters in length, one smoke on the south end of the box, another on the north end. Using my rockets as their target parameters, the Phantoms would streak in on the deck at high speed, dropping the sensors between the smokes. A pinpoint drop was vital to the folks at Task Force Alpha, so they could accurately time truck movements against known positions of each acoustical sensor. To make the system work, both FAC and fighters had to be right on the money.

With Jack orbiting in a ringside seat over the eastern ridge, we went to work on the Igloo White drop. Pressing in low and shallow, I laid both willie petes in a nice bracket. Next, Lead rolled in well to the south, hugging the deck as he zeroed in on the swirling white smoke. At release, Lead stroked both afterburners while pulling up and to the east into the blinding light of the morning sun. The wingman flew a carbon copy, and it was over, without a hostile shot being fired. While the fighters navigated to a waiting tanker for a poststrike refueling, I used the Covey discrete FM frequency to debrief Jack on the strike, putting particular emphasis on the requirement for absolute accuracy and on the risk the fighters took during their low-altitude, highly predictable run-in to the target box.

A few minutes later, Hillsboro asked me to check out two sets of map coordinates for possible enemy activity. I selected the one near Delta 87, location of the three 37mm guns with the endless supply of ammo. I asked Jack to investigate a section of a new road, Route 99, running along a flat plateau a few miles northwest of Delta 43. He banked off in that direction, and that was the last time I saw Jack Butcher.

The heavy foliage around Delta 87 yielded nothing. The trucks were down there all right, but I couldn't find their hiding place. After fifteen minutes of searching, I banked the Bronco around and started back up the Trail to see how Jack had made out.

I didn't give it more than a second's thought when Jack didn't answer my calls on company FM. My concern grew when he didn't come up on the UHF strike frequency or on Hillsboro's VHF frequency. Switching over to Guard channel, I still couldn't raise him. Since the chances of all his radios failing at the same time defied the odds, I tried a long shot, asking Panama if they had Covey 231 on their radar scope. Somehow, I knew their answer would be negative.

When I arrived over the general area of Jack's last known position, the morning sky was painfully empty. Below, a thin fog deck obscured the plateau containing Route 99. After calculating the terrain height, I rolled into a shallow dive, directly into the fog bank. I knew Jack had to be down there somewhere under that gray veil.

I coasted into the clear about a thousand feet above the ground. Within seconds, chills ran up and down my spine as the high-pitched shrill of an emergency beeper filled my helmet earphones. One quick jink to the north and I saw it, a burning pile of junk marked by thick black smoke, only a hundred meters west of the new road. There was no real question in my mind, but I circled down to the deck to make certain. Sure enough, I could still make out the numbers on the tail section, 693. It was, ironically, the very same OV-10 from my first trial by fire so many months ago, the same aircraft with the 23mm-induced broken wing spar, only recently put back in action.

As I plotted the coordinates of the crash site, a sound on the radio startled me. A garbled, slurred, almost unintelligible voice said, "Covey 221, this is 213. This is 213." I wanted to believe it was Jack's voice. It sounded a little like Jack, but the call sign was wrong. The voice had it reversed; his call sign was 231.

Disregarding the call signs, I answered, "Jack, this is Tom. Talk me into your location, buddy. I'm orbiting over the crash now. Which way?" In response, the wailing, pulsing beeper filled the airwaves with its forlorn sound. I pleaded, "Covey 231, this is 221. If you read me, turn off the beeper and come up voice."

With the emergency signal pounding in my ears, I felt myself turning into a crazy man. Jack was down there somewhere, counting on me to rescue him. This is what I did for a living. How many SF troops had I found in the jungle and plucked out? What was different about this one?

Why couldn't I find Jack? My chest felt like it wanted to explode in ten different directions.

I found it helped to talk out loud through the intercom, my own voice partially blocking the beeper. I reasoned with myself, "Okay, get organized. There's a slight breeze from the west. Watch the smoke. Jack's 'chute probably drifted to the east side of the road. Start the search pattern over there."

I ran a quick swing along the east side of the road at treetop level, looking down through the triple canopy for a telltale parachute. The only sign of life came from a flock of white birds, spooked into the air by the sound of the Bronco's whining engines. Every minute or so I called Jack on Guard, pleading with him to answer me. For my troubles, some impatient pilot, miles away and unaware of the situation, chimed in with a rude, "Get the hell off Guard!"

After crisscrossing the area numerous times, I finally saw evidence of human life. While reversing directions with a steep banked left turn, I spotted a slow-moving stream of .51-cal tracers arching up at me from the south. When I headed that way to investigate, I stumbled across a column of fifteen troops running down the center of the road, in the direction of the crash. With the left-hand set of M-60s armed, I rolled in on the running figures from behind, walking a long burst of fire into their midst. The two tail-end charlies collapsed as I zoomed a few feet over the heads of the remaining soldiers. As I yanked the aircraft through a tight turn to reengage, a loud tearing sound snapped my head around, just in time to see a string of tracers fill the airspace around me. For a brief second the flight controls seemed to bind, then broke free. Looking halfway back on the right boom, I saw the problem. Somebody down there was a damn good shot. Some kind of heavier weapon, probably a .51-cal machine gun, had stitched a row of ragged holes across the sides and bottom of the boom, almost ripping it in half, bottom to top.

In the ensuing confusion, my troops managed to blend into the brush alongside the trail, but the two bodies still lay where they had fallen. Something else had distracted me. For a few seconds, I couldn't figure out what it was. Then it hit me. There was no sound. The beeper had stopped. The silence was more deafening than anything I could remember.

As I started to search the west side of Route 99, Hillsboro advised, "Covey 221, I've got the help you asked for. Sandy Zero Three and Zero Four will meet you on Golf frequency." Looking down on my mission data card, I found the letter G and dialed in the corresponding UHF frequency. As I waited for the A-1s to check in, I couldn't for the life of me remember talking to Hillsboro about an SAR or A-1s.

Almost immediately the Sandys and I got off to a rocky start. After briefing them on the situation, I added, "Listen, gents, I know he's down there. How 'bout scrambling a Jolly and get him inbound while we continue the search."

Sandy Lead answered, "We can't commit the Jollies without an objective, and right now, buddy, you've got no objective."

I shot back, "For Christ's sake, Sandy. I talked to 231 on the radio. He's down there. I know it. In the hour it'll take the choppers to get here, we'll find him and have your objective. Now let's get on with it."

"Negative, Covey. I knew how you must feel, but no objective, no Jollies. And that's final."

His words stung me, setting off a torrent of rage fed by acute frustration. In an angry, bitter shout, I replied, "Hey, Lead. If you're gonna sit up there and quote regs to me, just take your wingman and get the hell out of here. I'll find him without your help."

The words were no sooner out of my mouth when I spotted a second group of bad guys trotting north along the road. Somewhat sarcastically I added, "I've got troops in the open down here, gents. If you're not gonna run an SAR, would you like to come down here and kick a little ass?"

With no further coaxing from me, Sandy Lead moved west about ten miles to the edge of the fog bank, reversed direction, then headed to me on the deck. As the big A-1H came into sight, I popped a quick smoke onto the road, scattering the troops in all directions. The Sandy flew several low passes, dumping rear-ejecting CBU-25 into their hiding places. When it was over, we counted two more bodies face down on the side of the road.

Sandy Lead covered me for several more minutes as I trolled the treetops looking for Jack. He knew what I refused to accept. With no voice or beeper for over an hour, the odds of finding Covey 231 were becoming bleaker with each passing minute. The A-1 jock trolled along with me, probably for no other reason than to pacify me. As I watched him work, as I watched him hang it out in the breeze, I sincerely regretted my earlier tirade—but not enough to apologize.

By the time Lead reached bingo fuel, much of the fog had burned off. The two A-1s rejoined, wished me good luck, then took up an RTB for their home base at NKP. Once more I took up the solo search for the missing Covey pilot. I would have given anything for the companionship and sharp eyes of Satan or Blister strapped in my back seat. Unfortunately, both of them had recently moved on to other assignments.

On one of my low circuits, the Bronco bucked again, this time from a big hole shot in the right flap. Reluctantly, I climbed a thousand feet to escape the worst of the small-arms fire. Given any kind of chance, I knew my beat-up OV-10 could get me home. Good old 693 had saved me once; now I counted on a badly wounded 701 to do the same.

In the excitement, the notion of running out of fuel never crossed my mind. I believed I could stay over the target as long as it took to find Jack and rescue him. My first inkling of a gas problem arrived with the new sector FAC sent to relieve me. When Lieutenant Bruce Young saw me down in the weeds, he stated, "Covey 221, this is 252. You've been out over four hours. Gimme a fuel check." My five hundred pounds of remaining fuel seemed to concern

Covey 252 more than it did me. As I briefed him on where I had already searched, Bruce kept repeating in an increasingly antsy tone, "Go home. Get out of here!"

The flight back to Da Nang was lonely and demoralizing. After a year of involvement in hairy rescues, I felt like a rookie for not being able to find Jack Butcher. I agonized over what his fate might be. The word going around was that the bad guys didn't take any prisoners in Laos, especially FACs. Preoccupation with those thoughts almost ended in disaster for me.

Without paying attention to what I was doing, I rolled into a left base to Runway 17 Left and threw the flap lever down. Before I could react, the OV-10 flipped the opposite direction, putting me into almost ninety degrees of right bank. In the mad scramble to feed in corrective left stick and rudder, I remembered the damaged right flap. I slammed the flap lever full up and wallowed back to the left before getting things under control. The alert tower operator added to my misery and embarrassment by asking, "Covey 221, are you experiencing control difficulties?" Replying with a sullen "Negative," I guided the crippled bird in for a relatively smooth landing and cleared the active runway. In spite of my distress at not being able to find Jack Butcher, I managed a weak smile as I watched the astonished faces of the maintenance folks staring in disbelief at my shot-up OV-10. And the ordeal wasn't over. I spent the rest of the day talking on the secure telephone with the Seventh Air Force command center, "Blue Chip," and with the Joint Personnel Recovery Center in Saigon. But rather than talking about what had happened, most of all I wanted another airplane so I could fly back out to Route 99 and continue the search for Covey 231. I knew the other Coveys meant well, but they just were not trained to fly low enough to find Jack. It was a bitter pill to swallow when the 20th TASS squadron commander refused to let me fly a second mission.

Much later, we found out that as Jack Butcher flew along Route 99, a round from a 37mm gun blew off the nose of his aircraft. He was captured moments after hitting the ground following ejection from his OV-10. Badly hurt, Jack was forced by his captors to talk to me on the radio despite a broken jaw. After a brief recuperation in a makeshift field hospital, the gutsy Covey escaped into the Laotian jungle on March 29, only to be recaptured a few hours later. Following extensive interrogation and a threatened execution by his North Vietnamese guards, the Covey once again escaped on May 9. During that evasion, SOG Bright Light teams led by the legendary Billy Waugh came within a whisker of rescuing Covey 231. Unfortunately, he was recaptured on May 19 and, following some brutal treatment, Jack was sent to Hanoi, where he remained until repatriation in March 1973, almost exactly two years to the day after his shoot-down. Jack Butcher was one of only nine U.S. airmen captured in Laos to make it back home. Hundreds of other pilots, aircrew members, and SOG personnel have never been accounted for.

April 1971

"Da Nang tower, Covey 221 three-mile initial—for the last time."

An indifferent American voice answered, "Da Nang landing Runway 17 Left. Altimeter three-zero-zero-two, wind one-four-zero at eight. Report a midfield break for departing traffic."

For some sentimental, incomprehensible reason only another pilot on his final combat mission could appreciate, the tower operator's unemotional response to my very last time in his pattern annoyed me. He obviously could have cared less about the end of my combat tour and all of the emotional baggage that went along with it. To the tower operator, April 4, 1971, was just another day at Rocket City, and Covey 221 was just another arrogant FAC bent on showing his fanny.

My own feelings, confused and exposed, didn't help matters any. My final visits to Quang Tri and to Phu Bai had been a lot tougher than I thought they would be. I felt a deep twinge of guilt and a definite tug at the emotions as I said good-bye to such old friends as First Sergeant Kim Budrow, RT leader Jim Butler, and Covey rider Jim Parry. We had gone through a lot together; I didn't know how to cut the cord and leave. I didn't want to leave. The only saving grace was that all of them would be leaving too. Following Lam Son 719, CCN had officially shut down, replaced by a temporary caretaker organization known as Task Force I Advisory Element. The Prairie Fire mission was over.

Shaking off the perceived snub from the Da Nang tower operator, I went through the checklist items in preparation for landing. I had gone through the same drill a thousand times before, and it had become second nature, almost an involuntary response. Yet on this final flight, each action seemed to take on a melancholy significance. Condition levers to takeoff and land. Power set at eleven hundred pounds of torque per engine. Airspeed 160 knots indicated.

At midfield I roll the Bronco into sixty degrees of left bank, then feed in the back pressure for a two-G, level, 180-degree turn. On downwind check below 155 knots, then gear lever down, my right thumb constantly flicks the trim button for a large dose of nose-up trim to compensate for the changing airspeed and angle of attack. Opposite the first yellow chevron painted on the overrun, the flaps go down as I bank into a descending final turn at 110 knots. Rolling out on final at three hundred feet, I slow the Bronco to 100 knots and hold that airspeed and angle of attack all the way to touchdown. The slight bump and the squeal of the main tires tell me I'm down, for the last time.

Taxiing toward the revetments, I could see the fire truck and an excited group of fellow Coveys. After I shut down and climbed out of the cockpit, the strange *fini* flight celebration began. In a ritual of unknown origin, named with the French word meaning "finished," the last flight party had become a tradition throughout Southeast Asia. The festivities got under way when the grinning firemen turned the hose on me full blast, soaking me in an instant with a heavy stream of Da Nang's famous brown water. Somebody produced several bottles of champagne, and everyone drank and shook hands with me, congratulating me on completing my tour. One of the Coveys even pinned a patch on my dripping wet flight suit: "Survivor, Southeast Asia War Games."

Everyone who was gathered on the hot concrete ramp at the north end of Da Nang's east runway seemed genuinely happy for me. In return, I smiled modestly, uncomfortable at being the center of attention, and secretly sad that the best flying job I could ever hope to have was over. For the party's sake, I acted happy right along with the crowd.

I had the feeling some of my buddies were doing a little acting themselves. Amidst the handshakes, back slaps, and bear hugs, I sensed they understood how I really felt. Their turn would come, and they too would experience the conflicting feelings about wanting to go home while wanting to stay. The only truly honest person at the party turned out to be the crotchety old maintenance line chief. As we shook hands, he said, "Captain, I'm glad you made it, but I can't say I'm sorry to see you go. You've been a one-man demolition derby on my flight line since you got here, breakin' airplanes and getting 'em shot up faster than we could fix 'em. You're a regular MA."

Unfamiliar with the term, I asked, "What's an MA, Sarge?"

Winking, he broke into one of his infrequent smiles and said, "Magnet ass."

The following day was dedicated to outprocessing. It came as a rude shock to find my new status carried no weight in the bureaucracy. When I tried to get the noncommissioned officer in charge of the personal equipment shop to sign off on my clearance form, he refused. He looked me right in the eye and said, "You've got three pair of binoculars signed out, and you only turned in one. Either give me all three pair or cough up eighty-five bucks each— your choice."

"Now wait a minute," I argued. "You know that both pair got shot out of my cockpit back in October. You were the one who issued me a new set the next day. They were combat losses, for crying out loud."

Looking bored with the conversation, the sergeant replied, "Call it anything you want, but my books have still got to balance. When you give me the glasses or the money, I'll sign your clearance sheet."

From the determined scowl on his face, I could tell the man wasn't about to budge or respond to logic. Trying to keep my irritation in check, I turned and walked out the door without a word to my tormentor. I spent the remainder of the morning at Covey Ops composing a letter from the head Covey to the personal equipment shop, explaining the circumstances surrounding the loss of the binoculars in question and further directing the NCOIC to keep the letter as documentation of a valid loss of government equipment.

Without saying a word, I strolled back into the personal equipment shop and carefully placed the letter and the clearance form on the counter, purposely keeping my gaze on the Air Force master sergeant's eyes. After a few uncomfortable seconds of ocular sparring, he grudgingly read the letter from Lieutenant Colonel Summers. Without looking up, he scribbled an unintelligible signature on the form and shoved it across the counter to me. He turned on his heel and walked away. I went out the door thinking that if an outsider had witnessed the little fiasco just transacted, he would have concluded the two of us weren't really fighting the same war. Looking down at the space on the clearance form, I couldn't help feeling the signature represented a very hollow victory. I had pursued the issue and won, yet the bested NCOIC—the same man who a week earlier would have moved heaven and earth to outfit one of "his" combat pilots—saw me now as an administrative loose end to tie up. I wasn't a part of it anymore, and it hurt. For his sake and mine, I should have simply paid the man the money.

Fortunately for me, things lightened up a little on April 6 when the Coveys threw one of their infamous "hail and farewell" parties, and as one of the departing honorees, I came in for more than my share of good natured kidding and abuse. In addition to speeches and the presentation of various going-away plaques, the Head Covey decorated me with the coveted "Brass Balls" award. But the climax of the evening occurred when several of my guests from CCN presented me with a gag "hero medal" that had everyone in the room rolling on the floor with laughter. The citation accompanying "Hero Medal Number One" read as follows:

"Captain Tom 'Tree Top' Yarborough, noted military

aviator extraordinaire, hero of the oppressed, and gentleman idol of women, distinguished himself while serving as a member of the Military Assistance Command, Studies and Observation Group, Republic of Vietnam, from July 1970 to April 1971. During that period Captain Yarborough was subjected to extrememly heavy and almost continuous drinking relationships with members of SOG's Mobile Launch Teams attached to CCN. Due to his outstanding ability to emulate the sordid and disgusting traits of his comrades, he developed the habit of consuming copious amounts of alcohol, thus perpetuating the best social traditions of the Air Force and Special Forces. He further exhibited unquestionable standards of bravery. On several occasions Captain Yarborough led dangerous reconnaissance patrols, originating from House Ten in Saigon, throughout the length and breadth of enemy and disease infested areas of Tu Do Street, where an amazing number of the ladies of the night seemed to be on a first name basis with him. He was also instrumental in the successful assault on a sinister establishment known as the 'Artistic Hand Massage Parlor.' On each of these forays Captain Yarborough always demonstrated the highest levels of gallantry and determination, in spite of being highly intoxicated. Additionally, during a long-range mission in Thailand, he single-handedly attempted to raze the the capital city, pillage the PX, plunder several jewelry stores, and deflower numerous virgins. In consideration of his exploits, it is hereby proclaimed that Captain Yarborough has brought much credit upon himself and a 'ti ti' bit upon the United States Air Force. He is therefore awarded the 'G.I. You Number Ten Cheap Charlie' Hero Medal Number One."

Two days later, on my last night at Da Nang, my final night as a Covey FAC, a thousand stray thoughts competed with my disorganized attempt to pack the trusty, old B-4 bag. As I folded up my flight suits and stuffed them into the zippered side pockets, a curious sadness gripped me. The faded green flight suits symbolized the end of the most intense, emotional year of my life. I had the odd sensation

of packing away those memories along with the flight suits.
I couldn't allow that to happen. I recalled my father describing World War II as the major global event and experience of his generation. Vietnam was mine. For the first
time I understood what he had been trying to explain.

My thoughts also brushed up against the dilemma most
of my Special Forces friends had already confronted. The
push-pull attraction and lure of combat reduced them to the
likes of the moth drawn relentlessly to the heat and danger
of the flame. Like the moth, the flame of battle in Southeast
Asia attracted the SOG troops, and it became the focus of
their existence—of my existence. Like them, the prospect
of returning to the States to perform mundane, routine training did not appeal to me. Had there still been a Prairie Fire
mission, I would have figured out some way to extend my
tour.

Shortly after one o'clock on the afternoon of April 9, a
mixed bag of soldiers, sailors, marines, and airmen climbed
aboard the Boeing 707—the Freedom Bird—for the
twenty-hour flight to Travis Air Force Base in California.
Saying good-bye in the terminal to my Covey friends, including Larry "Big Bippy" Thomas, Norm Komich, Henry
"Sugar Bear" Yeackle, and Rick "Salvo" Ottom, left a big
lump in my throat.

As I strapped into a seat by the window, a fellow Covey
finishing his tour sat down next to me. Not really expecting
an answer I said, "Chuck, this whole thing about a one-year
tour is dumb. Just when we get good at it, they send us home,
with no transition and no way to decompress. Why do I have
the feeling we're leaving with the job only half done?"

Squirming around, trying to fit his long frame into the
less than spacious airliner seat, Chuck responded, "Don't
think about it. It'll make you nuts."

As the big bird taxied out of the terminal area, the flight
attendant came up on the intercom. In a well-rehearsed but
sincere speech she told us, "Gentlemen, I can't begin to tell
you how proud we are of each and every one of you. It's
a real privilege and honor for this crew to fly you back to

the world." Following several administrative announce-
ments, the pretty flight attendant's face twisted into a dev-
ilish smile. "Military Airlift Command regulations prohibit
the serving or consumption of alcoholic beverages aboard
its flights; however, once we get airborne, if any of you would
like a cup of ice or a setup, just let one of us know." Predictably, the passengers responded with laughs and applause.

A few minutes later, when the Freedom Bird lifted off
Da Nang's west runway, the cabin resounded with more
applause, cheers, and rebel yells.

As the 707 banked around to the northwest to intercept
Airway Amber One, I had a great view of the dark green
foliage covering Monkey Mountain, of the yellow sand on
China Beach, of the gray concrete twin runways at the air
base, of the dark blue waters of Da Nang Bay. Far to the
west, veiled in a bluish haze, I could just make out the
fence—the annamitic cord of mountains separating Vietnam and Laos. The whole panorama had been my home
for a year of fifty-three weeks. Taking that one last look,
my mind flooded with thoughts of Da Nang, the Coveys,
and SOG. But the most vivid images glowing in my mind's
eye were of Prairie Fire. In uncanny detail I could still see
the faces of Satan, Blister, Evan Quiros, Mike McGerty,
Jim Smith, and Larry Hull: and I could recall every mission
we had ever run across the fence. Along with them, Prairie
Fire was history, and I had been there at the end. It was
time for me to go home.

Epilogue

Cruising north over the rugged Cambodian landscape, I had my OV-10, tail number 797, trimmed up for hands-off flight. One hundred miles in front of me lay Ubon Air Base, Thailand, destination for my last landing of the war. At 11:00 A.M. that morning, all direct U.S. combat involvement in Southeast Asia was officially to end. We were told we had to be out of Cambodian airspace by that hour—or suffer dire consequences. After controlling one air strike of A-7s near Kompong Cham, I was heading back across the fence for the final time. Absentmindedly I listened over the radio as each of the other FACs and fighter pilots checked out with Cricket, the EC-130 airborne battlefield command-and-control ship for Cambodia. Making no attempt at originality, I muttered the same farewell as all the other pilots: "So long, Cricket. See you next war."

Somewhere inside the EC-130 the controller answered, "Take care, buddy. Thanks for the good work."

After 608 combat missions in the Bronco, it was hard for me to comprehend the idea that it really was over. I had felt the same way more than two years earlier, leaving Da Nang at the end of my first tour. Yet there had been plenty of war to come back to when the dull, stateside training missions and post-Vietnam depression drove me up the wall. After the intensity of Prairie Fire, a routine existence as an Air Force pilot wasn't satisfying—I had to get back in the fight. Yet my feelings had nothing to do with being a warmonger or a glutton for punishment. The second tour was an attempt to recapture the excitement and camaraderie of flying for SOG. It had been another chance to do what I did best: fly combat.

As the flight north continued, with the warm sunshine beating into the all-glass cockpit, it occurred to me that I had seen about as much as a pilot could through the gunsight of an OV-10. I had seen the deactivation of Prairie Fire, with all its secrecy and high drama. I was airborne over I Corps on December 18, 1972, listening in disbelief as the B-52s participating in Linebacker II fell prey to SA-2 SAMs over Hanoi. I had been in action on January 27, 1973, when the Paris Peace Accords on Vietnam ended the U.S. war in that ravaged country. I had controlled air strikes on the Ho Chi Minh Trail on February 22, 1973, the last official day of the war in Laos. I had commanded the first strike package in support of ship convoys on the Mekong River attempting to run the gauntlet of fire to the starving people in Phnom Penh; in one five-hour period we controlled over 230 individual strike sorties against enemy positions along the Mekong. Now, on August 15, 1973, I was again a witness to history as the United States ended its combat role in the last of the three war-torn countries, Cambodia.

The touchdown on Runway 23 at Ubon was a grease job. A smooth final landing at the end had to be a good omen—or was it? Clearing the runway at midfield, I thought about my first landing there three years earlier under tougher circumstances. I thought about the battle-damaged right wing and the broken wing spar. Had it really been over three years?

Taxiing into the revetment area, I found it difficult to get caught up in the exuberance infecting the younger pilots, the very same pilots I had taken under my wing months earlier, the same young pilots who had hung on every word of my ample supply of war stories. While they performed a halfhearted ritual celebration of the moment by running their aircraft smoke generators at full blast, engulfing the ramp with billowing clouds of white-gray smoke, I caught myself contemplating the finality of the

event. It really was over. I felt it this time. But in the smoke
and laughter and handshakes on that blistering hot ramp at
Ubon, I genuinely felt something else, an unsettling feeling
gnawing deep in the pit of my stomach. The American public, disenchanted and upset by the mounting casualties,
higher taxes, and no prospect of a solution in sight, saw fit
to turn against the war—and in many cases, against the
warriors they had dispatched to do the fighting. As a result,
we were pulling out and leaving our Vietnamese, Laotian,
and Cambodian brothers-in-arms to go it alone. While most
Americans felt no personal attachment to these Southeast
Asian warriors—the ARVN, Montagnards, Hmong, and
Khmers—those of us who had fought beside them right up
to the very last minute felt firsthand the guilt and shame of
deserting our allies. We may have been ordered to leave
the battlefield, but we would never forget our friends who
would continue the fight until they won—or until they died
trying.

On that final day of the war, I did allow myself a single
celebration. When somebody on the flight line handed me
a magnum of champagne, I unhesitatingly lifted the bottle
in a toast that nobody there that day understood except me.
Letting my thoughts drift back some two years, I said simply, "To SOG, the finest men I've ever met and the best
damned warriors in the world." Later that night, fortified
with several large glasses of scotch, I tried to forget the
ignominy of my second combat tour while simultaneously
reflecting on the first. Again the focus was SOG, always
SOG. The men of that supersecret organization were, in my
estimation, the best troops the Army had ever produced.
Just a handful of Green Berets created a legend that would
live forever. As part of that legend, SOG became the most
highly decorated American military unit of the Vietnam
War. Statistically, they paid an enormous price, suffering
wound rates of over one hundred percent. The men of SOG
also became the ultimate personification of the phrase "Gallantry in action, above and beyond the call of duty." Twelve

SOG warriors received the Medal of Honor. Many more deserved it.

On reflection, I was immensely proud of having been associated with Operation Prairie Fire. On most of those missions across the fence I had made a difference. With a lot of help and luck, I had managed to mature from rookie FAC to combat-experienced veteran. Yet based on my experiences after my first tour, I knew nobody at home would applaud or cheer or care. But I also knew something more important, something that I would carry with me for a lifetime. I knew that in spite of the bone-jarring fear and the physical challenge of participating in life or death battles, I was part of a profession that put duty, honor, and country above self. Inside me, there was a deep satisfaction and pride in serving as a United States Air Force forward air controller.

As a fitting end to the final day of my war in Southeast Asia, I pulled out an old diary entry I had written two days before the end of my tour as a Covey FAC back at Da Nang. Reading the words again, I instinctively realized that one day I needed to tell my story to the world, a story about SOG—and the best job I ever had.

Da Nang, 2305 Hours, 7 April 71
A Whiskey Front Examination of What's Important

Considering my somewhat hard-core patriotic upbringing as an Army brat, I have been genuinely surprised by an unexpected swing in my feelings about priorities. Here in Vietnam, I've found that I rarely reflect on the larger implications of the Cold War. And I don't often stop to think about love of country or devotion to duty and flag, although they are as much a part of me as my own heart and soul. Instead, I have found myself thinking about a far more transcendent feeling that ironically has probably been present on every battlefield in practically every war. Stationed in this deadly place, those of us at the point of the spear come to realize that instead of fighting for our country, we fight mainly for our buddies. We kill for each other, die for each other, sacrifice for each other, and weep for each other. The circumstances ultimately cause us to love each other as brothers. Using that yardstick for measurement, I seem to have found, as incomprehensible as it may sound, more pure love in Vietnam than in any other place I have ever lived or visited. The discovery has changed me profoundly—far more so than any of the burns or shrapnel wounds that have scarred the flesh of my idealistic young body. Armed with new insight, I don't regret for a moment being here in Vietnam, because it has afforded me the honor and privilege to serve with the finest men I have ever met. I am proud to have these warrior-friends as part of my essential framework; I would rather die than let them down.

GLOSSARY

A-1 SKYRAIDER: A Korean War–vintage prop fighter capable of carrying large ordnance loads. Used extensively for search-and-rescue missions as well as in support of long-range reconnaissance teams.

A-4 SKYHAWK: A single seat light attack aircraft used by Navy and Marines.

A-6 INTRUDER: Sophisticated, all-weather attack jet flown by Navy and Marines.

A-7 CORSAIR II: A single seat jet attack aircraft used by both the U.S. Navy and Air Force.

AH-1 COBRA: Army helicopter gunship used extensively throughout Vietnam.

AK-47: The standard automatic assault weapon used by North Vietnamese and Viet Cong soldiers.

AO: Area of operations, usually a specific sector assigned to a FAC or ground unit.

ACROSS THE FENCE: Reference to crossing the border into Laos or Cambodia.

AIR AMERICA: The name of the CIA's proprietary airline.

ARC LIGHT: Code name for B-52 operations in Southeast Asia.

ARVN: Army of the Republic of Vietnam.

BAC SI: Vietnamese for "doctor." The medic assigned to Special Forces reconnaissance teams.

BARKY: Call sign of FACs assigned to the First Brigade, Fifth Mechanized Infantry Division, Quang Tri.

BARREL ROLL: Code name for USAF operations in northern Laos.

BDA: Bomb damage assessment, the reported results of air strikes.

BEEPER: A high-pitched, wavering radio tone broadcast on emergency frequencies, usually indicating a downed pilot.

BILK: Call sign of the FACs assigned to support the 101st Airborne Division, Hue Phu Bai.

BINGO: Radio term indicating the pilot has only enough fuel remaining to reach his home base safely.

BLACKBIRD: Slang term for USAF MC-130 aircraft in SOG's 90th Special Operations Squadron.

BLUE CHIP: Call sign for Seventh Air Force operations in Saigon.

BRIGHT LIGHT: Code name for a twelve-man Special Forces team dedicated to recovering POWs or downed pilots in Laos, Cambodia, or North Vietnam.

CANDLESTICK: Call sign for C-123K aircraft modified to perform FAC missions over Laos.

CBU: Cluster bomb unit. An area coverage, anti-personnel ordnance dropped by fighter aircraft, used extensively in Southeast Asia.

CCN: Command and Control North. The Da Nang–based regional headquarters for all cross-border operations, a subunit of Military Assistance Command's Studies and Observation Group. Similar headquarters operated from Kontum and Ban Me Thuot (CCC and CCS).

CHARLIE: A slang term for enemy soldiers, probably stemming from "Victor Charlie," the code words used for the letters VC, or Viet Cong.

COVEY: Call sign of the special-mission FACs flying sorties into Laos from Da Nang and Pleiku.

COVEY RIDER: Highly experienced Special Forces member who flew with Prairie Fire FACs to help direct air strikes and team inserts and extractions.

DAISY CUTTER: A fuse extender attached to the nose of a bomb.

DME: Distance-measuring equipment. A digital readout in miles from a specific navigation station.

DMZ: Demilitarized Zone. The no-man's-land between

North and South Vietnam at the 17th Parallel.

DUST-OFF: Call sign of Army UH-1 medical evacuation helicopters.

F-4 PHANTOM: State-of-the-art fighter bomber flown by Air Force, Navy, and Marines in Vietnam.

FAC: Forward air controller. In South Vietnam and Laos, virtually all air strikes were directed by FACs.

FLAK: Airbursts from antiaircraft fire.

FNG: A derogatory nickname for a new arrival to South Vietnam.

FOX MIKE: The code words for FM, or frequency modulation, the radio band used by Army units and FACs.

G: The force of gravity. When pulling off targets, pilots routinely encountered G forces four to six times their body weights.

GCA: Ground controlled approach (radar).

GUARD: A designated radio frequency for use in an emergency situation. While talking on other frequencies, pilots also monitored Guard.

HE: High-explosive, normally referring to rockets fired by fighters, FACs, or helicopter gunships.

HILLSBORO: Call sign of the orbiting EC-130 airborne battlefield command-and-control aircraft operating over Laos.

HO CHI MINH TRAIL: An extensive network of Laotian trails and roads used by the NVA to move men and supplies to South Vietnam and Cambodia.

HOLD-DOWN: A procedure in which one pilot keys or holds down his radio transmit button while a pilot in another aircraft homes in on the radio signal. A common practice among fighter aircraft attempting to rendezvous with a FAC.

HUEY: Nickname for the versatile UH-1 helicopter.

IGLOO WHITE: The electronic surveillance system designed to monitor truck traffic along the Ho Chi Minh Trail.

JOLLY: Call sign of Air Force HH-3 or HH-53 rescue helicopters, known as "Jolly Green Giants."

KARST: A large, irregular limestone rock formation, often

covered with jungle vegetation. Found throughout Southeast Asia, particularly in Laos.

KBA: Killed by air. Refers to casualties inflicted by aircraft.

KIA: Killed in action.

KING: Call sign of orbiting HC-130 aircraft responsible for coordinating all search-and-rescue operations for downed pilots.

KLICK: Slang for kilometer, a standard unit of measurement on tactical maps.

LAM SON 719: The ARVN invasion of Laos in February, 1971.

LAU-59: Designation for the rocket pods mounted on FAC aircraft.

LZ: Landing zone, usually an open area large enough to accommodate a helicopter.

MARK-82: A general-purpose five-hundred-pound bomb widely used on missions throughout Southeast Asia.

MIKE-MIKE: Slang for millimeter, as in twenty mike-mike cannon.

MISTY: Call sign for fast FACs flying the F-100 Super Saber.

MLT: Mobile launch team. CCN operated two permanent sites, at Quang Tri and at Phu Bai.

MOON BEAM: ABCCC EC-130 operating over Steel Tiger, the nighttime equivalent of Hillsboro.

NVA: North Vietnamese Army.

ONE-ONE: Designation for the SOG assistant team leader.

ONE-ZERO: Designation for the leader of a SOG reconnaissance team.

OSCAR DEUCE: Affectionate nickname for the O-2A FAC aircraft.

OV-IO BRONCO: a twin-engine light-attack aircraft used by forward air controllers.

PAVE WAY: Two thousand-pound, laser-guided bomb.

PIPPER: The aiming dot in the center of an aircraft gunsight.

PLAY TIME: The time that fighter aircraft can loiter over the target, normally five to ten minutes.

POW: Prisoner of war.

RPG: Rocket-propelled grenade used extensively by NVA forces.

PRAIRIE FIRE: Code word for cross-border ground reconnaissance missions. When used tactically by team leaders, the term indicated a dire condition requiring immediate extraction.

PSP: Pierced steel planking. Large sections of metal used for constructing temporary runways and ramps.

ROE: Rules of engagement. A lengthy, complicated list of limitations and conditions applied to a ground target before ordnance could be dropped.

ROLLING THUNDER: The American bombing campaign against North Vietnam from 1965 to 1968.

RT: Reconnaissance team. Each SOG team had a distinctive name, usually after a snake or a state.

RTB: Return to base.

SANDY: Call sign for A-1 Skyraiders dedicated to search-and-rescue missions.

SAR: Search and rescue.

SF: Special Forces.

SLICK: Affectionate nickname for the UH-1 Huey.

SOG: Studies and Observation Group.

SPAD: Call sign for the A-1 Skyraiders supporting SOG missions.

SQUAWK: An air traffic control term advising the pilot to set a specific sequence of numbers in the aircraft transponder. Once set, radar can interrogate the signal for positive identification.

STEEL TIGER: Code name for the southern panhandle of Laos containing the Ho Chi Minh Trail.

T-28 NOMAD: Two-seat prop trainer modified to carry bombs and rockets. The primary attack aircraft for the Royal Laotian Air Force.

TACAN: Tactical Air Navigation. A military navigation system designed to provide the pilot with bearing and distance from a ground station.

TAC E: Tactical emergency. RTs in Laos declared a TAC

E when their mission would be jeopardized without immediate close air support.

TASS: Tactical Air Support Squadron. All FACs were assigned to a TASS.

THUD: Affectionate nickname for the F-105 Thunderchief.

TIC: Troops in contact. A situation where friendly troops engage enemy forces in a firefight.

UHF: Ultra high frequency, the radio band used by most military aircraft. Also used on personal survival radios.

VC: Viet Cong, enemy soldiers.

VR: Visual reconnaissance, performed either on the ground or in the air.

WHIFFERDILL: Any improvised maneuver in an aircraft, usually involving a steep climb or dive.

WILLIE PETE: Slang for white phosphorous, the type of smoke rockets used by FACs to mark targets for fighter aircraft.

WINCHESTER: Pilots' slang for being out of ammunition or bombs.

X-RAY: Laotian nationals trained to fly with a FAC to validate sensitive enemy targets in Steel Tiger.

YANKEE STATION: Cruising area for the aircraft carriers of Task Force 77. Located approximately one hundred miles east of Da Nang in the South China Sea.

SELECTED BIBLIOGRAPHY

Benavidez, Roy, with Oscar Griffin. *The Three Wars of Roy Benavidez*. New York: Pocket Books, 1986.

Berger, Carl, ed. *The United States Air Force in Southeast Asia*. Washington, DC: Office of Air Force History, 1977.

Broughton, Jack. *Thud Ridge*. New York: Bantam Books, 1985.

Center for Air Force History. *USAF in Southeast Asia: Search and Rescue*. Washington, DC: Government Printing Office, 1992.

Churchill, Jan. *Hit My Smoke! Forward Air Controllers in Southeast Asia*. Manhattan, KS: Sunflower University Press, 1997.

Clodfelter, Mark. *The Limits of Air Power: The American Bombing of North Vietnam*. New York: Macmillan, 1989.

Conboy, Kenneth, and James Morrison. *Shadow War: The CIA's Secret War in Laos*. Boulder, CO: Paladin Press, 1995.

Drury, Richard. *My Secret War*. New York: St. Martin's Press, 1979.

Fall, Bernard. *Hell in a Very Small Place*. New York: J.P. Lippincott, 1967.

Flanagan, John. *Vietnam Above the Treetops*. New York: Praeger, 1992.

Generous, Kevin. *Vietnam: The Secret War*. New York: Gallery Books, 1985.

Guilmartin, John, and Michael O'Leary. *Helicopters: The Illustrated History of the Vietnam War*. Toronto: Bantam Books, 1988.

Halberstadt, Hans. *War Stories of the Green Berets*. Osceola, WI: Motorbooks International Publishers & Wholesalers, 1994.

Harrison, Marshall. *A Lonely Kind of War*. Novato, CA: Presidio Press, 1989.

Herring, George. *America's Longest War: The United States in Vietnam, 1950–1975*. New York: Random House, 1979.

Hubbell, John. *P.O.W.* New York: Reader's Digest Press, 1976.

Karnow, Stanley. *Vietnam: A History*. New York: Viking Press, 1983.

Kissinger, Henry. *White House Years*. Boston: Little, Brown & Co., 1979.

Moore, Harold, and Joseph Galloway. *We Were Soldiers Once . . . and Young*. New York: Random House, 1992.

Moore, Robin. *The Green Berets*. New York: Crown Publishers, 1965.

Morrocco, John. *Rain of Fire: Air War, 1969–1973, The Vietnam Experience*. Boston: Boston Publishing, 1986.

Momyer, William. *Airpower in Three Wars*. Washington, DC: Office of Air Force History, 1978.

Nolan, Keith. *Into Cambodia*. Novato, CA: Presidio Press, 1990.

———. *Into Laos*. New York: Dell Publishing Co., 1986.

Plaster, John. *SOG: A Photo History of the Secret Wars*. Boulder, CO: Paladin Press, 2000.

———. *SOG: The Secret Wars of America's Commandos in Vietnam*. New York: Simon & Schuster, 1997.

Reese, James, ed. *The Rustics: A Top Secret Air War in Cambodia*. Destin, FL: The Rustic FAC Association, 1999.

Robbins, Christopher. *The Ravens*. New York: Crown Publishers, 1987.

———. *Air America*. New York: G.P. Putnam's Sons, 1979.

Schemmer, Benjamin. *The Raid*. New York: Harper & Row, 1976.

Schlight, John. *The Years of the Offensive, 1965–1968*. Washington, DC: Office of Air Force History, 1988.

Shultz, Richard. *The Secret War Against Hanoi*. New York: HarperCollins Publishers, 1999.

Simpson, Charles. *Inside the Green Berets: The Story of the U.S. Army Special Forces*. New York: Berkley Books, 1984.

Singlaub, John, with Malcolm McConnell. *Hazardous Duty*. New York: Summit Books, 1991.

Stanton, Shelby. *Green Berets at War*. Novato, CA: Presidio Press, 1985.

Stoffey, Bob. *Cleared Hot!* New York: St. Martin's Press, 1992.

Sutherland, Ian. *Special Forces of the United States Army*. San Jose, CA: Bender Publishing, 1990.

Thayer, Thomas. *War Without Fronts: The American Experience in Vietnam*. Boulder, CO: Westview Press, 1985.

Thompson, James. *Rolling Thunder: Understanding Policy and Program Failure*. Chapel Hill: University of North Carolina Press, 1979.

Thompson, Leroy. *US Elite Forces—Vietnam*. Carrollton, TX: Squadron/Signal Publications, 1985.

Tilford, Earl. *Setup: What the Air Force Did in Vietnam and Why*. Maxwell Air Force Base, AL: Air University Press, 1991.

Westmoreland, William. *A Soldier Reports*. Garden City, NY: Doubleday, 1976.

USAF Operations in Laos: 1 January 1970–30 June 1971. Honolulu: Headquarters, Pacific Air Forces Corona Harvest, 1972.

U.S. Air Force: The Cambodian Campaign, 29 April–30 June 1970. Honolulu: Headquarters, Pacific Air Forces, 1970.

Waddell, Dewey, ed. *Air War—Vietnam.* New York: Arno Press, 1978.

Zaroulis, Nancy, and Gerald Sullivan. *Who Spoke Up? American Protest Against the War in Vietnam, 1963–1975.* New York: Holt, Rinehart, and Winston, 1984.

INDEX